Read these testimonies and more about how God's kingdom manifests on earth in tangible ways:

Healings and Creative Miracles

- "The eye is back!" exclaimed the stepdaughter of a man who'd had his right eye surgically removed due to irreparable injury. After his step-daughter and her church believed for the man's healing, he was given a brand-new eye supernaturally by God.

- A twenty-one-year old man suffered from achondroplasia, a genetic condition that is the most common type of dwarfism. After receiving prayer for a creative miracle, he reported that he had been touched by God's fire, and he could move his arms, which had previously had only limited mobility. Then, during the following year, he grew five inches in height as a tangible manifestation of the kingdom of God on earth!

- A woman responded in faith to an altar call for those who were HIV-positive. When a minister declared healing over her, she felt heat flowing through her body. The following day, she went to be retested, and the results were negative! She testifies that she received "joy, health, and everything I needed!"

Salvation and Victory over Sin

- A young man had used and sold drugs, prostituted himself with men and women, been in trouble with the law, and suffered from psychological imbalance. One day, he was alone in his room, desperate and depressed, when Jesus called him by name and said, "I have given you many opportunities, but you have turned your back on Me. This is your last chance to choose correctly." That night, the power of God delivered him. "I am a different person today," he says. "I do warfare against the enemy of our souls and uproot him from the territory that belongs to Jesus."

- A successful and wealthy attorney felt "an unmistakable emptiness from which I could not escape. I…could not understand why I was so often sad, depressed, and fearful." An ever-pres⋯⋯⋯⋯⋯ rang in her mind: *Is this all there is to life?* After respondi⋯ kingdom of God, she says, "Jesus melted my ⋯

I began my own personal relationship with Him, as I felt His presence for the very first time in my life....Jesus Christ filled that void inside of me."

+ A Major League Baseball player focused only on his success and ran away from his relationship with God. "Then, my friend took me to the baseball chapel," he says, "where I gave my heart to Jesus. I do not know how to explain it, but I felt that a heavy burden had been lifted from my soul....The hatred, hard feelings, resentment, bitterness, and more began to go away....Family, ministry, friendship...all has been restored!"

Deliverance from Demons and Oppression

+ During a spiritual retreat, a woman who was in bondage to rejection, abandonment, and guilt was led to renounce her bondage through prayer. "When I finished," she says, "I felt every oppression leave me. Today, I feel free of that generational curse of abandonment. The pain in my heart disappeared!"

+ "I was empty and wanted to die," said a young man who was diagnosed with schizoaffective disorder and obsessive-compulsive disorder and was told he would be on medication for the rest of his life. Then he responded to an altar call to accept Jesus. "I felt like a new, changed man," he said. "That night, I felt electricity going up and down my body." This young man has been off of his medication for nine years now, and he continues to be free of depression.

+ A woman in the Middle East had been violently demon-possessed for thirty years. A chain was fastened around her stomach, and the chain was attached to a hole in the wall, to keep her from harming others. The atmosphere was charged with spiritual opposition. After a pastor commanded demons of fear and suicide to leave the possessed woman, in Jesus' name, and after the woman's cousin prayed, sang, and worshipped God, the woman calmed down. For the first time in three decades, her ropes and chains were removed, and she began to behave normally. She ate her dinner calmly, and she slept on a bed with her clothes on.

Prosperity

+ "Lord, You promised that I would live in abundance!" prayed a man who had given to God sacrificially and trusted Him to provide for his family's financial needs. His savings were down to $1,200, and he had bills to pay. When he asked his wife to get the small box that contained their savings, she said, "There is $11,200!" Ten thousand dollars had been supernaturally placed inside the cashbox.

+ A pastor and his wife were activated in the supernatural power of the kingdom of God. They prayed for a man who had a debt of half a million dollars because his accountant had not paid his taxes, and they believed for the cancellation of the debt. The miracle took place! First, the man was notified that the debt had been reduced by half. A month later, he received notification that the rest of the debt had been canceled.

+ A family faced impending foreclosure on their home because the father's work hours had been reduced, making it impossible for them to meet their mortgage payments. "We began to declare a miracle from God," they said. They were certain that He would provide. Not long afterward, God spoke to a family friend in prayer, saying, "They will not be left homeless, because you will give it to them." The friend gave them $95,000 for the purchase of their home.

Resurrection Life

+ A couple's premature baby was stillborn, and they had to wait twelve hours before receiving permission to see their daughter's body in the morgue. When their church heard the news, they began to intercede for the family. The parents were finally allowed into the morgue, where their child's body had lain for half a day at extremely low temperatures. The woman took her daughter's cold hand in hers to say goodbye. Suddenly, they heard a weak sound, and the baby moved. God had raised her! The baby was immediately taken to the neonatal unit, where doctors confirmed that her vital signs were normal.

+ A pastor and his wife were sent to pray for a man in the hospital, yet they arrived at the room just after he had died. They laid hands on his dead body, declaring that God would resurrect him, but they walked away sad when they did not see him raised up. After they gave condolences to the family, the man's son said, "What are you talking about? My father is not dead!" While that fact was confirmed, another family was shouting with joy, saying that *their* father had awakened from the dead. The desk clerk had directed the pastor and his wife to the wrong room! The other man for whom they had prayed was now totally healed and telling everyone that Jesus had resurrected him! He and his entire family received Jesus as their Savior.

- A pastor preached to his church about stepping out in faith to pray for healings, miracles, and resurrections. Two young girls, ages fourteen and fifteen, took hold of that word. A week later, their grandmother suffered a severe heart attack and died. The two girls ran to her, scared but full of the boldness of the Holy Spirit. After they prayed, the grandmother's vital signs returned! The doctor could not understand how a ninety-year-old woman could have survived such a severe attack.

THE KINGDOM of POWER

HOW TO DEMONSTRATE IT
HERE & NOW

GUILLERMO MALDONADO

WHITAKER
HOUSE

Unless otherwise indicated, all Scripture quotations are taken from the *New King James Version*, © 1979, 1980, 1982, 1984 by Thomas Nelson, Inc. Used by permission. All rights reserved. Scripture quotations marked (NLT) are taken from the *Holy Bible, New Living Translation*, © 1996, 2004, 2007. Used by permission of Tyndale House Publishers, Inc., Carol Stream, Illinois 60188. All rights reserved. Scripture quotations marked (KJV) are taken from the King James Version of the Holy Bible. Scripture quotations marked (AMP) are taken from the *Amplified® Bible*, © 1954, 1958, 1962, 1964, 1965, 1987 by The Lockman Foundation. Used by permission. (www.Lockman.org). Scripture quotations marked (NIV) are taken from the *Holy Bible, New International Version®*, NIV®, © 1973, 1978, 1984 by the International Bible Society. Used by permission of Zondervan. All rights reserved. Scripture quotations marked (NASB) are taken from the *New American Standard Bible®*, NASB®, © 1960, 1962, 1963, 1968, 1971, 1972, 1973, 1975, 1977 by The Lockman Foundation. Used by permission. (www.Lockman.org). Scripture quotations marked (PHILLIPS) are taken from *The New Testament in Modern English*, © 1958, 1959, 1960, 1972 by J. B. Phillips, and © 1947, 1952, 1955, 1957, by The Macmillan Company.

Boldface type in Scripture quotations is the author's emphasis.

Some definitions of Hebrew and Greek words are taken from the electronic version of *Strong's Exhaustive Concordance of the Bible*, STRONG, (© 1980, 1986, and assigned to World Bible Publishers, Inc. Used by permission. All rights reserved.), the electronic version of the *New American Standard Exhaustive Concordance of the Bible*, NASC, (© 1981 by The Lockman Foundation. Used by permission. All rights reserved.), or *Vine's Complete Expository Dictionary of Old and New Testament Words*, VINE, (© 1985 by Thomas Nelson, Inc., Publishers, Nashville, TN. All rights reserved.).

Dictionary definitions are taken from *Merriam Webster's 11ᵗʰ Collegiate Dictionary*, electronic version, © 2003.

THE KINGDOM OF POWER: HOW TO DEMONSTRATE IT HERE AND NOW

Guillermo Maldonado
13651 S.W. 143rd Ct., #101 • Miami, FL 33186
http://kingjesusministry.org/
www.ERJPub.org

ISBN: 978-1-60374-744-8 • eBook ISBN: 978-1-60374-739-4
Printed in the United States of America
© 2013 by Guillermo Maldonado

Whitaker House
1030 Hunt Valley Circle
New Kensington, PA 15068
www.whitakerhouse.com

Library of Congress Cataloging-in-Publication Data (pending)

1 2 3 4 5 6 7 8 9 10 11 21 20 19 18 17 16 15 14 13

Contents

1

The Kingdom of God
Is Within You

Jesus made this remarkable declaration to His disciples: *"Do not fear, little flock, for it is your Father's good pleasure **to give you the kingdom"*** (Luke 12:32). This statement applies to Jesus' followers today, as well. No matter what troubles or fears we may contend with in our lives, God has given us His kingdom, which shines powerfully into the darkness of our world, sweeping away sickness, sin, demons, lack, and even death. I invite you to enter into God's kingdom of power so that you may see it demonstrated in the here and now!

There is a striking image of the earth at night that was produced by NASA through combined satellite data. Each white dot of light in the image represents the light of an individual city or other light source, and the collective lights of various metropolitan regions show up as brilliant patches of illumination.

Besides creating a beautiful picture, the manifestation of lights on satellite "maps" like this one communicate information about the lifestyle of people across the globe. They chart urbanization. They reveal nighttime electricity consumption. And they are sometimes used to indicate economic development and other social factors in various countries and regions. Researchers call this "luminosity data." [1]

1. geology.com/articles/satellite-photo-earth-at-night.shtml; geology.com/press-release/world-at-night/; http://www.flickr.com/photos/wwworks/2712986388/.

Lights Shining in the Darkness

[Jesus said,] *You are the light of the world. A city that is set on a hill cannot be hidden....Let your light so shine before men, that they may see your good works and glorify your Father in heaven.*

(Matthew 5:14, 16)

Jesus described His followers as having "spiritual luminosity." What if we were able to "map" the radiance of God's light emitted from believers throughout the earth, so that the degree of luminosity indicated people's spiritual condition and activity for God? We would be able to detect...

+ the nations or regions where God's light is shining the brightest on earth today.

+ how far and to what degree we have spread the kingdom of God throughout the earth.

The combined "spiritual luminosity data" of Christians all over the world would tell us to what extent we are shining *"as lights in the world"* (Philippians 2:15). If we are truly letting our light shine, we should see "patches" of brilliant spiritual light in our cities, states, regions, and nations. Believers joining together in unity as "shining cities" can dispel the spiritual darkness wherever they live, work, and travel.

Shining from the Inside Out

On the NASA satellite map, the white dots of light are clearly visible. However, we cannot see the electricity that produced those lights because it worked unseen within numerous generators.

In a similar way, our spiritual light is "generated" from within us. When we are born again (see John 3:1–21), God comes to dwell inside us through the Holy Spirit, and the kingdom is established within us. Jesus said, *"The kingdom of God does not come with observation; nor will they say, 'See here!' or 'See there!' For indeed, **the kingdom of God is within you**"* (Luke 17:20–21).

If no electricity were generated or used on the earth, our physical world would be much darker at night. When there is a major electrical blackout in cities or regions, the brightness on satellite pictures is diminished. Likewise, if the light of God within us is diminished, for various reasons, we will emit a weak spiritual light, and God's kingdom will not advance in our lives—or in the world.

Yet when the kingdom of God is flowing in us and through us by the supernatural power of the Holy Spirit, it is like a great generator. This happens when we learn how God's kingdom functions and then act on its principles. Then we will shine! We will give glory to God as we light the way for others to receive the kingdom of God in their own lives, producing miracles and transformation.

---

*The kingdom of God must first come within us,
so that it may be manifested externally.*

I was ministering recently at a meeting in Dallas where many miracles and healings took place under God's anointing. Pastor Damion of Phoenix, Arizona, was in attendance. He is under the covering of a church associated with our ministry, and he testified of a miracle involving a woman in his congregation. This woman's stepfather lives in Detroit and worked for an electric company. He had been beaten with a metal pipe because he had refused to do something illegal in relation to his job. As a result, his right eye had to be removed, and the eye area was sutured shut. Pastor Damion received a phone call from the woman in his congregation asking him to please keep her stepfather in prayer.

This pastor had been teaching his congregation some of the principles in my book *How to Walk in the Supernatural Power of God*. One Sunday, he was moved by God to play a recording of one of our ministry's services, which he downloaded from our Web site. He had remembered my mentioning something about playing such recordings during a service, because the spirit of healing and deliverance would remain in the atmosphere, producing additional healings and deliverances for those with the faith to receive them. After a powerful time of worship, Pastor Damion played the recording in faith, with the expectation that something would happen. Toward the end of the recording, I prayed, and during this part of the church service, the woman felt God prompting her to place her hand over her right eye as a prophetic act to accelerate the healing of her stepfather in Detroit. She believed, and the rest of the church believed with her, that something would happen.

Thirty minutes after the church service ended, Pastor Damion received a phone call from this woman, who was screaming into the phone. He thought something bad had happened, but she said, "The eye is back!" This is what had transpired: That morning, her stepfather was still in the hospital, and when the doctor was checking his sutures, he noticed something moving under the sutured eyelid. The doctor said that couldn't be, so they opened it up, and there was an eye! This man was able to see shapes and shadows, such as a newborn baby sees before his vision is fully developed. Later, he was able to see perfectly. God had created a new eye where the other one had been removed due to the severe damage it had sustained.

The stepfather was not a believer, but after this powerful miracle, he got saved and is now on fire for God. What's more, the man's stepdaughter has been able to become pregnant, after having been told by her doctors that she couldn't have children. In addition, the man's other daughter, who lives in Detroit, was healed of Crohn's disease. This is what the kingdom of God produces as it is demonstrated on earth!

The Kingdom of Power

Many of us have heard teachers and pastors talk about the kingdom of God, yet few of us have had a deep revelation and understanding of what it is, so we miss out on its truths and benefits. We fail to understand its potency for changing lives. As you read this chapter, ask God to give you a revelation of His kingdom, with its power and characteristics. God's kingdom is a reality that we can receive and enjoy today.

God's Sovereign Government

What is God's kingdom? It is His sovereign government on earth. In the New Testament, the Greek word for "kingdom" is *basileia*, which means "royalty," "rule," "a realm" (STRONG, G932), or "sovereignty," "royal power" (NASC, G932). It comes from the root word *basileus*, which relates to the idea of a "foundation of power" (STRONG, G935).

An earthly kingdom is the influence, dominion, will, and lordship of a king or prince over a certain territory for the purpose of governing its inhabitants. There can be no king without a dominion and subjects. The kingdom from heaven—the kingdom of God—is His realm and His foundation of power on earth. It is His dominion or lordship, in which He establishes His will here and now through the redeeming work of His Son Jesus Christ in the lives of His people. God governs over territories, entities, and human beings; He rules over sickness, poverty, and oppression. He is sovereign over His spiritual enemy, Satan (the devil), who seeks to spread his own kingdom of darkness in the world to counteract God's kingdom of light.

Everything a king rules is called his dominion or territory.

God is the Supreme Ruler of the universe, including our world, and He wants us to be active participants in spreading His kingdom here. *"The earth is the Lord's, and all its fullness, the world and those who dwell therein"* (Psalm 24:1). God's invisible, eternal, and permanent kingdom impacts the visible, physical, natural world by means of men and women who are born by the spirit into His kingdom.

Wherever God's kingdom governs, it is visibly demonstrated, and every work of the enemy must depart because darkness cannot remain in the same territory occupied by His light. For example, when the kingdom of God comes upon an individual, then sickness, sin, wickedness, and any other work of hell must flee.

I was ministering at a conference at the largest church in Peru, and we held a miracle and healing service. It was there that I met seven-year-old Loretta Ismaeles, who was born without a thyroid gland. This illness causes dwarfism and other symptoms, including a lack of hair. Loretta suffered daily from weakness and sleepiness. She would tell her mother that she wanted to be healed; she didn't want to spend the rest of her life taking pills, which had been prescribed by the doctor to keep her illness under control.

This little girl attended the miracle and healing service with her mother, and as I was ministering, Loretta felt fire rise to her heart and into her mouth, and she exhaled it. She believed that she was exhaling her various infirmities. When she went to the altar to testify of her healing, I asked one of the doctors to check her throat and look for a thyroid gland. The doctor examined her and felt the gland! God had created a new thyroid within her. Loretta cried from happiness. She checked the gland herself and jumped for joy when she felt it. She was happy knowing that she was healed, could stop taking the medication, and would no longer have to deal with the daily lack of strength and other symptoms. This was a visible demonstration of the presence of God's kingdom of power in our world today, bringing His will of healing and wholeness to the earth.

The kingdom of God is the manifestation of the spiritual realm that demonstrates His lordship, dominion, and will.

The Kingdom and the Church

To understand the kingdom of God, we must realize that it is not the same thing as the church. Today, many pastors, teachers, and believers miss the clear revelation and intent of the Scriptures regarding the kingdom. Jesus spoke of the kingdom more than one hundred times, while He referred to the church only twice. Following His crucifixion and resurrection, He remained on earth for forty days before ascending to heaven. What did He do during this time? He instructed His disciples *about the kingdom.* (See Acts 1:3.) Jesus is God the Son (fully God and fully Man), and after He fulfilled His mission on earth, God the Father established Him as Ruler over the world. As it says in Revelation 11:15, "*The kingdoms of this world have become the kingdoms of our Lord and of His Christ, and He shall reign forever and ever!*" God gave Jesus all authority in heaven and on earth. (See Matthew 28:18.) He is our Lord and King, and through Him, the kingdom of God is spread throughout the world.

Consequently, the church is composed of those who have been redeemed through the death and resurrection of Jesus and who are called to expand His kingdom, just as Jesus did when He lived on the earth. The church is not the kingdom but rather the *agency* through which the kingdom is extended.

Most of us have much more knowledge about the doctrine and culture of our individual churches and denominations than we do about the kingdom of God. Yet the church must always be subject to the purposes of the kingdom. No Christian church or ministry should conduct itself according to its own agenda. In the supernatural realm, we should be governed by a kingdom mentality rather than a democratic mind-set.

The Kingdom of God and the Kingdom of Heaven

Another misunderstanding about the kingdom is the meaning of the phrase "kingdom of God" versus the phrase "kingdom of heaven." In Scripture, these phrases are often used interchangeably. Yet, even though they are similar, I believe each implies something specific. The kingdom of heaven is a spiritual location called "heaven," from which God rules and influences the earth and the entire universe. This is God's dwelling place or atmosphere where His throne, court of angels, elders, and so forth, are found. (See, for example, Revelation 4:9–10.) The Father's seat of glory and power is surrounded by *"unapproachable light"* (1 Timothy 6:16).

The kingdom of heaven is the dominion of God.

The kingdom of heaven is invisible, but it impacts the visible world as the kingdom of God. Everything that takes place on earth to advance the kingdom must first be revealed, declared, and decreed in heaven. The kingdom of God extends the dominion and authority of the King to the world. It is the realm where His will is obeyed, producing a heaven on earth.

We can say that the kingdom of God is the atmosphere produced by our relationship of obedience and submission to Him. The spiritual and emotional atmosphere of any given place is the result of relationships. For example, when good relationships exist among the members of a household, a positive atmosphere can be perceived in their home. We experience something similar wherever the will of God is obeyed and His kingdom takes dominion over a territory, place, or person. If we have a right relationship with our heavenly Father, we will experience the spiritual atmosphere of heaven on earth, and we can convey that atmosphere to those around us.

In this book, our focus is the kingdom of God—how God wants believers, as the church, to continue to expand His reign on earth through our authority in King Jesus and our power in the Holy Spirit.

The kingdom of God is His will and dominion exercised on earth as it is in heaven.

Qualities of the Kingdom of God

Let us explore several distinguishing qualities of the kingdom of God so that we may act on them as we advance His kingdom on earth.

1. It Is a Supernatural Kingdom

Jesus said, "My kingdom is not of this world." (John 18:36 NIV)

God's kingdom is not physical, nor does it have an earthly capital, like Rome was the capital of the Roman Empire. It is a supernatural, or spiritual, kingdom. Its capital is in heaven, from which God reigns.

The capital of God's kingdom is in heaven.

Because the kingdom of God is not of this world, it doesn't arrive through natural means. We will not see a physical building, army, or anything of that sort descend from heaven. As we have noted, God's kingdom is within you and me—and it is among us and our other brothers and sisters in Christ—wherever we go. It is the life of God exercising its influence on earth as the power of the Holy Spirit works through our humanity.

The kingdom reveals itself visibly through miracles and signs of God's unconditional love. For example, when a person is delivered from demonic influences, we see physical evidence of the arrival of the kingdom of God and its collision with the kingdom of Satan; there are often symptoms such as convulsions as the latter is cast out of the individual's life. Moreover, the day will come when the kingdom of God will arrive visibly for every eye on earth to see when Jesus returns physically to establish His government on earth. (See, for example, Revelation 1:7; 1 Thessalonians 4:16–17.)

2. It Is a Kingdom of Power, Not Just Words

> *For the kingdom of God is not in word but in power.*
>
> (1 Corinthians 4:20)

The kingdom of God was never meant to be proclaimed with words alone, in an abstract way. Neither was it to be communicated as something that will come only in the future. It was always meant to be announced with power, and in the present—in the now. The apostle Paul wrote, *"For our gospel did not come to you in word only, but also in power, and in the Holy Spirit and in much assurance"* (1 Thessalonians 1:5). Many preachers talk about the kingdom, but they have no accompanying demonstration of what they teach. This shows they lack revelation of the true qualities of God's kingdom. It is easy to preach something that cannot be proven because, that way, we don't put our reputations at risk. But each time the kingdom is preached, there must be a visible demonstration of God's power to heal the sick, deliver the captives and the oppressed, and save the lost. Consider Jesus' ministry:

> *And Jesus went about all Galilee, teaching in their synagogues, preaching the gospel of the kingdom, and healing all kinds of sickness and all kinds of disease among the people.* (Matthew 4:23)

Each time the kingdom is preached,
it must be manifested with a visible act of power.

You may know that the meaning of the word *gospel* is "good news." So, what should happen when we proclaim the *"gospel of the kingdom"*? The same good things that happened when Jesus preached. He demonstrated the power of the kingdom with miracles, signs, healings, and the casting out of demons. Each time He announced the good news of the kingdom, these five entities, which have plagued humanity since the fall of man, could not remain:

+ Sickness
+ Sin
+ Demons
+ Poverty
+ Death

Sickness, sin, demons, poverty, and death all proceed from Satan's kingdom; therefore, each time Jesus confronted them with the superiority of God's kingdom, they experienced total defeat. Unfortunately, there are many theologians and preachers today who have never witnessed healing or the casting out of demons because they have only a mental knowledge of the kingdom, not an experiential knowledge of it. They have not witnessed God's power manifesting in visible ways.

At a miracle crusade at our church, I preached about the power of God and then ministered that power to others in a demonstrable way. Among those in attendance at the meeting was a woman named Madeline who was pregnant and had received a bad diagnosis concerning her baby. When she had gone for her first sonogram, the medical personnel had detected that her baby was missing its right kidney. Madeline was sad but began to pray for a miracle. The following month, she had another sonogram, and the doctors confirmed that the baby's right kidney had not formed. But Madeline did not give up. She continued to fight the good fight of faith.

In the midst of this distressing situation, she attended the healing crusade, believing for a creative miracle. I gave an altar call for everyone who needed a creative miracle, and Madeline was one of the first to respond. I declared the word, and she took hold of it, crying and believing that God had done the miracle. During the ninth month of her pregnancy, she went to have her last sonogram, and the doctor said he did not understand what had happened. What had not existed before was there now: the baby's right kidney had appeared! To the glory of God, after the birth, Madeline joyfully and gratefully testified that her daughter was healthy and had all of her organs. The supernatural power of the kingdom had performed a creative miracle that medical science was unable to produce.

The revelation of the message of the kingdom we proclaim can be proven by the visible manifestation of God's power, dominion, and authority.

---

3. It Is an Unshakable Kingdom

We are receiving a kingdom which cannot be shaken.

(Hebrews 12:28)

Our world is being shaken in many ways. The skies, the seas, the ground, the global economy, world leaders and governments, individual churches, denominations, and ministries are all being shaken. There is only one secure place for us to be: in the kingdom of God. If we are under its covering and authority, we cannot be shaken. Sickness will not be able to defeat us, poverty will not have lordship over us, economic crises will not rob us of our peace or our daily bread, moral corruption will not take hold of our children, and natural disasters will not devastate us. We will prevail over all things because of the covering, or protection, of God's unshakable kingdom.

> *Therefore whoever hears these sayings of Mine, and does them, I will liken him to a wise man who built his house on the rock: and the rain descended, the floods came, and the winds blew and beat on that house; and it did not fall, for it was founded on the rock.*
>
> (Matthew 7:24–25)

4. It Is a Kingdom Whose Reality Is Experienced Here and Now

Repent, for the kingdom of heaven is at hand. (Matthew 4:17)

When Jesus preached about the kingdom, He referred to it mainly in the here and now, saying that it *"is at hand,"* or *"has come upon you"* (Matthew 12:28), or *"has arrived among you"* (verse 28 NLT). He taught relatively little about the kingdom as the eternal future. He expressed the concept as a present reality, where there is no past or future—just an eternal now. Jesus said that the kingdom was *"at hand"* because heaven was on earth. He didn't tell people to wait for death to enjoy the kingdom in heaven; His message was that the kingdom had arrived and could be received.

Some people think that the kingdom of God consists only in the forgiveness of sins and a future in heaven. It is much more! Such people have repented enough to be forgiven and saved, but they haven't repented to the point where they can see the kingdom manifested abundantly in their lives. Full repentance, as we will see shortly, means a complete change of mindset. Forgiveness is just an entryway into a kingdom that is infinite, eternal, and of unlimited power.

Likewise, throughout history, the church as a whole has limited itself because it has often regarded the kingdom as either a past event or a future reality, without having a revelation of its present existence. It has frequently seen eternity as something we will experience after we die or after Jesus returns, when, in actuality, eternity always exists in the now. In the eternal now, eternity is past, present, and future put together. The church has also often shied away from supernatural manifestations, for reasons that we will address in a later chapter.

For now, it is important to know that the kingdom of God on earth was established by Jesus, and, when He returned to heaven, He delegated authority to the church to continue expanding the kingdom in the here and now, in the "present" of each succeeding generation of believers. The kingdom brings everything each human being needs, such as salvation, healing, deliverance, prosperity, and purpose. It is to be experienced today, and it is to be applied to each circumstance we are undergoing at this moment.

The kingdom of God is an eternal reality that can affect any present situation, here and now.

Throughout the New Testament, we read of the kingdom being brought to earth. Therefore, when I am ministering and meet a person suffering from cancer, I remember that cancer does not exist in heaven. I pray for that person, and the cancer leaves. I don't have to wait for Jesus to return to either receive healing or minister healing, because I am a carrier of God's kingdom who visibly manifests His power here and now.

It is the same for all of the leaders in my ministry. While my wife, Ana, was ministering to thousands of people at a conference in Argentina, she met a woman named Alejandra who had arrived wearing a scarf to hide her baldness. Alejandra testified that she had undergone three operations in the past twelve months to cure the breast cancer that threatened her life. Her left breast had been removed, and she was undergoing chemotherapy, which had caused the loss of her hair. She had discovered a lump on her breast the size of an egg while she was breastfeeding her newborn daughter, and the doctors had confirmed that it was cancer. "When I heard the news," Alejandra said, "all I knew to do was to hold on tight to God and say, 'Lord, I give You my life.' I was expecting my miracle, so I never let go." That was her faith affirmation.

During the conference, God's presence was very strong. While Pastor Ana walked up and down the aisles, she laid hands on Alejandra's shoulder and declared her healed. "I didn't feel anything at that moment," Alejandra said, "but when I returned to the doctor for further testing, everyone was surprised to discover that the cancer had disappeared!" But the miracle doesn't end there. After the three operations, her left breast looked like a tiny mass the size of a raisin. Everything down to the bone had been removed, including muscle tissue. She was unable to lift her left arm or do anything else with it because it would swell due to the lack of ligaments. Although she was grateful to the Lord for her healing from cancer, she was still unhappy. She did not want to see her body as it was. Her husband, Juan, continued the story by telling us, "I said to God, 'This is not the God I know! I want a new breast for my wife!' Then I made a covenant, believing He would do it. One morning, she said to me, 'Look!' When I looked, her breasts were the same! The only visible mark was a small scar caused by the surgery. God created a new breast! This is a true miracle of God and total restoration. The Lord reconstructed her breast; this is something that is not often seen!" The visible manifestation of the power of God is in the "now," and Alejandra is complete, as if cancer had never invaded her body.

The kingdom of God has come, is coming, and will come.

The Character of the Kingdom of God

How can we recognize that God's kingdom has truly arrived in our midst? We can tell by experiencing, and living according to, the character of His kingdom.

For the kingdom of God is not eating and drinking, but righteousness and peace and joy in the Holy Spirit. (Romans 14:17)

The kingdom of God doesn't consist in material things or mere words but in three main characteristics—righteousness, peace, and joy—which are found only in the Holy Spirit.

1. Righteousness

Living in righteousness means several things: (1) Being in good standing with God by the forgiveness and redemption we receive through Christ's death and resurrection. (2) Acting in the same ways that God acts, as it says in Micah 6:8: *"What does the LORD require of you but to do justly, to love mercy, and to walk humbly with your God?"* (3) Submitting yourself to be accountable to God for your thoughts, words, and actions, and allowing Him to correct you and to guide you in *"paths of righteousness for His name's sake"* (Psalm 23:3).

There is no righteousness outside of God's kingdom, only rebellion.

To be within the kingdom of God, we must be righteous, regardless of which denomination we are affiliated with or what we might call ourselves. We can belong to a church that is Pentecostal, Baptist, Methodist, or something else, but if we have not submitted to the government of God, then we are rebels and unrighteous. Only those who are within the kingdom can know righteousness; outside of it, Satan rules us. The good news is that everyone who repents can receive the righteousness that comes through Jesus Christ, in which we can enter the kingdom of God and have true, eternal life.

2. Peace

And the government will be upon His shoulder. And His name will be called Wonderful...Prince of Peace. Of the increase of His government and peace there will be no end. (Isaiah 9:6–7)

Isaiah the prophet proclaimed an essential sign of the Messiah (Jesus Christ) and the essence of the good news He would bring to earth: the *government* would be upon His shoulders. He would take over the governance of human beings, all of whom have been lost under their own governance since humanity first rebelled against God. We will explore this topic in more detail in the next chapter. The government of King Jesus brings true and lasting peace to all who submit to it.

> ### *Peace is possible only when one lives under submission to the kingdom, or government, of Jesus Christ.*

The Hebrew word for "peace" is *shalom*, which can mean "completeness," "soundness," (NASC, H7965), and "safe," with connotations of being "well" and "happy" and of "health" and "prosperity" (STRONG, H7965). Peace and other life-giving benefits come as a result of our having been justified by Jesus Christ.

One measure of the success of a government is the peace enjoyed by its citizens. And true peace on earth comes from the kingdom of God. Therefore, it is in vain that nations seek peace outside His kingdom.

> *Has not the LORD Almighty determined that the people's labor is only fuel for the fire, that the nations exhaust themselves for nothing? For the earth will be filled with the knowledge of the glory of the LORD, as the waters cover the sea.* (Habakkuk 2:13–14 NIV)

History has shown that peace cannot come in the absence of a righteous government; thus, the words *righteousness* and *peace* will always be related; one cannot exist without the other. We cannot experience true peace without having righteousness. Jesus wants to reign over the human race to bring it both righteousness and peace.

> *The work of righteousness will be peace, and the effect of righteousness, quietness and assurance forever.* (Isaiah 32:17)

Rebels do not enjoy peace! We can be "religious" and still have a rebellious nature. Trying to keep all the rules or practicing religious rituals does not bring righteousness. In Luke 15, in the parable of the prodigal son, the older brother stayed home and kept every one of his father's rules. However, in his heart, he was as rebellious as his wayward brother. The father's welcoming celebration for the younger brother, who had repented, exposed the condition of the older brother's heart. (See verses 25–32.) Peace is one of the primary needs of all human beings, and we can understand why people feel uneasy, unhappy, and miserable when they are not in relationship with God and are leading lives that are contrary to His kingdom. Receiving peace with God through Jesus Christ brings an end to our rebellion and misery.

> *"Peace, peace to him who is far off and to him who is near," says the Lord, "and I will heal him. But the wicked are like the troubled sea, when it cannot rest, whose waters cast up mire and dirt. There is no peace," says my God, "for the wicked."* (Isaiah 57:19–21)

Why are the oceans always "uneasy," choppy, and in constant movement? Scientists have discovered that the seas continually react to various forces. The gravitational influences of the moon and the sun produce high and low tides. Currents also contribute to the movement of the water. Tides cause the water to move up and down, while currents move the water back and forth.[2] The state of an individual who is separated from God is an uneasy restlessness, similar to the churning waters of the ocean. He is unable to find peace and never feels satisfied.

Has the world ever been as uneasy as it is today? Look around and observe how people determinedly and even obsessively seek pleasure. What produces this relentless pursuit if not uneasiness, dissatisfaction, and lack of peace? Often, people say things like "Let's take our minds off our problems and just go do something!" "I can't stand being home by myself," or "I feel like I'm going crazy." Some people try to find relief from their uneasiness by constantly going to parties or engaging in other pleasure-producing practices. They have a constant desire to see or experience something new and fresh. The modern term for this behavior is "escapism." People want to escape reality. Because they are agitated, they seek ways to "feel something good" or situations in which they can let go of what troubles them. They

2. http://oceanservice.noaa.gov/navigation/tidesandcurrents/.

try to stimulate themselves through amusement, adventures, and strong emotions. These endeavors express the fundamental uneasiness that is produced by the negative spiritual, emotional, and physical forces at work in their lives.

The apostle James wrote that the person who doubts the reality of God and His truth is *"like a wave of the sea driven and tossed by the wind.…He is a double-minded man, unstable in all his ways"* (James 1:6, 8). Many people feel pulled between good and evil, between knowing that they should do what is right but liking what is bad and destructive. Yet everyone has a need for peace, and we will never feel satisfied without the peace of God. As I said earlier, the only way to find peace is to submit to God's government and receive His righteousness through Jesus Christ. When righteousness enters our hearts, its produces eternal peace, rest, and security.

3. Joy

Do not sorrow, for the joy of the LORD *is your strength.*

(Nehemiah 8:10)

The kingdom of God also brings us joy! There is a difference between happiness and joy: happiness belongs to the realm of the soul, while joy belongs to the realm of the spirit.

Happiness is connected with external circumstances. Depending on the nature of those circumstances, we feel happy or sad. Many people believe that having a nice car, a new house, and a high-paying job with enough money coming in to cover all their bills will bring them happiness. If they achieve these things, they are temporarily happy. However, the state of various life circumstances—finances, relationships, health, and so forth—often changes, which means that their happiness is constantly in jeopardy.

In contrast, joy is always related to a stable source that never changes, does not vary, and is not affected by external forces. This source is God and His unshakable kingdom. Regardless of the circumstances we might be experiencing, His joy is our strength. We simply have to make sure we keep ourselves under submission to King Jesus and His kingdom; then, we will have peace and joy in the Spirit of God.

4. The Holy Spirit

The Holy Spirit is the Administrator and Executor of the kingdom. He is the only One who can reveal the things of the kingdom and of its King. (See, for example, 1 Corinthians 2:11–12.) When we receive the Holy Spirit, we become carriers of the kingdom of God, which is revealed in and through us by the Spirit.

Without the Holy Spirit, there is no kingdom or government of God.

The Holy Spirit is always at work in the lives of God's people who yield themselves to Him. He produces great spiritual activity, manifesting miracles, healings, signs, and wonders. He generates the supernatural both within the church and in the kingdom at large. If the Holy Spirit were to be removed from our midst, we would be left with only a theoretical, theological, and historical kingdom without power, one that would be unable to produce change or transformation in people. Righteousness, peace, and joy are possible only where the Holy Spirit operates.

The church deceives itself when it talks about the kingdom of God and Christianity but fails to allow the supernatural power of God to be revealed in people's lives. How is it possible for us to preach the kingdom of God while at the same time ignoring, rejecting, and criticizing the things of the Spirit? How can we teach on the kingdom without mentioning being filled with the Holy Spirit? How can we proclaim a kingdom of power without producing healings, miracles, signs, and wonders as visible proof? How can we welcome the kingdom and not give the Holy Spirit the freedom to move among us?

We must seek to manifest the kingdom, in all its fullness, in our own lives and in our world. During a miracle crusade in South America, I met Efraín Sigala. He had spent twenty years of his life connected to an oxygen tank, and he was tired of living that way. He couldn't work (he had been a pastor), and he was hardly able to walk, so that he had been declared handicapped. Every day, he felt faint. He would pray to God for strength to keep going.

Though Efraín was a Christian, he didn't know the supernatural power of God, and he didn't know about my ministry. However, some of his friends, who were also pastors, told him how the Spirit of God moves during my services, and they paid for an entry ticket so he could attend our meetings. Full of expectancy, Efraín declared that he would return home totally healed. During the time of ministry, while I prayed for a baby and a woman who was having difficulty breathing, Efraín said to his wife, "The time has come." He made his way to the altar and shared his story. He explained that he had pulmonary fibrosis, which had caused inflammation and scar tissue in the pulmonary walls, damaging his vocal cords. He had a hard time breathing, and his body was functioning at a low capacity. Also, a valve in his heart was blocked, and the doctors suspected that he had cancer.

I prayed for him and, in the name of Jesus, I cursed the sickness and decreed the spirit of life and the health of heaven upon his body. Suddenly, he began to tremble under the power of the Holy Spirit. When he stopped shaking, his eyes shone brightly. As an act of faith, he removed his oxygen mask and breathed in deeply several times. Immediately, he started to move and walk without a problem. He was healed! He walked the entire platform and even ran across it. His skin had been yellowish before the miracle, but now it had a healthy pink glow. Efraín was the epitome of happiness! His lungs were healed, and he has not needed the oxygen tank since. He also regained full use of his limbs. This is true Christianity—the power of God visibly manifested through us, His children.

The supernatural demonstration of the kingdom comes only by the Holy Spirit, not by theology or doctrine.

Praying for the Kingdom to Come

Your kingdom come. Your will be done on earth as it is in heaven.
(Matthew 6:10)

The Lord's Prayer, which Jesus taught His disciples, deals with worshipping God the Father, having communion with Him, and bringing

His kingdom to earth. Note that the first request, after *"Hallowed be Your name"* (Matthew 6:9), is *"Your kingdom come."* God's kingdom should be our top priority.

Furthermore, this prayer confirms where the kingdom should manifest—*"on earth."* Again, many Christians believe that the main purpose of the kingdom is to take them to heaven; instead, it is clear that the purpose of the kingdom is to bring heaven to earth! We must understand that our King's will, dominion, and lordship must be carried out on the earth here and now, the same way they are carried out in heaven.

All other prayers are secondary to this purpose, as well as all of our personal needs, problems, trials, and difficulties. After we have prayed for God's will to be done on earth as it is in heaven, then we can pray for our *"daily bread"* (Matthew 6:11). However, most Christians place their problems and personal needs ahead of the kingdom of God. They don't realize that this is precisely the reason why their needs are not being met: their priorities are not in order. (See Matthew 6:31–33.)

When the kingdom is a priority in our lives—when we worship God, serve others, heal the sick, testify of Jesus, deliver the oppressed, give offerings, and take the gospel wherever we go—our needs will be supplied. We should pay close attention to the way this portion of the Lord's Prayer is expressed: *"Your kingdom come. Your will be done on earth as it is in heaven."* These statements do not come across to me as passive requests but as assertive ones. Later on, Jesus said, *"From the days of John the Baptist until now, the kingdom of heaven has been forcefully advancing* ["suffers violence" NKJV], *and forceful men lay hold of it"* (Matthew 11:12 NIV). We are to "seize" what is in heaven and bring it to earth. As we pray, we pull to earth whatever is in heaven: health, deliverance, peace, joy, forgiveness, miracles, healing, prosperity, and so much more! When we depend on the realm of God, we can visibly bring forth whatever is needed.

Heaven is the pattern, or model, that we need to bring to our environment. When we find people with arthritis, diabetes, cancer, or any other sickness, we must remember that sickness does not exist in heaven, and we must "pull" the kingdom of heaven to earth, so that its power can manifest and people can be healed and set free in the name of Jesus.

The Lord's Prayer deals with worshipping God the Father, having communion with Him, and bringing His kingdom to earth.

How to Enter the Kingdom of God

To this point, we have learned what God's kingdom is, where it is found, and its main qualities and characteristics. Now, we will discover how to fully enter into it. Salvation through the work of Jesus at the cross is part of God's provision, but there is also something we must personally do.

1. Be Born Again

Jesus answered, "Most assuredly, I say to you, unless one is born of water and the Spirit, he cannot enter the kingdom of God."   (John 3:5)

The kingdom of God is entered by spiritual birth, and this *"new birth"* (1 Peter 1:3 NIV) gives us citizenship in it. We cannot enter the kingdom by being religious; by belonging to a denomination, ministry, or sect; by being affiliated with a particular philosophy; by knowing the theology of salvation through the cross; or by any other means. A total separation from the curse of sin must take place; the umbilical cord of iniquity that connects us to sin and the rebellious nature must be cut. The kingdom is not a mere "remedy." It involves becoming a new creation. (See 2 Corinthians 5:17.)

There is no entry into the kingdom of God except by the new birth.

2. Repent

Now after John [the Baptist] was put in prison, Jesus came to Galilee, preaching the gospel of the kingdom of God, and saying, "The time is fulfilled, and the kingdom of God is at hand. Repent, and believe in the gospel."   (Mark 1:14–15)

John the Baptist prepared the way for Jesus' coming by calling the people to repentance. Jesus couldn't present Himself to the Israelites as the

Messiah while the people's hearts were not ready to repent—this being the first condition or requirement for receiving Him.

In the above passage, the word *"preaching"* comes from a Greek word meaning "to herald (as a public crier), especially divine truth"; subsequently, it can mean "to preach," "to proclaim," or "to publish" (STRONG, G2784). Jesus' ministry continued where John the Baptist's ended. There was no variation in the message they proclaimed; both called people to repentance. Why? Because the kingdom of God had arrived, and, again, the people's hearts had to be ready to receive it. Being born again takes place only by repentance.

Repentance is the unalterable condition for preparing to receive the kingdom and for being born into the kingdom.

In the economy of the kingdom, we must humble ourselves before we are exalted, we must give in order to receive, we must serve in order to be great, and we must die in order to live. (See, for example, Matthew 23:12; Luke 6:38; Matthew 20:26; John 11:25.) Accordingly, we must die to our own "government"—to our selfish desires, opinions, and personal "vote"— surrendering ourselves to God, so that we may truly live in Him and in His kingdom.

What Should We Repent of, and Why?

All we like sheep have gone astray; we have turned, every one, to his own way; and the LORD has laid on Him [Jesus] the iniquity of us all.   (Isaiah 53:6)

As we will see in chapter 2, every problem and difficulty we face began when the first human beings departed from God's government and tried to live according to their own ways. God called this departure "iniquity," "sin," and "rebellion." All human beings have inherited this nature of iniquity, sin, and rebellion. The only solution for our problems is to reenter the kingdom. Yet there is so much rebellion today that many people do not even want to hear the word *government* in relation to God. They don't view the arrival of the kingdom of God as good news because they don't want to repent, or change their wrong thoughts and ways.

Iniquity is equivalent to rebellion and all of its consequences.

True repentance involves a new frame of mind that reflects a change in attitude. This change is evidence of the work of the Holy Spirit upon a person's heart, which eventually results in a new way of life for that person. Repentance is not an emotion, although it may also be expressed through the emotions. Rather, when we realize our true, bankrupt spiritual condition before God and the rebellious nature that has led us away from Him, repentance is the decision we make to turn 180 degrees and walk in the opposite direction—toward Him. Repentance also indicates our decision not to rule ourselves any longer but to be ruled by God, according to His government. Thus, repentance causes sin to die. Although repentance is required for entering the kingdom, we must also constantly seek to renew our thoughts and ways in accordance with God's thoughts and ways and daily submit our lives to Him, so that we will continue to walk in the right direction.

Every human being is a rebel by nature,
expressing that rebellion through thought, choice, and deed.

You might not be a thief, a liar, an adulterer, a killer, or a perpetual evildoer, but the instant you entered this world, you did so with a rebellious nature; you were born in iniquity. (See Psalm 51:5.) The Bible says *"all have sinned and fall short of the glory of God"* (Romans 3:23). In one sense, committing iniquity is inevitable for us, because iniquity comes through our bloodline. However, God has also given us a conscience and the ability to reason, which help show us right from wrong. More than that, He offers us His own Holy Spirit to live within us and enable us to obey Him. We can choose to live in iniquity, or we can repent and enter the kingdom of life. We have to come to our senses by recognizing the truth about ourselves and our sinful lifestyle. Then, we must turn around and go the other way.

"Come now, and let us reason together," says the Lord, *"though your sins are like scarlet, they shall be as white as snow; though they are red*

*like crimson, they shall be as wool. If you are willing and obedient, you
shall eat the good of the land."* (Isaiah 1:18–19)

What Does It Mean to Repent Wholeheartedly?

To repent wholeheartedly means to recognize that we have lived independently of God. Basically, this means that we have ruled ourselves and gratified our sinful nature by living as we pleased; by doing, thinking, and feeling what we wanted, as well as by prioritizing our own desires and standards for personal gain and satisfaction. We became our own authority, deciding what career path to follow, what business to start, where to live, whom to marry, and so forth, without consulting God. This is why many of us go from failure to failure, wondering why we were born and if there is any meaning to life. We wonder why we are depressed or why so many young people choose suicide, believing it will end the terrible void in their lives. The "freedom" to live as we want to, which we fight so hard to defend, has left us without purpose in life.

For our repentance to be genuine, we must place ourselves, from this day forward, under God's authority and government, allowing Him to have full reign in our lives. Every decision we make must be based on kingdom principles and commandments. Because we now live to please the King, we will not do anything without His consent, authority, and guidance. This is true repentance!

---

*The evidence of repentance is change, and change is not change
until there is genuine transformation.*

Many people in the church today have never truly repented. Their condition is evident by their constant rebelliousness and their bouts of anger, depression, selfishness, and so forth. They lack peace and cannot fully receive the righteousness that God has provided for them in Christ. The power of the kingdom is available to those who have fully repented and renounced their rebellion against God. Then, and only then, can they claim His promises of salvation, healing, deliverance, righteousness, peace, joy, and prosperity. We must also realize that our freedom and supernatural provision in Christ are not an excuse for us to live as we wish. Rather, they enable us to enjoy the benefits of the kingdom at the same time as we minister them to others.

In my more than twenty years of experience in dealing with people in ministry, I have come to the conclusion that most people's problems are caused by a lack of wholehearted repentance. When people are led to repent fully, many of their problems cease to exist, because an individual who repents no longer resists God. Instead, he says, "Lord, here I am. I will do whatever You ask me to do." Whenever we teach people about God's kingdom but neglect to tell them about obedience, submission, and being under His government, we have failed to communicate the essence of the kingdom.

Whether you are a Christian or not, and whether you attend church or not, if you identify with this rebellious lifestyle of separation from God and see yourself as lost and directionless, not knowing the purpose for which you were born; if you feel you want to end it all because life seems too much for you; if you are sick and medical treatment has not brought relief or healing—it is time for you to experience the kingdom of God, here and now, with the manifestations of His power. Repent of your past lifestyle; renounce sin, iniquity, and rebellion against God; and return to Him. He wants His kingdom to manifest in you. He wants His realm to spread to others through you, bringing righteousness, peace, and joy in the Holy Spirit. If you desire to be reconciled to God and are willing to submit to His government, you can pray this prayer of repentance and receive forgiveness so that you may enter into the kingdom of God in all its fullness:

> Heavenly Father, I recognize that I am a sinner, and I repent of my lifestyle, which is contrary to You and Your kingdom. I turn away from all my sins and rebellion, and I desire to follow You wholeheartedly. With my mouth I confess that Jesus is the Son of God, and I believe in my heart that You, Father, raised Him from the dead. In the name of Jesus, I am saved. Let Your kingdom manifest in my life. Use me to spread Your kingdom wherever I go. Amen!

The Priority of Seeking the Kingdom

Seek first the kingdom of God and His righteousness, and all these things shall be added to you. (Matthew 6:33)

We have learned that there is no righteousness or peace outside of God's kingdom, because rebellion produces only chaos and destruction. The only way to be righteous is to receive the righteousness of Jesus by faith and to be in submission to the kingdom of God. Every need that arises will be supplied if our priorities are in order. When I focus on and align myself with the priorities of the kingdom, God's order comes into my life, and His promises to supply me with food, drink, clothing, a bed to sleep in, a roof over my head, money, and more are activated. I have proven this principle in my own life and ministry for many years.

We are to manifest, or bring forth, the reality of God's will, lordship, and dominion to earth wherever we encounter those who are experiencing hard times. Sickness, oppression, poverty, sadness, divorce, depression, crimes, wickedness, and murders do not exist in heaven. To end or prevent such things in the life of a person, family, church, city, or nation is to establish the kingdom of God on earth. When something is not aligned with God's will, depending on what it is, we must make it a priority either to realign it or to remove it.

I practice kingdom living in my daily life, but I am not the only one! I am constantly training and equipping disciples to take the kingdom everywhere they go. In our family and ministry, we see thousands of people receive salvation, deliverance, and restoration through my wife and through our ministers, elders, deacons, mentors, and House of Peace (the church's home fellowship ministry) leaders, as well as through the pastors under our spiritual covering and our disciples around the world. In the name of Jesus, they deliver people from homosexuality, lesbianism, bestiality, pornography, masturbation, incest, theft, abandonment, witchcraft, and addictions, such as those to alcohol, prescription medications, and illegal drugs.

We have seen Jesus heal people of cancer, AIDS, hepatitis, arthritis, diabetes, lupus, bipolar disorders, schizophrenia, and much more. Many people have experienced creative miracles, such as receiving new organs where they were missing them, and the restoration of cleft palates. Why is this happening? Because we believe that heaven is a reality that can be lived here and now.

Two of my spiritual children are pastors of a church in Spain, and they do the same supernatural works that I do. A young lady named Gabriela Asencio, who is now a bank consultant and humanities student, visited their congregation. She told them she was living in "hell" due to anorexia, bulimia, a bipolar condition, and severe depression. In the past, she would often hurt herself and had tried several times to commit suicide, and she also had been in a psychiatric ward several times. The doctors told her that she would never get better and would have to take prescription medication for the rest of her life. This medicine made her drowsy and sometimes even caused her to lose consciousness. When she woke up, she would again lose control.

These pastors in Spain ministered inner healing and deliverance to Gabriela, and the power of God delivered her! Now, she is completely healed and full of the Holy Spirit. She testified, "My life revolved around my sickness. I couldn't enjoy anything and had no dreams, plans, or projects. I felt alone and would spend days planning how to hurt and kill myself. I hated my family. I would often not eat because I felt guilty, and if I ate, I couldn't control my desire to vomit. During the worst times of anorexia and bulimia, I couldn't buy clothes for myself or even look at myself in the mirror, not even to clean myself. I couldn't study, relate to people, or forgive or love anyone." Now, Gabriela studies, works, serves, and loves the Lord and other people. She is a mentor who ministers deliverance and affirms others.

If you decide to receive the revelation in this book and dare to make the establishment of the kingdom of God your priority, in the name of Jesus, you will see miracles begin to take place. The invisible kingdom will manifest in the visible realm, bringing transformation to people's lives.

I encourage you to make this decision and to manifest the kingdom everywhere you go. Where there is spiritual darkness, remove it; where there is sickness, cast out the spirit of infirmity. The kingdom of power is within you. The only thing you need to do is to demonstrate it here and now!

2

The Original Mandate of Dominion

God's plan of expanding His kingdom over the earth through human beings did not begin with our redemption in Jesus. It is not just a response to the fall of mankind. It is an eternal purpose, and God's plan has been in effect since before the beginning of creation.

In this chapter, we will learn about the dominion God gave the first human beings, Adam and Eve, and about His intentions for the earth. We will explore how Satan entered Eden to tempt Adam and Eve, and how they fell from their dominion. We will see how Jesus' sacrifice on the cross restored our relationship with our heavenly Father and enables us to fulfill our dominion purpose. And we will be challenged to change our mind-set to avoid the "pull back" or "retraction" mentality, so that we may receive an expansion mentality. No longer do we need to be dominated and controlled by circumstances, problems, and Satan. We can live a victorious life and once again exercise the dominion that Adam and Eve lost.

There is much evidence of the advancement of God's kingdom today. Consider the story of Paulo DaSilva, one of my spiritual sons. Although he was raised in a Christian home in Brazil, by the age of sixteen, Paulo had lost his way. He spent two years involved with drugs, lies, and violence until he had a personal experience with God and returned to church. He studied theology, became a pastor, and worked hard to win souls, so that his congregation grew to 450 members. But stagnancy set in, and his church stopped growing. Instead of having joy and energy, he felt sad and tired.

Then, he discovered the supernatural power of God's kingdom, and as he demonstrated it, God released growth in his church. He now has over 1,300 active members, and he baptizes hundreds of new believers every month. His ministry has also established six new churches in Brazil in less than two years. The miracles he is seeing are amazing. God is healing people of cancer, AIDS, and various other infirmities. Marriages are being restored, and people are being delivered from addictions and are experiencing financial prosperity. The youth of the church are now on fire for God, ministering the supernatural everywhere they go. And the leadership of the church is being transformed as people learn to walk in kingdom power. You can do the same!

Let us now turn to the origins of our kingdom authority and power.

Our Sovereign Creator

In the beginning God created the heavens and the earth. (Genesis 1:1)

The first verse in the Bible is brief, but it conveys deep meaning to us. The Scriptures begin by explaining the origins of mankind. They tell us where we—not God—come from. The words *"in the beginning"* refer to time, and God is not subject to time; rather, He is the One who created it. Therefore, Genesis refers to the beginning of our universe and of humanity.

The Hebrew word translated *"God"* in Genesis 1:1 is *Elohim.* It is the name for God associated with Him as the Creator.[3] God gave further revelation of Himself when Moses asked Him what His name was. He answered, *"I AM WHO I AM"* (Exodus 3:14). As one Bible dictionary says, this response "is more than a simple statement of identity....It is a declaration of divine control of all things."[4] God is self-existent. He does not depend on anyone or anything else to exist. The name *"I AM"* encompasses each aspect of God's nature, as well as all the other names by which He is called in His Word.

---

3. www.hebrew4christians.com/Names_of_G-d/Elohim/elohim.html; www.abarim-publications.com/Meaning/Elohim.html.
4. *Vine's Complete Expository Dictionary of Old and New Testament Words*, 13–14.

In Genesis, God did not introduce anyone or anything before Himself: *"In the beginning God...."* And this is the way it should be, because only God can reveal Himself and His works to us. Note that He specifically presents Himself here as the Creator, revealing one of His most important aspects, one that no one else possesses or can duplicate.

No other being, and no other reality, came before God. When nothing of our universe existed, He began to create, and the first thing He created was the heavens—our universe and atmosphere—and the earth. Remember that the seat of God's throne in heaven is the source from which all of the resources of the earth (and the rest of the universe) are found, since God's will was for heaven to come to earth and be duplicated here. After creating the physical world and the animals, God created man and woman as the crown of His creation and put them in charge of manifesting His glory on this planet.

Created in God's Image and Likeness

Then God said, "Let Us make man in Our image, according to Our likeness...." So God created man in His own image; in the image of God He created him; male and female He created them.

(Genesis 1:26–27)

The word *"image"* is translated from the Hebrew word *tselem*, which can mean "resemblance" or "representative figure" (STRONG, H6754); it also has "the sense of essential nature" (VINE, H6754). Human beings have the essential nature of God.

The word *"likeness"* is from the Hebrew word *demuwth*, which can mean "resemblance," "similitude" (STRONG, H1823), "shape; figure; form; pattern." This word "signifies the original after which a thing is patterned" (VINE, H1823). I think *The Living Bible* best captures the sense of Genesis 1:27: *"Like God did God make man."* God created man like Himself. The I AM took man from His substance. We could also say that He reproduced Himself in man. Man is meant to be on earth as God is in heaven.

To help us understand this remarkable truth, let us look at a natural example. When parents engender a child, they produce another human being whose genes come from them. The genetic makeup of my sons, Bryan and Ronald, comes from both their mother, Ana, and me. They belong to our bloodlines, and they are the continuation of the Maldonado family here on earth. In a similar way, since we were created out of the essence of God, we have His "genes." We are not "gods"; we are not divine. However, we have God's nature and characteristics. That is why we read in the Scriptures that human beings were created to be *"a little lower than God [Elohim]"* (Psalm 8:5 NASB).

Several Bible versions translate *Elohim* in the above verse as *"angels"* or *"heavenly beings,"* but I believe it's appropriate to translate the word as *"God,"* as the *New American Standard Bible* has it. God created mankind in His own class and category; He created us in His lineage.

Man is meant to be on earth as God is in heaven.

There are a number of significant ways in which we are like our Creator. Let us look at a few of them. First, *"God is Spirit"* (John 4:24), and the essence of men and women is spirit. (See, for example, Ecclesiastes 12:7.) Man is a spirit with a soul who dwells in a physical body. Second, God thinks, imagines, generates ideas, and makes plans; human beings do the same using the physical brains He has given us. Third, God expresses emotion, and human beings express emotion. Fourth, God experiences pain when He is rejected and betrayed, and He also loves, gives, and forgives; humanity does the same. Fifth, God has the ability to hate—He doesn't hate any person, but He does hate sin. People also have the ability to hate, although, because of the fallen nature, this quality has often been distorted and abused; it has been the motive for terrible conflict and destruction in the world.

No created being besides man possesses all the above qualities, because we human beings are the only ones whom God created in His image and likeness. Again, please understand I am not implying that human beings are God but that they are of the same "species" as He. Adam and Eve were the extension of God, and they were intended to make of earth what heaven is like.

Created to Have Dominion

Then God blessed them, and God said to them, "Be fruitful and multiply; fill the earth and subdue it; have dominion over the fish of the sea, over the birds of the air, and over every living thing that moves on the earth." (Genesis 1:28)

People were created to *"have dominion,"* or to rule. They were God's legal representatives to apply or enforce His kingdom laws on earth.

Some time ago, I was invited to preach in Rosario, Argentina, at a three-day event for Christian leaders. Before going, I spent several days in the presence of God, fervently seeking His face, His direction, and His guidance for that trip. When I arrived in Argentina, I spent more time seeking His face, praying in the spirit, worshipping, and interceding, until I clearly heard His voice, saying, "I am going to do something unusual." On the last day, we had scheduled an evening meeting in a bullring—with stone seating and sand—but it was raining, and the hosts thought it was better to cancel it. The rain was coming down hard, and much of the equipment and many of the lights that had been previously installed in preparation for the crusade were damaged.

The rain stopped, and everything was wet, but the people still came, and the place was filled. When it was my turn to minister, the pastor hosting the event said to me, "Hurry up, because the rain is about to start again. Just make a quick prayer for the sick." As soon as I took the microphone and started to welcome the people—over twelve thousand who had come from different parts of the country—the rain started to pour down hard. Dark clouds covered the bullring, and the rain was relentless. At that instant, the Lord guided me to say a very simple prayer: "Lord, thank You for the natural rain You give us, but we do not want natural rain. We want You to pour out spiritual rain."

Instantly, the rain stopped, the dark clouds disappeared, and the sky was clear and full of stars. It was such an incredible moment that everyone there who was seeking a miracle was deeply touched. God did an unusual sign by instantly stopping the rain! He also demonstrated a principle of dominion in which the natural world is subject to God's will through people whom He uses as His instruments. I was able to preach, minister healing and miracles, and even speak prophetic words over the country. And, that night, we witnessed incredible miracles.

Among the many testimonies we heard, I especially remember the two given by people for whom God created new kidneys. One was a young lady who had been born with only one kidney; the other was a man who'd had one of his kidneys removed. The man was totally surprised at what had happened, and he cried and thanked God for the miracle. He testified that although his kidney had been removed, he could now feel it inside. To confirm what he felt, after the crusade, he went back to the doctor, who confirmed that he did have a brand-new kidney!

Another powerful testimony came from a man who had been missing bone in his heel due to a congenital malformation. God did a creative miracle and filled in the bone in his foot. What is more, the man's daughter received the same miracle at her home, hundreds of miles away from where the crusade was taking place. In addition, a woman testified that she was healed of cardiac arrhythmia. Many more testimonies of powerful miracles were shared that night—testimonies that demonstrate God's desire to spread His kingdom throughout the earth.

Let us now learn more about the dominion that God gave to Adam and Eve.

"Be Fruitful, Multiply, and Fill the Earth"

The mandate God gave humanity began with *"Be fruitful and multiply; fill the earth…."* Here, again, we see the concepts of both our calling to expansion and our representation of God's image. Human beings were meant to continue to fill the earth with God's kingdom through succeeding generations born from Adam and Eve and their children.

I believe that dominion was the highest level of spiritual power given to man—it is a "territorial power." Therefore, the first thing Adam and Eve had to know was their territory. We cannot rule over a territory that we are ignorant of or uninformed about.

> *Then the LORD God took the man and put him in the garden of Eden to tend and keep it.*　　　　　　　　　　　　　　　　　　(Genesis 2:15)

After creating Adam, God put him into the environment of His presence. The word *"Eden"* means "pleasure" or "delight." The word *"garden"* signifies "enclosure" or a "fenced" place. It comes from a root word meaning "to hedge about"; it is something that "protects," "defends," "covers," or "surrounds." When we are in God's glory, we are surrounded by and protected by God's presence.

The garden of Eden was the base of operations, or starting point, that God gave human beings, because they were always meant to have His glory as their habitation. From this point forward, they were to expand God's rule throughout the earth, bringing that glory with them.

We should understand that even though Eden was the place from which everything began, it is mentioned few times in Scripture. It is not even mentioned again in Genesis after the first several chapters. From my research, I have concluded that Eden was not a physical location on earth; rather, it was an open door, or entryway, into heaven. It was an environment that was a "gate" or "portal" to heaven because God manifested His glory there. Adam moved wherever the glory or presence of God moved. Later, other people, including Jacob, had encounters with the presence of God, and these encounters did not occur at one stationary place on earth. In Jacob's case, while he stayed overnight in a city called Luz, he had a dream in which he saw a ladder from heaven that descended to earth. He called the place in which he had this dream "Bethel," meaning "house of God." (See Genesis 28:17.) Bethel was, in a sense, Jacob's "Eden."

The prevailing principle of the kingdom of God is permanent expansion. Likewise, expansion should be the mind-set of the church—never decrease, shrinkage, or stagnancy. For example, our ministry has sustained continual expansion during our years of service to God and His kingdom. We began with twelve people who met in the living room of my house, and our numbers increased to forty within three months. As a result, we moved to a small meeting place, but the congregation quickly grew to 150, so we found ourselves in need of a building expansion. By the time this expansion was completed, we had grown to 250. A year later, we had 650 members. Eighteen months later, in fulfillment of a prophetic word, we purchased a former Jewish synagogue, which quickly started filling to capacity each Sunday so that we had to have five services to accommodate the 5,000 people who were then attending. Kingdom dominion was an important factor in our growth, because God had given us a specific territory into which we were to expand in His name.

Only four years after founding the ministry, we received another prophetic word instructing us to purchase new land. After another four years, we began construction on an enormous church with the capacity for 6,000. Today, we have more than 20,000 active members, including the founding church and our "daughter" churches. In conjunction with our kingdom expansion, we have traveled to over 50 nations, more than once, to manifest the supernatural power of God. We also reach millions of people in many nations with the message and power of God through the media—television, radio, the Internet, and magazines. And we currently offer spiritual covering to over 100 churches around the world, including daughter churches and satellite churches that are associated with us—in addition to all the other congregations that are connected with them.

> *The prevailing principle of the kingdom of God is permanent expansion.*

All this has occurred since the establishment of our ministry less than twenty years ago. The spiritual training and equipping we have given to thousands of leaders have multiplied this expansion, because these leaders carry God's supernatural power to their cities and nations, where they, too, multiply themselves by investing in others' lives. In a similar way, our University of the Supernatural Ministry trains people in the fivefold ministry of apostles, prophets, pastors, teachers, and evangelists. (See Ephesians 4:11.) Kingdom expansion is ongoing in our ministry, and the fruit of our labors is incalculable, due to our exercise of dominion within the particular territory God has given us. Yet we are still not satisfied! We keep moving forward to accomplish our next goals, which will lead to greater levels of kingdom expansion. I tell you all of this to emphasize that the book you are reading is not about theories but rather knowledge gained from personal experience. Everything that I teach in these pages, our ministry has experienced. Thousands of people have seen and heard the manifestations of God's kingdom in our services and through our broadcasts.

"Subdue the Earth and Have Dominion"

Two additional words in Genesis 1:28 define the mandate that God gave human beings at creation: *"subdue"* and *"dominion."* The word *"subdue"* is translated from the Hebrew word *kabash*, which literally means "to tread down" and conveys such ideas as "conquer," "subjugate," "bring into bondage," "force," "keep under," and "bring into subjection" (STRONG, H3533). *Subdue* is a term often related to military power that indicates the force to overcome or bring under control.

The word *"dominion"* is translated from the Hebrew word *radah*, and this word, also, means "to tread down." It has such connotations as "subjugate," "come to have dominion," "prevail against," "reign," "bear rule," "rule over" (STRONG, H7287), and "dominate" (NASC, H7287a). Many of these senses imply compelling someone to do something by force, to place underfoot, or to enslave. We cannot talk about the meaning of the kingdom of God without including the subjugation of Satan and his works.

God invested human beings with His power and authority so they could have dominion in three primary areas as they expanded His kingdom throughout the earth as His representatives and ambassadors: (1) rulership over creation; (2) power to perform the works of God; and (3) authority over Satan, demons, and any other spirits. Human beings were to rule over creation—over nature, space, time, and matter. They were to be kings over creation—under God. In line with this, they were given power to perform all the works God called them to do. This ability is similar to what Paul wrote thousands of years later about those who have been redeemed by Jesus Christ: *"For we are His workmanship, created in Christ Jesus for good works, which God prepared beforehand that we should walk in them"* (Ephesians 2:10). Humanity also had authority over Satan and his demons, having the power to exercise dominion over the enemy and subdue him. As we will see later in this chapter, in a tragic decision, they chose not to use their authority, and this is the origin of mankind's myriad problems.

Dominion is the highest spiritual power given to man, because it is territorial power.

Understanding Dominion Principles

What did it really mean for mankind to rule over the earth? Here are some essential principles to help us understand what dominion is all about—what it meant for Adam and Eve before the fall, and what it means for us who have been restored to our rule through Jesus Christ and are expanding God's kingdom throughout the world. Understanding dominion will enable us to avoid pitfalls that can derail our purpose.

1. Man Was Created with an Instinct for Power

In the beginning, God gave Adam a built-in desire and ability to rule. This is why many people's greatest desire is for power. Everyone has the instinct and need to exercise power. If anyone says otherwise, he is deceiving himself. God designed us with this instinct, which goes beyond reason or choice. I believe it is similar to the instincts in animals. For example, God created birds with the instinct to fly, and so He gave them wings and feathers to enable them to do so. He created fish with the instinct to swim, and so He designed them with scales and gills, which allow them to breathe underwater. When God created mankind, He gave men and women a spirit of leading and ruling; thus, He designed them with the ability to think, to address challenges, and to be creative, and He gave them the desire to exercise their power.

This inherent desire is the reason why some people become desperate when they lose control of their lives in various ways. Many of them are willing to sacrifice everything to regain power—or to feel that they have. I have seen this in my own experience dealing with presidents and prime ministers, senators and congressmen, governors and mayors, CEOs and entrepreneurs, leaders in sports and entertainment, and so on. People desire high positions because of the power they can obtain. For example, some governmental roles do not offer great salaries, but they do offer a great amount of influence and authority. Leaders in these positions often feel important when others defer to them and call them by their titles.

Those who seek out such leaders and defer to them are usually not attracted to the individuals who hold the positions as much as they are attracted to the power they possess. Many of us do the same thing on a smaller scale in our everyday lives. Why do we go to the doctor when we feel sick? Because the doctor has knowledge and skills that were acquired by extensive study and training, and therefore has the power to heal us.

Unfortunately, due to the fall, most of us don't understand what true power is. Many people seek to fulfill their desire for power from the wrong sources, such as religion, witchcraft, a pursuit of fame or great accomplishments, academic degrees, wealth, and more. The power they attain through these avenues is not ultimately satisfying because it is only temporal and does not reflect the life and purpose of God's kingdom.

When God designs something, He equips it with the ability to accomplish its purpose. This is why human beings have an instinct for power.

2. Leading Is Not the Same as Ruling

Next, we must learn the difference between leading and ruling. Most people don't understand the distinction, especially in our Western society. Here is the difference, which I will explain more fully below: We lead when people follow us of their own free will and give us permission to guide them. We rule when people do not want to follow us, even though they may know we are carrying out God's will. When we rule, we have to make decisions that go against people's feelings and desires, in order to be obedient to God.

Jesus gave us the pattern for leadership. For instance, He washed His disciples' feet as an example that we should serve one another (see John 13:3–17), and He said that whoever desires to become great must become a servant, just as He did not come to be served but to serve. (See Matthew 20:25–28.)

We lead by means of spiritual fatherhood, relationships, service, and example when people follow us willingly.

Some believers think about their God-given assignment of dominion solely in terms of leadership, when it also includes the necessary aspect of ruling. As a result, they have an incomplete concept of dominion. Ruling is needed in situations and spheres where leadership may not apply, because the people we are accountable for are not willing to follow God's purposes. You guide or lead people only when they are willingly submitted to you. In ruling, you don't give people any option; you do not ask for their permission. An illustration of this concept is ancient Rome. The Romans did not lead; they ruled, and that is why they were able to conquer territories.

We must first offer leadership to those who are our responsibility, as Paul encouraged Timothy: *"Do not rebuke an older man, but exhort him as a father, younger men as brothers, older women as mothers, younger women as sisters, with all purity"* (1 Timothy 5:1–2). However, when we face determined resistance from those under our care, we must exercise rule. In these situations, we can't always ask for people's opinions, because knowing God's will is enough—if this is what God wants, then this is what needs to be done.

When you don't rule, you abdicate your authority,
and your anointing diminishes.

Here are several examples to help us better understand the difference between leading and ruling. First, when there is a clash between the kingdom of heaven and the kingdom of darkness, then rule and subjugation of the enemy are absolutely necessary. Obviously, we will never be able to "persuade" the devil to do right, and we will never be able to influence him for good by setting a godly example. He is completely rebellious against God and will never change in this regard. Ruling and subduing are our only options with Satan.

Second, within a family of husband, wife, and children, the Scriptures say that the husband is the head of the home (see Ephesians 5:23), and he is the one who must seek God's direction for the family and exercise leadership by his example. Both parents are to teach and train their children, but the father is generally the one who must discipline the children when they refuse to be obedient. This is when ruling rather than leading, as we have defined it, is necessary. If a father continued to meet his children's physical and emotional needs but never corrected them when they required it, he would be doing them a great disservice, and he would not be following the command of Scripture. (See Ephesians 6:4.)

God's original intent for His government was priority and order. Even in equality of ministry, there is priority.

As the head of the home, the husband/father sometimes has to make decisions for the good of the family that are not popular. When Adam accepted the fruit that Eve gave him, he followed her lead instead of exercising the rule that God had assigned to him. Sin did not take place when Eve ate the fruit but rather when Adam ate it, because God had made him the highest authority on earth, under His sovereign rule. God had created Adam first out of the dust of the ground, and Eve was formed from the "rib" or "side" of Adam. Although they were to jointly exercise dominion over the earth, Adam, as the head, had the final authority. Unfortunately, he did not exercise it. He surrendered to the woman's feelings and desires instead of governing and saying "No!" to the devil's suggestion and to Eve's offer of the fruit.

Adam was evicted from the garden of Eden for not ruling when he was supposed to.

A third realm that helps us to understand the difference between leading and ruling is the church. Leading according to Jesus' example—including demonstrating unconditional love and sacrifice, and performing healings and miracles out of deep compassion for people's needs—is essential for those who are in positions of authority in a local church. When people observe leaders who minister in this way, as Jesus did, they will be drawn to the message that is presented to them from God's Word. There are instances, however, when we need to follow Jesus' example of ruling. He preached, taught, healed, and addressed numerous questions as He exercised leadership. Yet, when He encountered greedy and hypocritical religious leaders, He exercised rule. For instance, when He saw the money changers treating the temple like a marketplace, He drove them out, restoring order to God's house. (See Matthew 21:12–13; Mark 11:15–17.)

Let us look at another example of ruling from the early church. The apostle Paul dealt with a situation of sexual immorality in the Corinthian church in which a man was openly sleeping with his father's wife and was unrepentant. The church was looking the other way instead of addressing the issue. Paul's instruction was to put this man out of the church in hopes that he would be forced to come to his senses and repent, and thereby be spared the judgment of God. (See 1 Corinthians 5:1–5.) The Corinthians followed Paul's advice, and the discipline worked.

By the time Paul wrote his second letter to the Corinthians, the man had thoroughly repented. This illustration teaches us the true intent of ruling in relation to other people (as opposed to Satan). Ruling is not meant to punish—it is meant to correct, while also restoring godly order. The Corinthians turned out to be so zealous in their rule that they had continued to shun this man even after he had repented. So, after acknowledging their obedience, Paul had to instruct them to forgive the man, accept him back into their fellowship, and demonstrate the love of Christ to him, so that he wouldn't be overcome by sorrow and so Satan couldn't use the situation to take advantage of them. (See 2 Corinthians 2:4–11.) Similarly, the Scriptures say that God disciplines us for our good, so that we may share in His holiness. (See Hebrews 12:5–10 NIV, NASB.)

We rule with authority over those who are under our care but who refuse to follow us of their own free will.

3. There Is a Difference Between Dominion and Authority

In order to fulfill God's dominion mandate, it is also necessary to know the difference between dominion and authority. Sometimes, people use these words interchangeably in relation to God's command in Genesis 1:28, but they have distinct meanings. To understand the distinction, let us consider the implications of our calling.

God gave Adam and Eve and their descendants the whole earth as their territory, with the garden of Eden—the presence and glory of God— as their base of authority. Yet no one person, alone, could *"fill the earth and subdue it"* (Genesis 1:28). The dominion mandate is a collective mandate.

Together, human beings were to fill the earth and subdue it, each performing the unique purpose for which he or she had been created, as they all worked in unity to fulfill God's purposes.

In a similar way, through our redemption in Christ, God has assigned each of us a portion of "territory," or "territorial power," where we can exercise the measure of our dominion on earth. This dominion is based on the faith, anointing, and gifts He has given us. Our words and actions are most effective when we are in the territory God has assigned to us and are seeking first His kingdom.

This territorial power is not symbolic. It is a reality in which we must live. Neither is the territory in which we are to be fruitful random or general. Rather, it is specific. To use an illustration from the legal system, a Miami, Florida, police officer does not have the authority to arrest a criminal in the State of California because the officer's territory of dominion is Miami. Outside of that city, his power is inapplicable, because it is not within the realm of his jurisdiction. However, suppose law enforcement officials in a city in California called upon a Miami police officer to provide counsel and advice because they were having difficulty solving a crime in that state, and they needed his knowledge and expertise in a certain area. The Miami policeman would then be functioning outside of his primary territory. Although he still would not be able to make arrests or exercise other legal power there, he would be assisting and supporting the California officials within their jurisdiction.

With this as background, we can define *dominion* as a person's total territorial power from God, while *authority* relates to a delegated power to "legally" operate in another person's territory. Authority is the lawful right to enforce obedience and to act as God acts. Someone who exercises dominion has received the territory to which God has assigned him and has come to know and understand his purpose in relation to it. He is therefore able to delegate authority to others to use his power, name, word, anointing, and resources to exercise an aspect of dominion in that territory. Although each of us has an assigned territory, we will also, at various times and seasons of our lives, be operating under delegated authority within someone else's territory, so that God's work can be accomplished in the world.

Dominion is an absolute territorial power, but authority is the lawful right to exercise it.

Let me give you a practical example of the relationship between dominion and authority. As children grow, their parents delegate authority to them so they can carry out certain tasks within the home or accomplish assignments outside of the home, in accordance with their ages and abilities. The children complete their tasks under their parents' authorization and supervision. While the parents delegate authority to their children to prepare them for life, they continue to have dominion in the home.

No one with delegated authority is greater in authority or "above" the one who delegated power to him, because the one who delegated it has the dominion. God has assigned that person to the territory and planted him there; hence, he has territorial power. The person with the dominion did not receive it by personal choice; rather, he was given it by God.

When we have the responsibility of dominion, we should be cautious about choosing those to whom we delegate our authority and deciding how much of that authority we delegate. Sometimes, people believe that because they have been sent to do something, they already have dominion, when, in reality, they have only delegated authority. They are in a trial period designed to test their obedience, faithfulness, and loyalty. People who think they are not accountable to anyone else simply because they have been given limited rule are out of order and are operating under the spirit of rebellion.

For a person to delegate authority, he must be in dominion.

When people do not submit to God and the delegated human authority He has placed in their lives, they become vulnerable to the spirit of vengeance and the enemy's attacks. Submission to God is the number one rule that must be observed to keep the enemy from entering our lives.

When we act with God's authority, we are not acting as mere men but on God's behalf. A spiritual battle ensues every time we want to remain natural people when God has given us His authority to be supernatural. Once more, to be supernatural means to act like Him. As Jesus is, so are we in this world. (See 1 John 4:17.) When we exercise God's authority, sickness and demons have to leave because we are God's representatives on earth, either by dominion or by delegated authority.

The continuance of a person's power is determined by that person's submission to authority. A person who is not under authority is not under spiritual protection.

---

4. Wrong Motives and Illegitimate Means Are Unlawful Grounds for Ruling

To exercise true dominion, we also need to be careful not to abuse our authority. Let us review what Jesus said about leading and serving:

But Jesus called [His disciples] to Himself and said, "You know that the rulers of the Gentiles lord it over them, and those who are great exercise authority over them. Yet it shall not be so among you; but whoever desires to become great among you, let him be your servant. And whoever desires to be first among you, let him be your slave; just as the Son of Man did not come to be served, but to serve, and to give His life a ransom for many." (Matthew 20:25–28)

God's motivation in governance is always the will of God and the good of the people. When people rebel and break His kingdom laws, He has to rule them, with the intention that they be brought back to His will. Again, it is one thing to be dominated and quite another to be governed. We will be either governed by God or dominated by the devil; there is no neutral ground. Satan is an illegitimate ruler motivated to kill and destroy. (See John 10:10.) He will never govern for the good of people, and his methods are always deceit, control, and lies. (See John 8:44.)

People who are controlled by the fallen, carnal nature often have faulty motives and reasons for exerting power, so they tend to employ illegitimate means, such as manipulation, domination, and control. Wherever we encounter any of these three characteristics, we should recognize that a spirit of rebellion is operating behind it. God never manipulates or dominates people.

Governing doesn't mean acting like a dictator. It often requires great wisdom and self-control. A dictator subjugates people in order to carry out his own will, rather than God's. He wants to wield power rather than serve the people and lead them into the blessings that God pours out upon the obedient. The dictators in our world overpower people and subject them to poverty, control, and injustices.

Men and women were created to *have dominion over* their environment; they were not designed to *be dominated*, to be controlled and suppressed. God did not design us to live like this, and it has no part in our dominion mandate. Jesus came to earth to restore human beings to dominion so we could rule over sicknesses, circumstances, and Satan and his demons; so we could have power over alcohol addiction, drug abuse, bad thoughts, and anything else that causes us to move away from God's will. Dominion was not given to us so that we could subdue other human beings—only the enemy. If God gives us authority in other people's lives, it is only to govern, guide, and direct them, never to put them under subjection. It was the entrance of sin into the world that led people to control and subjugate other people.

Those who are rebellious against God and His delegated authority are being influenced by the fallen nature, as well. They find the idea of governance offensive because they want to be able to do anything they desire. There is a rebel in each human being; therefore, a true leader has to decide to do what God commands, and he must be able to discern when to lead and when to rule. For example, when we know the truth about God's will on a specific spiritual matter but fail to act on it, people under our care will often end up leading us in the direction they want to go—which may not be God's way.

True spiritual maturity is character submitted to spiritual authority.

Today, we see a number of governmental officials in the nations of the world submitting to peer pressure. They compromise their principles and thereby become politicians without any convictions. They are guided solely by the demands of the people rather than by God's will.

In the family, parents are not governing their home well when they allow their children to do whatever they want, to be disrespectful, and to break the rules of the household. When children's rebelliousness is tolerated, they will walk all over their parents. Tragically, they will come to rebel not only against the head of their household but also against God. Parents must take firm action—the action of ruling—in order to make their children's paths straight. If they don't do this, they will have to deal the consequences, which may include their children's drug habits, jail sentences, and lives of promiscuity and failure. Children need their parents' rule; it is to their benefit.

When God spoke to me to build a church debt free, without bank loans, I shared this vision with my family and closest leaders. The project would cost millions, and, at the time, we did not have the money to construct it. However, those were God's orders. Five couples among my closest leaders were not in agreement with this project. They did not support me because, according to them, I was acting according to personal ambition and not according to God. Yet, in my heart, I knew that building the church was God's will. In that instance, I had to exercise rule. I did not allow these five couples to lead me. I told them that if they wanted to follow me, they were welcome; but, if not, then I would build the church with the rest of the people. These couples left the church, and I followed God's orders. The building was constructed debt free, and God provided all the money we needed, minute by minute and day by day. We have become role models to many other pastors who are building their churches debt free. I made a decision to rule, and the result was that God was glorified.

5. The Principle of Multiplication Is Eternal

When we understand the first four aspects of dominion, we also must keep in mind that there is an eternal principle of multiplication of the kingdom that explains why Adam and Eve were to *be fruitful and multiply* (Genesis 1:28). As we have noted, Eden was only a point of departure; it was not meant to be an end in itself. God told Adam and Eve to expand Eden—His presence and glory—throughout the world. He did not want them to settle for less than that or to conform to any other way of living. God's kingdom is a limitless kingdom. It is an ever-expanding realm. It has always existed, it exists now, and it will continue to expand throughout eternity in ways we cannot now know or imagine.

The devil is aware that the more the kingdom of God expands on the earth, the closer he is to his end, because both kingdoms cannot occupy the same territory. This is why he implemented a plan of disobedience against Adam and Eve to stop God's purpose. Satan's strategy has not changed since that time. He is always fighting to keep God's people from expanding His kingdom. He wants to restrict us and prevent us from advancing. He devises plans not only to contain us as individuals but also to contain our families, churches, and businesses. For this reason, we must discern his plans, avoid falling into his traps, and learn to rule over him, so that God's purposes can be carried out in the earth. Therefore, let us investigate how and why mankind fell from dominion and then learn from this revelation, that we may remain strong and effective in the dominion we have regained through Christ.

How Mankind Fell from Dominion

To comprehend why God gave Adam and Eve dominion power over Satan, and why they fell from this dominion, we must look at Satan's background and motivations. He had been created by God as an angel called Lucifer, or "light." However, he rebelled against God and was expelled from heaven, along with a third of the angels who had joined him. Some theologians and Bible scholars have concluded that Satan's rebellion and expulsion from heaven took place between the first two verses of Genesis 1—between *"In the beginning God created the heavens and the earth"* (verse 1) and *"The earth was without form, and void; and darkness was on the face of the deep"* (verse 2). I share this view, and it is from this perspective that I will discuss the significance of these events in relation to humanity's dominion mandate.

Satan had already been expelled from heaven when Adam and Eve were created, and his kingdom of darkness and destruction was in operation. The devil had seized the territory of earth, and God allowed him to do this—for His own purposes. It is essential to recognize that Satan is never stronger than God. He is a created being, and he was thrown out of heaven after he rebelled. God always has total control over everything He creates.

Genesis 1:2 says that *"darkness was on the face of the deep,"* meaning that the earth was in chaos and darkness because Satan had seized it; the presence of his kingdom always results in such disorder and destruction. But Genesis 1:2 also says, *"And the Spirit of God was hovering over the face of the waters."* Even in the midst of the darkness, God's power to create was present, because the territory of earth did not belong to Satan. He was a usurper. Under the influence of God's Spirit, the earth received light, order, and life. The waters parted, dry land appeared, and plants and animals were brought into being. Finally, God created man and placed him in Eden—in the midst of His glory. As we have discussed, from there, man would extend God's kingdom throughout the whole earth, ruling it as God rules heaven. In this way, God gave human beings dominion not only over the natural world and everything in it, but also over the enemy, who was still present on the earth. They were to subdue him and his kingdom—to bring him under control by spiritual force.

God's original intention was for human beings to be the agents that would carry out heaven's laws on earth.

Yet the devil desired to shroud the earth in darkness once again. To do this, he had to recover his rule by taking the territory away from man, since God had granted man authority over it. Satan's plan was to make human beings fall from the glory of God by means of rebellion and disobedience— the same way by which he had fallen. So, he "prowled around" the earth, seeking to devour God's supreme creation. (See 1 Peter 5:8 NIV.)

> *Now the serpent* [Satan, in the form of a snake] *was more cunning than any beast of the field which the LORD God had made. And he said to the woman, "Has God indeed said, 'You shall not eat of every tree of the garden'?"* (Genesis 3:1)

The Bible is silent as to when or how Satan entered Eden. The only thing that is on record in Scripture is Adam's surrender to temptation. We must again understand that if Satan entered Eden, the dwelling place of God's glory, then God had allowed him to do so. God didn't intervene, because He had given that territory to Adam and Eve. Yet, in His sovereignty, God was fulfilling His purposes even in the midst of Satan's temptation.

Since the serpent gave a distorted summary of God's instruction, let us review what God actually said to Adam: *"And the* Lord *God commanded the man, saying, 'Of every tree of the garden you may freely eat; but of the tree of the knowledge of good and evil you shall not eat, for in the day that you eat of it you shall surely die'"* (Genesis 2:16–17).

My spiritual perception is that this was not the first time Satan had approached Eve in the form of the serpent and engaged her in conversation in an effort to tempt her. I say this because when a person sins, it does not usually happen overnight. The Bible teaches that sin is a seed—a thought or desire—that is entertained and meditated upon until it is planted in the heart and finally results in action. I believe the devil took over the serpent's body in order to tempt humanity repeatedly, because the enemy does not possess a creative weapon. He cannot create; he can only imitate. This is why one of his main strategies has always been persistence. When we read this account in Genesis, we realize that Eve's answer was not one that came from a person who was awed or surprised. It appears that she was used to these visits and discussions. It is easy to understand how, by continual persistence, the deceiver wore down her resistance.

It is likely that Adam was present each time the serpent spoke to Eve, and that he, too, was being tempted. Eve was just the first to surrender to the temptation. The Scriptures say that she was *"deceived"* (see Genesis 3:13; 2 Corinthians 11:3), but that Adam *"was not deceived"* (1 Timothy 2:14). However, Adam did not try to stop Eve from eating the fruit; instead, he surrendered to temptation, as well. When Adam knowingly sinned, the earth became cursed. (See Genesis 3:14–24.) Satan thus made himself the earth's legitimate governor—legitimate not because God gave him this authority but because Adam surrendered it to the kingdom of darkness due to his sin.

If Adam had cast out the devil from the garden, the devil would have had to flee. (See James 4:7.) In the New Testament, when Satan prompted

Peter to try to deter Jesus from dying on the cross for our sins, Jesus responded, *"Get behind Me, Satan!"* (Matthew 16:23). This is what Adam should have done. I believe that Adam knew his enemy well, and he also knew that his enemy's suggestion was wrong. God had given Adam the authority and power to resist, yet he went ahead and disobeyed God anyway. Similarly, there are certain circumstances in our lives in which God will not intervene because He has already given us the dominion—the power and the authority—over them through Jesus.

The Four Stages of Adam's Fall

What was the process by which Adam fell from the dominion, authority, and power God had given him for the purpose of governing the earth? We can identify four stages that led to Adam's descent. From my experience in ministry, this is the same pattern the enemy encourages in the lives of men and women in the body of Christ today in order to destroy them through temptation, so it is essential that we be fully alert to it.

1. Adam Was Aware of His Coexistence with Evil

And out of the ground the LORD God made every tree grow that is pleasant to the sight and good for food. The tree of life was also in the midst of the garden, and the tree of the knowledge of good and evil.

(Genesis 2:9)

When Adam was placed in the garden, he was aware of the presence of the enemy's kingdom. He knew that good would be coexisting with evil on earth—at least for a while. At the same time God bestowed dominion on Adam, He gave him instructions about what to do with evil. These instructions were to subjugate and rule it. Adam had the ability to resist and conquer Satan and his kingdom when confronted with temptation, because he had not yet sinned. Since he was aligned with God and His Spirit, evil had to submit to his rule.

To coexist with evil doesn't mean to tolerate it.

Satan then came and discussed God's commandments with Adam and Eve in a way that was intended to confuse them and weaken their spiritual resistance. Again, in such a situation, Adam's job was to place Satan underfoot and force him to submit, to dominate him and bring him under subjection. This was because Adam's purpose was to carry out God's will by governing, protecting, and spreading His kingdom on the planet.

2. Adam Began to Tolerate Evil

Then the serpent said to the woman, "You will not surely die. For God knows that in the day you eat of it [the tree of the knowledge of good and evil] your eyes will be opened, and you will be like God, knowing good and evil."   (Genesis 3:4–5)

When did Adam go from coexisting with evil to tolerating it? When he began to entertain temptation instead of taking dominion and immediately casting out the serpent from Eden. By dwelling on Satan's statements, he gave the evil one the right to touch his life and to encroach on his relationship with God.

Jesus sent messages of admonition and encouragement to believers in seven different churches in the first century, and these messages are recorded in the book of Revelation. In His message to the church at Thyatira, He said that He had a few things against them. One of these things was that they tolerated a woman named "Jezebel." This may have been her real name, or the name may have been used to connect her with Jezebel from the Old Testament, the wife of King Ahab, who led the Israelites into false teaching, idolatry, and immorality. Jesus said, *"You tolerate that woman Jezebel, who calls herself a prophetess. By her teaching she misleads my servants into sexual immorality and the eating of food sacrificed to idols"* (Revelation 2:20 NIV). Similar to the church at Thyatira, Adam and Eve tolerated the serpent, Satan, and allowed him to influence them spiritually. This was unnatural, because, in the physical world, no normal person would tolerate having a venomous serpent invade his home. His first instinct would be to eliminate it before it bit, poisoned, and killed someone.

The evil you tolerate will become the evil that destroys you.

Each of us tolerates certain sins and wrong elements in our lives, even though we know they displease God—evil thoughts, attitudes, actions, and habits; people who are detrimental to our spiritual and emotional health; and more. Many of us don't realize that, by tolerating them, we are following in the footsteps of Adam and giving the enemy the right to invade our "Eden" and erode our fellowship with God, so that our access to His presence is blocked.

When our relationship with God deteriorates, or we find ourselves being spiritually attacked in an area of our lives, we must ask ourselves some hard questions: How did the enemy gain a foothold in our home life or our finances or our business? Could it be that we stopped tithing our income and ceased honoring God with our money? How did Satan afflict our bodies with sickness or disease? Could it be that we tolerated a sickness or mistreated our bodies so that they became ill? How did Satan invade our church, city, and nation? In what way have we given him the legal right to afflict us? What authorized his attack against us? I believe that if we seek God with integrity and humility, He will give us the answers. If we repent, the blood of Jesus will cleanse us (see 1 John 1:7–9), and we will be able to recover our Eden and take back the dominion rights the enemy has stolen from us. Later in this chapter, and also in the next chapter, we will see how Jesus won back these rights for us and how we can enter into His victory.

A person's disobedience is the devil's legal authorization to attack him.

3. Adam Lost the Fear, or Reverence, of the Lord

The fear of the LORD is to hate evil; pride and arrogance and the evil way and the perverse mouth I hate. (Proverbs 8:13)

To fear the Lord is to reverence, honor, and respect Him. It means to be in awe of Him. Adam went from coexisting with evil to tolerating it, and from tolerance of evil to losing the fear of the Lord, which guards us against yielding to evil. When Adam became indifferent to the dangers of evil, he soon entered into a relationship with it. Evil is not held back if we lose our reverence for the Lord. God's Word tells us that if we fear the Lord, we will hate evil—not allow it to influence us!

Losing the fear of the Lord leads to a loss of sensitivity to evil; we no longer see its dangers and consequences, and we compromise the truth.

4. Adam Finally Sinned

So when the woman saw that the tree was good for food, that it was pleasant to the eyes, and a tree desirable to make one wise, she took of its fruit and ate. She also gave to her husband with her, and he ate.

(Genesis 3:6)

Here we see the final stage in Adam's descent. He went from coexisting with evil to tolerating it to losing the fear of the Lord to falling from God's glory into the curse of sin. In this way, human beings lost their dominion and their life in the presence of God. What is more, they lost the territory He had given them, and they entered into Satan's bondage. In essence, Adam gave the enemy the keys to his life, and that is how Satan took over the rulership of the earth. Jesus called the devil *"the ruler of this world"* (John 12:31; 14:30; 16:11), and Paul echoed this description by referring to him as *"the god of this world"* (2 Corinthians 4:4 KJV, NASB).

Today, the same sad descent and subsequent surrender to temptation takes place in the lives of millions of people. The strategy of the deceiver is to wear us out mentally, emotionally, and physically until we finally give in and fall. Just as Adam and Eve should have rebuked and subdued the serpent the first time it showed up, that is what we must do with Satan when we are tempted. If you are being tempted today, my advice is not to tolerate those thoughts but to exercise the authority that Jesus gave you to cast them out and to subdue the wicked one under your feet. (See Romans 16:20; 2 Corinthians 10:5.) Satan and his demons observe us and know our weaknesses. They wait for the opportune moment to tempt us in our weakest area, often by deceit, until we lower our guards and submit.

The devil will not stop until he sees you fall down, so do not argue with him or entertain his ungodly suggestions. You must rebuke him—cast him out—immediately! Regardless of how logical or good those thoughts or arguments might seem as you try to rationalize them, his goal is to destroy you—to kill you.

The Catastrophic Result of Adam's Sin

The dire consequence of Adam's willful disobedience was that human beings now had a sinful nature, which was inherited by every person of every succeeding generation of the human race. When Adam and Eve sinned, they did not consider the consequences of their actions and the effect they would have on their descendants. In my view, they were not used to thinking in terms of the future, because everything in the presence of God is in the eternal "now." Yet, because they sinned, their children and their descendants were born under the curse of sin, with a legacy of rebellion and iniquity.

Because of the fall, people's lives have become dominated by many harmful things, such as drugs, bad habits, a lust for money, an unhealthy desire for fame, and the torment of demons. They are mainly dominated by their own fleshly desires. Humanity went from being God's governor on earth to being ruled, manipulated, and controlled by the enemy of his soul. God's plan for humanity was frustrated for a time, but since nothing ever surprises Him and nothing ever puts an end to His plans, His purposes could not be thwarted. By all appearances, it seemed the end for mankind, but God had already designed a plan of redemption through the blood of the perfect Lamb, who would pay the price for our sin and restore us to dominion over the enemy and his kingdom of darkness.

We have an all-knowing God—He knows the past, the present, and the future of both time and eternity. If you are experiencing difficult times in which God's plan for your life seems paralyzed, or if you are frustrated over a particular emotional, physical, or spiritual problem, what you are going through has been foreseen by God; therefore, He already has a solution to your problem, just as He had for the woman in the following testimony.

Not long ago, I traveled with my ministry team to bring the supernatural power of God to the city of East London, South Africa. Hundreds convened at one of the churches there, and sitting among the audience at one of the meetings was Penelope Quluba, a woman who had been diagnosed with colon cancer three years earlier. Doctors had told her that the cancer was aggressive and could not be removed. They also said she would eventually become paralyzed and experience kidney failure. The only option was to put her on radiation and chemotherapy and let the cancer take its course. In addition, Penelope had to undergo surgery to have a colostomy bag inserted. As a result, she felt self-conscious because not only was she sick; she also carried an unpleasant odor.

After her diagnosis, Penelope regularly spoke healing over her body, declaring the Word of God and telling her body that it was the temple of the Holy Spirit and had not been created with aggressive cancer or a colostomy bag. By the time of the meeting in East London, she was due to have more surgery because she had completed the chemotherapy, and the doctors needed to see what was happening in her colon. I gave an altar call for those who had cancer or HIV. Penelope made her way to the altar, where I laid hands on her and declared her healed in the name of Jesus. Two weeks later, when she visited the hospital for the first time since the ministry event, the doctors were baffled when they found no trace of cancer! They removed the colostomy bag and put everything back to normal. Penelope is now free of cancer and full of vitality by the grace of God.

Jesus Restored Humanity to Dominion

When God came to earth in His Son Jesus Christ, Satan was the earth's "landlord"—humanity had to pay him "rent" in the form of suffering the rule of his kingdom of darkness. Yet the Son of God willingly separated Himself from His glory and majesty in heaven to be conceived by the Holy Spirit in the womb of a virgin in order to save us from our bondage. Jesus was begotten of God by the power of the Holy Spirit, but He also needed to be born of a woman to be fully human as well as fully God. (See Isaiah 7:14; Luke 1:35.)

Adam's experiences with the devil in the garden of Eden were very different from Jesus' experiences with the devil thousands of years later in Palestine, even though there were some important similarities. Adam dealt with a being who had been thrown out of heaven and had no legal status on earth. Satan had not been given dominion over anything. (See Revelation 12:9.) He was and will continue to be a liar, a thief, and a destroyer. Yet, through Adam's sin, he was able to take over legal possession of the territory of earth.

Jesus, therefore, came into the world to deal with a being who had usurped mankind's authority and established himself as the one in charge. Jesus confronted him in spiritual warfare as a Man and not as God, because, if He had done so as God, the devil never would have been able to try to oppose Him. He would have been immediately defeated without any problem. The point is that, by God's decree, dominion over the earth had been given to human beings. This is why Satan had to defeat Adam, a man, in order to rule the world. It is also why Jesus had to come to earth as a Man to destroy the works of the devil and conquer him forever.

There is another significant difference between the experiences of Adam and Jesus. Adam was created and placed in Eden as an adult man. He received direct, revealed knowledge from God about the earth and his role in it, and he was surrounded by the Father's glory. Jesus came to earth as a baby. He had to grow physically, mentally, and spiritually, and He had to come to understand, by means of His physical senses, how the natural world functions. He received spiritual revelation from continually seeking the Father through prayer and communion with Him, spending hours and hours in God's presence. While Adam was tempted by Satan in the middle of a garden full of delicious fruit ready to be eaten, Jesus was tempted by Satan after spending forty days fasting in the desert.

How Jesus Dealt with the Devil

Then Jesus was led up by the Spirit into the wilderness to be tempted by the devil. And when He had fasted forty days and forty nights, afterward He was hungry. (Matthew 4:1–2)

In these verses, we learn that Satan tried the same tactic with Jesus that he had used with Adam: tempt Him to make Him sin and then defeat Him. The devil tempted Jesus three times, and each temptation was directed toward His identity as the Son of God. It is interesting to consider that Jesus had the power to do everything the devil asked Him to do, but He did not do it because the temptation was not a valid foundation on which to manifest the power of God.

The Father had not given Jesus authority and power just to establish His identity but to defeat the devil's kingdom. Jesus did not need to prove anything to the devil. He simply refuted the three temptations with the Word of God, thereby defeating him. Then, Jesus returned from the desert *"in the power of the Spirit"* (Luke 4:14) to begin His mission. Jesus conquered Satan as a Man to demonstrate that it is possible for a human being to overcome temptation through the power of the Holy Spirit. The Spirit had descended on Jesus at His baptism, just before His temptation experience in the desert. (See, for example, Matthew 3:16.) And Jesus was empowered by the Spirit after the devil's temptations. Through the Spirit, Jesus accomplished what Adam had failed to do.

Later, Jesus died on the cross as our Sacrifice; He was buried, descended into hell, thoroughly defeated Satan by taking back the keys of death and hell, and was resurrected victoriously in order to reestablish the dominion, power, and authority that humanity had lost in Eden. Believers continue to deal with Satan's temptations and attacks, but ever since Jesus' resurrection, Satan has been functioning as an illegal ruler on earth, just as he was in Adam's time before the fall. More than this, the enemy's power has been defeated. He no longer has authority over us, unless, like Adam, we grant it to him again. In each temptation and circumstance we face, we have the choice of defeating the enemy or giving in to him. When we give in to him, we allow him to gain a foothold in our lives.

Take Back Your Dominion

And Jesus came and spoke to [His disciples], *saying, "All authority has been given to Me in heaven and on earth."* (Matthew 28:18)

Satan will continue to tempt people for as long as he can—until the culmination of all things when Jesus returns—in order to try to recover dominion of the earth. However, if we know our identity in Christ and are willing to cast the serpent out of our Eden, Satan cannot defeat us. Paul said, in essence, that he would not allow anything to dominate him that didn't build him up in Christ. (See 1 Corinthians 6:12.) The only authority the devil can try to exercise is the one we allow him to have. *"Do not give the devil an opportunity"* (Ephesians 4:27 NASB). Because of Jesus, every believer has the power to bind what needs to be subdued and to loosen what needs to be released on earth. (See Matthew 16:19; 18:18.) However, we have to remain under the authority of our heavenly Father, living in obedience to Him, as Jesus did, as well as to our delegated human authorities.

The devil's plan was to contain Adam's Eden and keep it from expanding. He tries the same thing with us today.

We must not tolerate sickness, sadness, depression, poverty, fear, or other evil strategies designed to destroy us. Some people cannot subdue or bind sickness because it has become the norm for them; thus, they have given the keys of their health to the enemy. We must be prepared to subjugate and dominate every work of the devil. *"For this purpose the Son of God was manifested, that He might destroy the works of the devil"* (1 John 3:8).

What Jesus accomplished for us is powerful; it enables us to defeat Satan in the midst of our difficult circumstances in a fallen world. Jesus not only restored the original dominion we lost, but He also promises us a resurrection life that is *"more than all we ask or imagine"* (Ephesians 3:20 NIV).

I was recently invited to minister at a conference in Dallas, Texas. One evening when I was not scheduled to preach, I went to receive from God myself. At the end of the service, a woman came up to me and said that her doctor had told her she needed two knee replacements because she no longer had any ligaments in her knees and the bones were worn. She was in intense pain, and the only solution was a miracle. I discerned such a faith in her that, as I was leaving the meeting, I declared her healed, and she instantly received her healing! She started moving her legs and running, which she could not do before. She explained that the doctor had said that if she wanted to bend her knees and run, she would require brand-new knees. As she wept and cried, she said, "I can't believe it; I have brand-new knees."

If you have allowed the devil to enter your Eden, and if temptation has destroyed your will; if you have lost your dominion and given it over to the enemy—today, Jesus gives you a new opportunity. Repent and ask

God to forgive you through Christ's sacrifice on the cross for your sins. Decide now to take back your dominion through Jesus' resurrection power, whether it is dominion over your character, your attitudes, or even criminal behavior. Take back your rule in relation to addictions to alcohol, illegal drugs, or prescription pills; take authority over sickness, illicit sex, fear, depression, anger, bitterness, unforgiveness, a spirit of suicide, bickering, or gossip. Right now, renounce and rule over these things. God has given you dominion over all of Satan's works and over the sinful nature!

Ruling in the spirit realm starts with ruling our own spirit.

Jesus said, *"From the days of John the Baptist until now the kingdom of heaven suffers violence"* (Matthew 11:12). I believe this means that when we begin to remove Satan's kingdom, he fights for his life. Jesus said that when the word of the kingdom is preached, the devil comes immediately to snatch it from those who do not understand it. (See Matthew 13:19.) The enemy doesn't want to be forced out of the territory of people's lives. All the spiritual and physical battles people have fought on earth—from the garden of Eden through today—have been battles over territory. Even in our personal lives, the greatest battles we fight relate to the territory of our lives and ministries. When we minister, we become a threat to Satan because we are removing his kingdom of darkness from people and places in which he has held a stronghold. A true proclamation of God's kingdom will bring a clash with Satan's kingdom. When we see demons being cast out by the Spirit of God, the kingdom has arrived among us. (See Matthew 12:28; Luke 11:20.)

Jesus also said, *"The ruler of this world is coming, and he has nothing in Me"* (John 14:30). There was nothing of Satan's nature about Jesus, and we should root out anything of the enemy's nature in us. Let us live a new life according to the righteousness, peace, and joy of the kingdom of God. When we repent and ask God wholeheartedly for His kingdom to reign in our lives, He will release the spirit of dominion over us. We must rule over the entire territory He has given us, beginning with our own spirit, soul, and body.

Since before the creation of the world, God has had wonderful plans for the human race. Perhaps His heart was saddened more than at any other time in human history when Adam fell from his dominion of the earth in Eden and handed over that rule to Satan. Humanity has continued to stagger under Satan's kingdom of darkness ever since. However, through history, the love of God has always sustained and provided for His people, and He fulfilled His plan to redeem all human beings through Christ. Jesus came to earth and changed everything, making all things new again. (See Revelation 21:5.) Since then, we have been given access to grace and power for personal transformation through the Holy Spirit, as well as the ability to bring the kingdom of God to the world around us. Let us live in the reality that our dominion has been regained, and that God's kingdom will continue to increase for all eternity.

3

Jesus' Resurrection Established His Kingdom and Dominion Over the Kingdom of Darkness

This chapter contains an essential biblical truth that has produced extraordinary changes in many people's lives. It has transformed them and enabled them to transform others. It is the truth that Jesus reigns in resurrection power, and that, through Him, we can reign in the same power that raised Him from the dead as we expand His kingdom!

The resurrection makes Christianity unique from all other religions of the world because the followers of those religions know that their leaders are dead and buried. But Jesus is alive, and His resurrection power is still in force as He saves, heals, and delivers people all over the earth.

In the Bible, there are several passages that mention people who died and were resurrected, including the son of the widow of Nain (see Luke 7:11–16) and Lazarus (see John 11:38–44), yet their resurrections were different from Jesus' resurrection. They died as sinners and were raised from the dead with the same sinful nature. Furthermore, they died again and will remain in that state until Jesus returns. Christ, on the other hand, lived a completely sinless life, and, after He died with all the sins of humanity upon Himself, He was gloriously raised from the dead without sin. He continues to live today—and forever—to give life to all who believe in Him.

Often, when we hear the message of Christ's resurrection preached in churches, it is presented solely from a historical point of view without revelation. Consequently, we do not often witness God's power manifesting among His people. To benefit from this power, we must have the revelation of His resurrection in the "now."

Through His resurrection, Jesus validated His deity, His kingdom, and His dominion over Satan's kingdom. The resurrection is not a myth or a legend. It was a historic event that established a "before" and "after" in the history of humanity. It marked a line between Satan's dominion over the earth and Christ's conquest of Satan, His eternal reign, and the reestablishment of mankind's dominion over the earth. It inaugurated a new era in which human beings were freed from bondage to Satan so they could become God's children and friends. There are so many outcomes and benefits of the resurrection that it would be impossible to enumerate them.

The following is the testimony of a woman who experienced transformation through the power of the resurrection.

"I was abandoned when I was only a baby, and I was raised by a stepmother who mistreated me. I did not understand why this had happened to me. In time, I learned that my sisters had also been abandoned. I grew up without a personal identity and without love. One day, my stepmother grabbed me by the hair and yelled at me, saying, 'You are not my daughter!' At that moment, I understood why I was not loved, and the pain in my heart increased even more. I left home when I was fifteen and eventually became a single mother. In the years that followed, I had several men in my life, but they, also, abandoned me. I had two children with the last man I lived with, but he rejected our first son, refusing to recognize him as his child. He mistreated him, making him feel inferior; this was a repeat of my own childhood.

"One day, I decided to leave everything behind and never return, so I went to live alone in Miami. I abandoned my children in the same way I had been abandoned. After I had been living in the United States for some time, someone invited me to King Jesus Ministry. There I met God and opened up my heart to Jesus. It was then that I understood I was in bondage to rejection, abandonment, and guilt.

"During a spiritual retreat hosted by the church, I was led to renounce this bondage through prayer. When I finished, I felt every oppression leave me. Today, I feel free of that generational curse of abandonment. The pain in my heart disappeared! Now, I plan to return to my country. I want to see my children and be the mother to them that they need but that I could not be for so long. I have peace and joy. The love of God has enabled me to give what I could not give. I was delivered of the spirit of lust that had made me follow after any man who crossed my path. Now, I live a full and happy life. My children will not suffer anymore, because the generational curse of abandonment has been broken!"

The fruit of this woman's deliverance is a transformed life, changed values, and the desire to be restored to her family. The power that operated in her is the power of the resurrection. This same power can operate in you, too—right now!

Let us ask the Holy Spirit to reveal the power of Christ's resurrection for our lives as we progress through this chapter. Please pray the following out loud:

Holy Spirit, You are the Administrator and Executor of the power of Christ's resurrection. I ask You to enlighten my understanding with the spirit of wisdom and revelation, so I can know the power of the resurrection, apply it to my life, and release it over others who are in need. In the name of Jesus, amen!

We will now look at three ways in which Jesus suffered death on our behalf so that we could experience His resurrection life.

Jesus Suffered Three Deaths on Our Behalf

Jesus is called the *"last Adam"* (1 Corinthians 15:45). As the Son of God, He identified with the first Adam and every one of his descendants who has ever lived, or ever will live, by becoming a human being and enduring everything that human beings experience. His life was an act of substitution that reached its climax on the cross, when He died in our place for our sins. (See Isaiah 53:6.) Regardless of how we may categorize various sins as being greater or lesser, all sin leads to death. (See James 1:15.) But Jesus "tasted" death so we could receive eternal life. (See Hebrews 2:9.)

To be our Substitute, Jesus had to undergo the three types of death that every human being was destined to endure (without His redeeming work on the cross) due to Adam's rebellion and the entrenched sin nature inherited by the whole human race: (1) physical death, (2) spiritual death, and (3) the "second death."

1. Physical Death

The first death that Jesus experienced was that of His physical body.

And when Jesus had cried out with a loud voice, He said, "Father, 'into Your hands I commit My spirit.'" Having said this, He breathed His last. (Luke 23:46)

Jesus had been arrested, interrogated during the night, condemned to death, mocked, tortured with beatings, pierced by a crown of thorns, and crucified until He succumbed to death. When Jesus took our place on the cross, it was not just a symbolic or theoretical act. He totally identified with our humanity and carried our sins and sinful nature on Himself. In the moment He physically died, His human spirit and soul separated from His body. His body was buried in a tomb, where it remained for three days, but His spirit continued on and carried out tasks to complete His mission as Savior of the world.

In the exchange that took place at the cross, Jesus carried the consequences of our disobedience so that we could receive the benefits of His obedience.

2. Spiritual Death

Jesus enjoyed no special favor or experience with the Father just because He was God's Son. Though He was divine, He was also human, as much as you or I, except that He was without sin. As a human being on earth, Jesus' life depended upon His relationship with the Father. Likewise, we believers have no life in ourselves but only in our relationship with the Father through Christ. (See John 6:57.)

Sin separates human beings from the life of God. (See Isaiah 59:2.) Therefore, the first consequence Jesus experienced when He took upon Himself on the cross all the sins of humanity was that His relationship with God was severed. He was cut off from life, union, and communion with the Father. This severance from God is the nature of spiritual death. Since all of humanity was spiritually dead in trespasses and sins, Jesus endured spiritual death for us. *"For [God] made [Jesus] who knew no sin to be sin for us, that we might become the righteousness of God in Him"* (2 Corinthians 5:21).

Jesus allowed Himself to be totally and genuinely abandoned by the Father for our sake. When He cried out on the cross, *"My God, My God, why have You forsaken Me?"* (Matthew 27:46), this was the first time He prayed without receiving an answer. Why was His prayer not answered? Because our sin in Him had broken His relationship with the Father.

The same truth applies to us, even as believers. God never loses the power or ability to hear the prayers of His people. But we may not receive answers to our prayers when we have sin in our lives, because our sin separates us from Him.

Only sin, or iniquity, can separate a person from God.

---

3. The "Second Death"

The Gospels don't specifically disclose what Jesus experienced in the afterlife between His death on the cross and His resurrection, but we are given some revelation from the book of Psalms and certain New Testament passages, which we will look at in this connection.

Jesus taught, *"For as Jonah was three days and three nights in the belly of the great fish, so will the Son of Man be three days and three nights in the heart of the earth"* (Matthew 12:40). After Jesus died, His spirit descended into hell. In the Bible, the afterlife is sometimes called "Sheol," or "Hades." In Jesus' parable of the rich man and Lazarus, Hades is described as being divided into two regions: a place of torment (where the spirits of the unbelieving awaited their final judgment) and *"Abraham's bosom"* (where the spirits of the righteous awaited the completion of the Messiah's mission of salvation, so they could dwell in God's presence). (See Luke 16:19–31.) Jesus underwent the torment in Hades, or Sheol, that we would have received.

The *"second death"* is eternal separation from God's presence. This is permanent spiritual death in hell—the realm where people will suffer the wrath of God for every sin and iniquity committed. (See, for example, Revelation 20:11–15.)

Jesus had to taste this form of death because He had to receive the punishment we would experience without His redemption. He endured the wrath of God in the spirit realm for the sins and iniquities of the entire human race in order to save us from that place of torment. Though Christ's suffering on the cross was horrendous, His spiritual suffering in hell, of which few believers are aware, was even more terrible. We sometimes believe that His resurrection was easy, but we have to understand from where He was raised. Here is a verse from the Psalms that depicts Christ's experience in the place of torment:

> My flesh also will rest in hope. For You will not leave my soul in Sheol, nor will You allow Your Holy One to see corruption.　　(Psalm 16:9–10)

Where the verse says *"My flesh,"* it refers to Christ's physical body. While His spirit was in Sheol, His body rested in the tomb and did not decay. (See Acts 2:31; Ephesians 4:8–10.) Psalm 71 also gives us a sense of Jesus' time in hell:

> You have allowed me to suffer much hardship, but you will restore me to life again and lift me up from the depths of the earth. You will restore me to even greater honor and comfort me once again.
> 　　　　　　　　　　　　　　　　　　　　(Psalm 71:20–21 NLT)

In Sheol, Jesus' primary suffering, again, was His separation from the Father. The direct communication They had shared throughout Jesus' life on earth was broken. He was alone and in darkness. But Jesus did not lose faith. I believe that the following words apply to Him, even though they were written by David:

> O LORD, God of my salvation, I have cried out day and night before You. Let my prayer come before You; incline Your ear to my cry. For

my soul is full of troubles, and my life draws near to the grave. I am counted with those who go down to the pit; I am like a man who has no strength, adrift among the dead, like the slain who lie in the grave, whom You remember no more, and who are cut off from Your hand. You have laid me in the lowest pit, in darkness, in the depths. Your wrath lies heavy upon me, and You have afflicted me with all Your waves. (Psalm 88:1–7)

This psalm describes Jesus as the perfect Lamb carrying all the sins and iniquities of humanity and receiving the wrath of God, not in His body but in His spirit. He received each judgment in His spirit. We can't even imagine the torment He experienced. If we were to summarize these verses, Jesus was basically saying, "My spirit is surrounded with evil; it has reached Sheol—the kingdom of the dead. I have turned into a man without God, cut off from His presence. I have been placed in the abyss—the lowest place, the place of thickest darkness—enduring the impact of God's wrath, locked in a prison. I have been cut off from My friends and family." (See Psalm 88:18.) His "friends" were now the tomb and darkness.

In this condition, Jesus asked certain questions of God:

Will You work wonders for the dead? Shall the dead arise and praise You? Shall Your lovingkindness be declared in the grave? Or Your faithfulness in the place of destruction? Shall Your wonders be known in the dark? And Your righteousness in the land of forgetfulness? (Psalm 88:10–12)

These questions were answered masterfully by Jesus' own resurrection from the dead, through which the Father honored the Son. The answer to all of them is "Yes!" Realizing that Jesus triumphed over the foes of death and hell, which were unconquerable to mankind, is key to understanding His full work on the cross and His resurrection. God has worked wonders for those who were spiritually dead and have lived under the inevitability of physical death. His marvels and His righteousness are known by all who have been spiritually resurrected in Jesus and will experience physical resurrection when He comes again!

At the same time, Jesus' resurrection brought about the remarkable, immediate resurrection of certain people who had died in faith. The Scriptures tell us, *"Many bodies of the saints who had fallen asleep were raised; and coming out of the graves after His resurrection, they went into the holy city and appeared to many"* (Matthew 27:52–53). It's not clear what happened to these saints after this event, but they had been in Abraham's bosom in Sheol, and when they received the news of Jesus' victory over sin and death, they arose from their graves by that same resurrection power.

> *The resurrection is the manifestation of*
> *God the Father honoring His Son.*

Jesus Experienced Two Resurrections on Our Behalf

The verb *resurrect* indicates "to rise," "to awaken from death," or "to return to life." Jesus experienced resurrection in two distinct ways so that we could live a new life in Him.

1. Jesus Was Made Alive in His Spirit

For Christ also suffered once for sins, the just for the unjust, that He might bring us to God, being put to death in the flesh but made alive by the Spirit. (1 Peter 3:18)

The Greek word translated *"made alive"* is zoopoieo, which also could be rendered "vitalized," "given life," or "quickened" (STRONG, G2227). I believe the above verse is saying that Jesus was vivified, or made alive, in His spirit by the working of the Holy Spirit before His physical body was raised from the dead. I picture this vivification occurring in the following way: While Jesus was in Sheol, receiving the punishment for our sin, a meeting was taking place in heaven. God the Father and the Holy Spirit, with the angelic beings looking on, were discussing His death and what judgment He should receive for becoming sin for us. Suddenly, the Father, the Judge of the universe, said, "Jesus of Nazareth, My Son, is not guilty. He never committed a sin but rather bore the sins of the world. Therefore, We must raise Him from the dead." While Satan and his demons were in the midst of celebrating what they thought was their defeat of God's Son, a great explosion was heard throughout hell. The Holy Spirit descended to resurrect Jesus. The power of God came upon His spirit, which was instantly made alive. That was the initial resurrection He experienced. By the same power, we will all be resurrected one day! (See Romans 6:5.) For now, we have received a *"guarantee"* of our complete spiritual resurrection with the gift of the indwelling Holy Spirit. (See, for example, Romans 6:4; 2 Corinthians 5:4–5.)

Yet, even after His spirit was resurrected, Jesus had not finished His work in the depths of the earth.

> *By the Spirit…He [also] went and preached to the spirits in prison….* (1 Peter 3:18–19)

The word *"preached"* in the above verse is *kerusso*, which means "to herald (as a public crier), especially divine truth"; it indicates "to proclaim" and "to publish" (STRONG, G2784). I interpret *"spirits"* here to mean evil spiritual entities, or demons. As God's messenger, Jesus went to the place where the demons are incarcerated in hell. What did He proclaim to them in that place? He wasn't proclaiming the gospel for purposes of salvation but rather making an announcement. I believe His declaration went something like this: "Everyone, listen! Now I am the Lord of Lords and King of Kings. All authority has been given to Me. Therefore, I have the keys of hell and death. I have defeated Satan, and now I live forever!"

Jesus also preached to those who were in Abraham's bosom, for their salvation.

> *For this reason the gospel was preached also to those who are dead, that they might be judged according to men in the flesh, but live according to God in the spirit.* (1 Peter 4:6)

These people had died in faith, waiting for the redemption of the Messiah, just as is described in Hebrews 11:13–16. They were first to receive the good news of the resurrection. As we have seen, this was confirmed by the fact that a number of them came out of their graves when Jesus was physically resurrected.

Therefore, when the heavenly court abolished Jesus' death sentence and the Holy Spirit raised Him spiritually, Jesus declared God's faithfulness to those who had died waiting for the Messiah, and He also proclaimed His victory before His enemies.

2. Jesus Was Made Alive in His Body

After Jesus' spirit was resurrected, it returned to His body in the tomb, where He was physically raised from death to live forever as a new Man. Christ defeated death in all three of its forms—physical death, spiritual death, and the second death. Nothing could stop Him! He conquered sin, the devil and his demons, death, and hell. God *"loosed the pains of death"* (Acts 2:24) when He raised Jesus, and He will do the same for us!

Mosaic law established that two trustworthy witnesses were sufficient to verify a truth. (See, for example, Deuteronomy 19:15.) However, God gave us more than two witnesses in confirming the truth of His Son Jesus and His mission. First, we have the testimony of the Old Testament prophets concerning the Messiah's coming (see, for example, Isaiah 53; Hosea 6:2), and the Scriptures are the highest authority and the absolute truth inspired by God. Eleven of Jesus' disciples (Judas had died), who had lived with Him for three years and been taught by Him, testified to seeing Him raised from the dead. Beyond them, there were more than five hundred people who witnessed Jesus' physical resurrection. And Paul encountered Christ on the road to Damascus. (See, for example, John 20:19–29; 1 Corinthians 15:3–8.) To this list, we could add everyone who has ever had an experience with the resurrected Christ and whose testimony is confirmed by the transformation of his heart and life.

To sum up, I believe this is the order in which the resurrection and glorification of Jesus occurred: First, He was raised from Sheol in a spiritual resurrection; second, He was physically raised from the dead; and, third, the Father exalted Him to His right hand in heaven, giving Him authority over everything and everyone.

> *Jesus Christ* [is] *the faithful witness, the firstborn from the dead, and the ruler over the kings of the earth.* (Revelation 1:5)

Jesus was the first to be resurrected in glory. He was the *"firstborn from the dead."* When we identify with Jesus' death, burial, and resurrection, we are "born again," and we become a new creation. Only when this occurs can we receive, by the law of inheritance and identification, every benefit granted by the resurrection. (See, for example, John 1:12–13; 1 Peter 1:3.) We are spiritually made alive and resurrected with Christ so that we can be seated in heavenly places and rule together with Him. Praise God!

When we identify with Jesus' death, burial, and resurrection, we become a new creation to rule and reign with Him.

Fundamental Accomplishments of Christ's Resurrection

Jesus' resurrection from the dead is foundational to God's plan to rescue the human race and bring His kingdom to earth, because it accomplished the following:

- Restored us to communion with the spiritual life of God. Jesus' death and resurrection made us one with the Father again; we have been reunited with Him. (See 2 Corinthians 5:18; 1 John 1:3.)

- Implanted in our mortal bodies the resurrection life, which will fully manifest when Christ returns for His church, at which point our bodies will be glorified like His. (See Romans 8:11.)

- Returned us to eternity in the presence of God. This is the consummation of Christ's perfect work on the cross and His resurrection. (See 1 Thessalonians 4:17; Revelation 21:1–3.)

- Seated us in heavenly places to rule with Christ. After paying for our sins and being raised from the dead, Jesus sat down on His throne at the right hand of the Father as our High Priest. His sitting down represented the fact that He had accomplished His work. Under the Levitical priesthood (instituted under the law of Moses), the priests never "sat down," because the presentation of sacrifices offered for the atonement of sins was perpetual. However, Jesus sat down forever, symbolizing His authority, government, and reign, because His work was done. Once His atoning work was accomplished, He gave us back the dominion that Adam had lost and—even more remarkable—seated us together with Him in His heavenly rule. The Son of God is the only King who allows His subjects to reign with Him. This is our inheritance! (See, for example, Ephesians 2:5–6; Hebrews 4:14; 6:20; 7:26–28; 10:11–13.)

It is a fact that Jesus died on the cross,
but it is a matter of faith that He rose from the dead.

A woman named Amalia, who is a member of a church in Argentina that is under the spiritual covering of King Jesus Ministry, witnessed the power of the resurrection to raise her child from the dead. She'd had an at-risk pregnancy that had caused her to go into labor in her sixth month. The birth was complicated, and the baby girl was stillborn. The doctors held the infant under observation for several hours, but she was finally declared officially dead, and her body was sent to the morgue. When the church heard the news, they began to intercede for the family.

As soon as Amalia was able, she asked to see her daughter's body, but because of the many rules and regulations, she had to wait twelve hours before receiving permission. Finally, she and her husband were allowed to go to the morgue. The forensic doctor led them to a small box where the baby's body lay dead. When he opened the box, Amalia and her husband saw that the baby was wrapped in cloth. Amalia removed the cloth and took her daughter's cold hand in hers to say good-bye. Suddenly, they heard a weak sound, and the baby moved. She was alive! The impact of this experience was so great that Amalia was on the verge of fainting. When the forensic doctor saw what was happening, he started to cry. He couldn't get over his shock. The baby had spent twelve hours in the morgue at extremely low temperatures. She was immediately taken to the neonatal unit and given the attention she required. There, the doctors confirmed that her vital signs were normal.

When the director of the hospital heard what had happened, he suspended every doctor and nurse who had attended at the delivery, thinking the baby's parents would file a malpractice suit, because he did not understand how something like this could occur. Finally, everyone had to admit that what had happened had been a miracle of God. The baby girl had been raised from death by the power of the resurrection of Jesus Christ, while she'd been in the morgue lying in the box! The news went out to the media throughout the country and the world. Today, the baby, Luz Milagros, is with her family, growing strong and healthy. Similar miracles can happen in your life, in your family, and in your church as you apply the power of the resurrection to your circumstances.

Essential Revelations of the Resurrection

Much of the church has not understood the essence of Christ's resurrection due to a lack of revelation concerning its indispensable truths. The main purpose of this chapter is to open the eyes of God's people to the spiritual significance that Jesus has been gloriously raised from the dead and imbues us with His power!

1. The Resurrection Is Always Revealed by the Holy Spirit in the Now

"*Later He appeared to the eleven* [apostles]" (Mark 16:14). The Greek word translated "*appeared*" is *phaneroo*, which means "to render apparent." It indicates "to appear," "to make manifest," and "to show oneself" (STRONG, G5318). This word especially means "to be revealed in one's true character."[5] In other words, Jesus revealed Himself to His followers as the living Christ. Why was this necessary, if the apostles already knew Him? Because they knew Him in a human sense, or "*according to the flesh*" (2 Corinthians 5:16), but they needed to know Him in the Spirit, in all of His deity and majesty. They needed to acknowledge Him not as the earthly Christ but as the eternal Christ who, in and of Himself, has all power and authority. It is the lack of this revelation that causes people to think of the resurrection as mere historical information. Therefore, revelation of the living Christ distinguishes between those who believe in the resurrection for the here and now—the eternal present—and those who believe in it as a historic event. The former are activated and receive Jesus' supernatural power in their lives.

We cannot genuinely believe something, or value it, if we lack revelation concerning it.

5. *Vine's Complete Expository Dictionary of Old and New Testament Words*, 32.

Revelation is essential because, without it, our faith cannot operate. Anything we do without faith is a dead work. (See James 2:20.) Regardless of which stage of life or ministry we might be in, and regardless of the size of our ministry or the extent of our service to the church, every genuine work for God must begin with the revelation of the resurrected Christ for the kingdom here and now.

Every minister and ministry must be established on the revelation of the resurrected Christ in the now.

2. Jesus' Resurrection Is the Demonstration of His Love and His Power

Through Christ's sacrifice on the cross, we are forgiven, but through His resurrection, we begin to operate in His power. God *is* love, but He *has* power. His love is the source of His power; He has no other power besides love. When Satan saw Jesus Christ, he knew Jesus was God because of the pure and sacrificial love He demonstrated, which prompted Him to heal, save, deliver, and set the oppressed free. When Satan encounters genuine love, he knows power is connected with it. And the greatest demonstration of God's love was Jesus' death on the cross for mankind.

Yet the church has often made the mistake of stopping at the cross. We must transition to the resurrection. Yes, Jesus' death redeemed, rescued, and saved us. And, through the cross, we crucify sin and the flesh. However, the resurrection gives us a new and eternal life in God, one that replaces the old life, which has been crucified with Christ.

Jesus was resurrected! The message of the cross and the message of the resurrection must always be preached together. We will have a new dimension of God's power when we enter into a new dimension of His love. And, when the genuine love of God flows from us, it produces a demonstration of the power of the resurrection.

The cross is the demonstration of Christ's love.
The resurrection is the demonstration of His power.

As we receive the revelation of Christ's resurrection and truly live in it, we will witness miracles, signs, wonders, and the raising of the dead, which will advance God's kingdom on earth. Receive this revelation by the Holy Spirit right now! I declare that your eyes and ears are open to understand that Christ lives and that the power of His resurrection is active and available—here and now—as we see in the following testimony.

Stephanie González of Georgia was born with a cleft palate and deafness in her left ear. When she was just four months old, she had her first surgery for the cleft palate, which was successful. When she was several years older, she endured a very painful surgery in which part of her tongue was cut to further repair the cleft palate. This left her unable to speak for over two months. She was fed through a tube, and she was able to communicate only by writing. Her mother, Argelia, prayed, "Lord, I need to see Your work. I need to see a ray of hope, because I am losing her." Those were moments of anguish and desperation, but even in her delicate state, it was Stephanie who tried to console her mother by writing, "Mommy, I am fine. I will speak again. I promise. We will overcome this trial together."

Stephanie also underwent surgery to restore the hearing in her left ear, but the procedure did not work. Later, when she was having dental surgery, the doctor said that there was an infection in her right ear that was so bad, the eardrum had closed, and there was nothing he could do. The infection had perforated the cranium, and she lost the hearing in her right ear, also. She was totally deaf. Only a cranium implant or a miracle could restore her ability to hear.

Argelia was invited by her brother to a conference in Atlanta sponsored by King Jesus Ministry, and she brought Stephanie with her. However, she didn't understand that Jesus still heals, and she kept repeating, "No one can help me." She felt guilty, and she asked herself what she had done wrong to deserve so many years of sacrifice and pain with her daughter. She wondered what would happen in the future, and she worried that she would eventually lose her daughter.

But then, God did a creative miracle of healing at the conference! Today, Stephanie has perfect hearing in both of her ears, without implants, and she also speaks normally. Argelia is grateful for every person who prayed for them. She is very happy to know Jesus, and she affirms that "the miracle Jesus did on my daughter is priceless." Stephanie is very intelligent and has since earned several school awards and is doing better academically than the other students in her class. She even won an award for writing an essay entitled "My Life Story." Her testimony is a wonderful demonstration of Jesus' resurrection power to heal and restore.

The cross is a known historical fact,
but the resurrection must be revealed in the now.

3. Jesus' Resurrection Is the Foundation and Sustenance of Christianity

And with great power the apostles gave witness to the resurrection of the Lord Jesus. (Acts 4:33)

There would be no Christianity without Jesus' resurrection. This is the foundation of Christ's church. Without the resurrection to culminate the work of the cross, there would be no forgiveness of sin, and there would be no salvation, because it is resurrection power that activates that work. (See 1 Corinthians 15:17; Romans 10:9–10.) No amount of words, principles, laws, or doctrines can replace the work and power of Christ. People who have an encounter with the power of the resurrection say, "I used to be [and they mention some manifestation of the sinful nature or satanic oppression], but now I am a totally different person. The evil things I used to do, I no longer do."

The resurrection is the only source of power for transforming the heart.

4. If Christ Had Not Been Resurrected, Our Faith and Message Would Be in Vain

And if Christ is not risen, then our preaching is empty and your faith is also empty. (1 Corinthians 15:14)

If we don't believe that Jesus was raised from the dead or that His resurrection has living power for today, then what—and why—are we preaching to others? The early church testified and proclaimed the resurrection by releasing demonstrations of its power. If you are a pastor or an evangelist, let me ask you: When was the last time you preached about the resurrection? Have you been preaching about Christian principles but not explaining to people how they can have the power to obey them? The principles are important, but the only way for the power of God to be released is for people to receive the revelation of the resurrection for the here and now. Will people continue to be lost and sick if you preach the power of the resurrection? No! People will receive salvation, healing, and deliverance; they will be transformed and live in prosperity. These things come through faith in the risen Christ, who lives in the here and now—the eternal present. In the book of Acts, we read of great manifestations of the power of God—extraordinary miracles that occurred as a result of the disciples preaching the resurrection of Christ. I have seen the same in my own ministry. In my opinion, this is the main ingredient lacking in the church today.

5. The Resurrection Validates and Vindicates Christ as the Son of God

Jesus was judged and found "guilty" by two earthly courts—religious and secular—even though He was innocent. The human race as a whole rejected Him. (See Psalm 2:1–3.) But, as we have seen, God Almighty, from His Supreme Court, overturned the decision and, on the third day, vindicated Christ by raising Him from the dead. (See Acts 13:29–31.) To use a human analogy, this was similar to the Supreme Court of the United States overturning the ruling of a lower court and issuing a new ruling.

> *He who sits in the heavens shall laugh; the LORD shall hold them in derision. Then He shall speak to them in His wrath, and distress them in His deep displeasure: "Yet I have set My King on My holy hill of Zion."*
> (Psalm 2:4–6)

In the Bible, God's laughter is always an expression of victory, never of something humorous. The affirmation *"I have set My King"* refers to Christ being given all power and authority by the Father. Before the foundation of the world, Christ was the *"Lamb slain"* (Revelation 13:8) for our sins, and He was also anointed as King over all things, even though He had to come to earth to fulfill these heavenly realities.

If Jesus had not been resurrected, His identity as Lord and King would not have been verified. In a sense, the resurrection completely fulfilled the Father's decree in Psalm 2:7, *"You are My Son, today I have begotten You."* The Hebrew word translated *"begotten"* is *yalad,* meaning "to bear," "to beget," "to bring forth" (STRONG, NASC, H3205). With the new verdict of the heavenly Supreme Court, the Father eternally "brought forth" Jesus from within Himself as the Son of God.

Jesus' resurrection confirms that He is who He claims to be, because the tomb could not hold Him back. His resurrection proves His deity, His lordship, and His kingdom. In light of these facts, it is not enough to preach about the cross alone. The apostle Paul never saw the resurrected Christ with his own eyes, though he did encounter Him in brilliant light on the road to Damascus, and Paul talked far more about the resurrection than the cross. To Paul, the cross *and* the resurrection were not mere historic events but realities on which to base one's life and faith.

The resurrection is the validation and vindication of Christ as the Son of God and the confirmation of everything He claimed to be.

6. Christ Is the Only One with a Testimony of Being Raised from the Dead

The testimony of Jesus is the spirit of prophecy.   (Revelation 19:10)

Jesus was the first to be spiritually and physically raised from the dead. He was; He is; and He will come again to earth as Victor. (See Revelation 4:8.) The Old Testament prophecies of the Anointed One, or Messiah, point to Him. They confirm that He is God and Sovereign of the kingdom. If Christ had not been resurrected, it would have been a declaration that death had defeated Him, and He would not be different from any other prophet, teacher, or philosopher who has ever lived.

No religious leaders, prophets, or philosophers could truthfully testify to having lived a sinless life, been raised from the dead, and been glorified by God the Father. Everyone else is still dead: Buddha, Confucius, Muhammad, Karl Marx, Mahatma Gandhi, and more. Their followers admit this reality without a problem and even visit their grave sites each year. But the tomb where Jesus was buried was vacated! He lives! This fact places Jesus in a unique category; it also identifies Him and sets Him apart as God. Death, the tomb, and hell could not hold Him. (See Acts 2:24.)

Yet the authenticity of Jesus' testimony is under attack and persecution by the enemy in our day, just as it was in the first century. Because of the testimony of Jesus, Stephen was stoned to death, Peter was crucified, the apostle Paul was imprisoned and likely executed, and John was exiled to the Isle of Patmos. Satan is terrified of the testimony of the resurrection because he knows it has the power to overturn the kingdom of darkness.

We need to provide proof of Jesus' resurrection through the supernatural power of the kingdom of God. Suppose a defense lawyer was developing a case to present in court and was considering you as one of his witnesses. To be a useful witness, you would need to have some personal experience or evidence pertaining to the case to present before the judge and jury. If you didn't have any experience or evidence, it would be pointless for the lawyer to call you to testify. Similarly, a true witness to Christ is someone who has supernatural evidence of His resurrection. In the present-day church, many people's testimonies are fruitless because they proclaim Christ without any evidence. This is because, in ministry today, people are often evaluated according to qualifications that do not align with the standard of the Bible. It is easy to preach something that we have not experienced.

Are we being true witnesses? Where is our evidence of the empty tomb? Where is the proof, through supernatural miracles, signs, wonders, and the raising of the dead, that Jesus resurrected and is alive in our personal lives and ministries? Are we willing to risk persecution for preaching the complete message of the kingdom, the cross, and Christ's resurrection by releasing His supernatural power on earth?

Had Jesus not resurrected, He would be no different from any other prophet, teacher, or philosopher.

7. The Resurrection Established Christ's Kingdom and Destroyed Satan's Kingdom

Having disarmed principalities and powers, He made a public spectacle of them, triumphing over them in it. (Colossians 2:15)

When Jesus was publicly executed, His death on the cross must have appeared to be utterly humiliating. To add to His spiritual and physical suffering, He was mocked by the Roman guards who beat Him and by many onlookers at His crucifixion. However, it was actually Satan who was humiliated by Christ's victory over sin and death, and his defeat was publicly exposed by Jesus' resurrection. When Christ was raised from the dead, He confirmed His lordship, set up His kingdom as the legitimate government, and established dominion over Satan. If He had not been resurrected, He would have had no kingdom to rule, and Satan's kingdom would still have dominion over the earth. Praise God that Jesus rose from the dead and defeated Satan, taking from him all power and authority!

Every time we preach the resurrection, we remind Satan of his defeat.

8. Christ's Resurrection Won Our Salvation, Redemption, Justification, and Resurrection

Jesus Christ bought our freedom from the kingdom of darkness, in which we were slaves. Even though we were guilty, He redeemed us and declared us righteous in Him, as if we had never sinned. If Jesus had not resurrected, we would not only still be in sin, but we would also have no basis for redemption. (See Luke 1:68–69; 1 Corinthians 15:17; Romans 6:11.) As the first to be raised from the dead, Jesus is the head of a new race. (See Ephesians 2:15.) Just as we were included in Adam's fall from dominion and his death, we are included in Jesus' resurrection and His eternal life. Again, His resurrection guarantees our resurrection, as well! (See 2 Corinthians 4:14.) Our bodies will be transformed into glorious bodies, like Christ's, when He returns for His church. (See Philippians 3:20–21.)

9. The Resurrection Gives Us the Right to Rule Over Everything Jesus Conquered

For if by the one man's offense death reigned through the one, much more those who receive abundance of grace and of the gift of righteousness will reign in life through the One, Jesus Christ. (Romans 5:17)

Through His death and resurrection, Jesus conquered sin, death, hell, the devil and his demons, sickness, the old nature and the flesh, the world, fear, poverty, vengeance, rejection, curses, and much more. Everything Jesus Christ defeated is now subject to His dominion—it is a conquered enemy. I encourage you today to take authority and dominion through Christ over every enemy that was conquered by His resurrection.

10. The Message of the Power of the Resurrection Releases Miracles, Signs, and Wonders Here and Now

What did the disciples believe, and what did they preach? The reality and message of Christ's resurrection! *"And they went out and preached everywhere, the Lord working with them and confirming the word through the accompanying signs"* (Mark 16:20). Supernatural signs followed them to endorse their message.

Pastors Maiken and Raquel Suniaja of Venezuela are two of my spiritual children. For ten years, they were members of a church where the pastor was a very nice man but did not believe in the supernatural power of God. As a result, there was no fruit of the presence of the Lord in that place. One day, Maiken found our ministry's Web site, where he listened to my message "Accelerating in the Supernatural." What he heard opened his spiritual senses, activated him, and led him to make a radical decision. He heard God's voice saying that he should look for a location and establish a church. He did, and, from the beginning, God performed miracles to confirm the message of the gospel of the kingdom that he was proclaiming. Every time he finished preaching, he would minister the power of God, and the people began to be healed of cancer and other infirmities and to receive deliverance from various addictions.

Three months later, I met pastors Maiken and Raquel at an event in Caracas. There, they received greater activation. Since then, miracles and resurrections from the dead through their ministry have multiplied, particularly among infants. Pastor Raquel is a registered nurse who works in two clinics. One day, a pregnant mother arrived in the emergency room with the diagnosis that her baby had died in her womb. Several tests had been done, and the baby had been declared dead. Pastor Raquel said, "I remembered the teaching on the power of the resurrection and took God's authority. I placed both hands on the mother's womb and said, 'Your child will live.' I then rebuked the spirit of death from the child, in the name of Jesus. When the woman was wheeled into the operating room to have her dead baby removed, the surgical team found that it was alive!" The doctors and the mother could not get over their shock, and the news revolutionized the clinic.

Another time, a pregnant woman was brought to one of Pastor Raquel's clinics, and the doctors could not detect any vital signs in her; neither she nor her child had a heartbeat. Medically speaking, they were dead. Without giving it another thought, Pastor Raquel laid hands on the mother's forehead and decreed life over her, saying, "Resurrect, right now!" Within seconds, the woman's vital signs were normal, and the baby's heartbeat was detected.

In another case, a baby was stillborn. Pastor Raquel was assisting the pediatrician, who did CPR but was unable to bring the child back to life. The baby's skin was beginning to turn purple, and his body was rigid. Pastor Raquel said, "At that moment, the only thing I thought was that it was Jesus' turn to intervene. I laid hands on the baby's body and rebuked the spirit of death and declared resurrection and life over the boy." Praise God, after she prayed, a normal pink color returned to the baby's skin, and he was completely healthy. God had raised him from the dead! Pastors Maiken and Raquel Suniaja continue to demonstrate that God's presence is with them and that they have been anointed to manifest His glory.

*When the Holy Spirit reveals the resurrection,
it is confirmed with miracles, signs, and wonders.*

How to Walk in the Power of the Resurrection

Let us now look at key principles for living in the power of Christ's resurrection.

1. Die to the "Old Man"—the Flesh, or the Carnal Self

"I have been crucified with Christ" (Galatians 2:20) is a declaration of death to the "old man"—the flesh, or the carnal self—and the most important condition for the power of the resurrection life to manifest through us. We have often been taught to live for Christ, but the Bible also teaches that we must die to self in order to be able to live for Him. We must be "crucified" with Christ so that we can enter into His life.

I am not referring to a physical or spiritual death—Jesus paid the price of sin and death for us. Again, this is a death of the fleshly desires. Jesus' experience of death was unique, but all of us need to die to ourselves in order to receive and operate in His resurrection power. Whenever our carnal self, or sinful nature, gets in the way, it can block the power of God in our lives.

Many believers are incapable of manifesting the resurrection life because they have yet to die to self and make the choice to live according to the Spirit. The life of the kingdom has been made available to every believer by faith. When the resurrection life of Jesus is active within us, we can also minister it to others in healing and deliverance.

> [Jesus said,] *"Unless a grain of wheat falls into the ground and dies, it remains alone; but if it dies, it produces much grain. He who loves his life will lose it, and he who hates his life in this world will keep it for eternal life."* (John 12:24–25)

In Greek, there are various words that denote "life," depending on the particular sense that is being conveyed. In the above verse, the word translated *"life"* is *psuche*, which means "the soul" (NASC, G5590), or indicates "the seat of personality."[6] The soul consists of the mind, will, and emotions; it is the center of our feelings, desires, affections, and preferences.

I believe that in verse 25, Christ was basically saying that if we love our *psuche*—what we think, feel, and want—without pursuing what God wants,

---

6. *Vine's Complete Expository Dictionary of Old and New Testament Words*, 588.

we will die spiritually. But if we hate our lives, in the sense of turning away from *"the spirit of the world"* (1 Corinthians 2:12), we will receive eternal life. We cannot lead selfish lives and the life of the resurrection at the same time; it is impossible for us to manifest both at once. One must die for the other to live. We must die to the old life to give way to our new life.

We cannot manifest the power of the resurrection until we die to self.

When we die to self, another Person—Christ—begins to live in and through us. *"It is no longer I who live, but Christ lives in me"* (Galatians 2:20). We have become totally different people because we are dead to the sinful nature. Sin can't control us, because we no longer control ourselves. We no longer do exactly what we want or feel but what Jesus wants. When we reach this point, then we are ready to live by the faith of Christ. The supreme sign that Jesus was dead to His own *psuche,* or self, was manifested in the garden of Gethsemane, where He died to His own will before the crucifixion, praying, *"O My Father, if it is possible, let this cup pass from Me; nevertheless, not as I will, but as You will"* (Matthew 26:39). Jesus humbled Himself, and that is why God exalted Him.

Living the resurrection life is a matter of constantly choosing to deny ourselves: *"If anyone desires to come after Me, let him deny himself, and take up his cross daily, and follow Me"* (Luke 9:23). For Jesus to manifest His life through us, we must do His will, not our own. We must continually elect to think Jesus' thoughts rather than our own thoughts. This can be accomplished only through the power of His resurrection and by walking in the Spirit. (See, for example, Galatians 5:16–25.) The flesh instinctively wants to retake control, but if we daily decide to allow Jesus to live through us, we will produce abundant fruit.

We will live to the degree that we are willing to die.

The apostle Paul said to all Christians,

If then you were raised with Christ, seek those things which are above, where Christ is, sitting at the right hand of God. Set your mind on

things above, not on things on the earth. For you died, and your life is
hidden with Christ in God. (Colossians 3:1–3)

The emphasis here is not on faith but on reaching the end of one's self. Each one of us must come to the point at which, having tried it all according to our own abilities, we give up because there are no more alternatives but Christ. That is when we renounce our old lifestyle and say to our heavenly Father, "Lord, let Your life flow through me." We must die to self each day. This is a lifelong process. We will die ten thousand deaths to self before reaching our final destination.

Humility and surrender are the supreme signs that we have died to self.

When we die to ourselves, all resistance to change and transformation by God disappears. We stop fighting and surrender to Him. If we are still fighting, it means that the sinful nature is still dominant in us. When we totally surrender, we no longer resist God's will. We become His "property." We no longer care what people do to us or what a doctor's report says, because we trust fully in God's power. We are no longer afraid to take leaps of faith or great risks, because we know we have nothing to lose. Always keep this in mind: The more completely you die to self, the more the power of the resurrection will manifest in and through you.

2. Live by the Faith of Christ Within You, Here and Now

The believer's life of faith begins at the resurrection, after death to self. *"The life which I now live in the flesh I live by faith in the Son of God"* (Galatians 2:20). We cannot operate in faith if we are living in a natural, carnal state in which we are dominated by reason, time, and space. The flesh can't produce faith, because it is a heavenly *"substance"* (Hebrews 11:1), not a natural one. Hence our need for Jesus' faith, not our own.

Christ's faith dwelling in us is the resurrection life.

"Now faith is…" (Hebrews 11:1). When we die to self, we receive the faith of Christ, which is for the now, and we begin to flow in the power of

the resurrection that dwells within us through the Holy Spirit. When the flesh is alive, the impossible is very real, but when the flesh is dead, our reality is *"with God all things are possible"* (Mark 10:27).

Many believers fail in faith for the "now" because they try to believe before crucifying their egos. What their eyes see is more real than the invisible reality. But the supernatural, eternal dimension can be seen and believed only with God's faith, not with the flesh. Faith, therefore, is the evidence of resurrection power.

When Jesus died, He nailed the word "impossible" to the cross. It is only through the cross and the resurrection that we pass into the supernatural realm. The instant Christ was raised from the dead, everything became a possibility to those who believe. Now, we have the same life that operates in Christ!

Faith is the life of Christ in the believer that comes from His resurrection.

Having the faith of God gives us a celestial perspective, from which everything is possible. When we declare or decree God's truth, we do so from a position of ruling in heaven, together with the King. The heavens don't recognize the word *impossible* because there, everything is completed, healed, transformed, saved, and free. Christ lives in us by the resurrection; we are His dwelling place. This indwelling is different from a visitation, such as occurred in the Old Testament, when God came to His people for only limited periods of time. Now, He remains in us. And, when we minister to other people, He comes to them through us.

Because faith is for the here and now, we should not postpone doing anything in the present in hopes of doing it in the future. We can receive what we pray for this instant. We should no longer struggle to believe but simply surrender and humble ourselves and allow Jesus to live His life, His faith, and the power of His resurrection in us. There has to come a time in our lives when we are finally dead to sickness, criticism, rejection, unforgiveness, insecurities, fear, and so on. I declare an open heaven over your life, right now! From this day forward, Jesus lives His life through you. Allow Him to heal you, deliver you, and transform you.

Faith is now, when we die to self.

3. Receive Your Inheritance of the Resurrection by Faith

That you may know...what are the riches of the glory of His inheritance in the saints, and what is the exceeding greatness of His power toward us who believe, according to the working of His mighty power which He worked in Christ when He raised Him from the dead and seated Him at His right hand in the heavenly places.

(Ephesians 1:18–20)

The church was birthed from Christ's resurrection, and we are the continuation of His resurrection on the earth today. It is our inheritance in Him, but we can receive the riches and power of this inheritance only by faith. Jesus' resurrection power includes the manifestation of the former and latter glories together. (See Haggai 2:9.) The former glory includes all the supernatural acts that took place from the law and the prophets in the Old Testament through John the Baptist in the New Testament. Jesus was the bridge between the former glory and the latter glory. He ushered in the latter glory after His resurrection. This glorious movement was released in the upper room on Pentecost with the outpouring of the Holy Spirit.

We have the testimony of Christ—He is risen and alive! Therefore, we must demonstrate the resurrection with the combined power of the former and latter glories, which will manifest with an acceleration of salvations, miracles, signs, wonders, the casting out of demons, and the raising of the dead wherever we go.

If the revelation of the resurrection is absent, there will be no supernatural power in the church.

4. Know Christ in the Power of His Resurrection

That I may know [Christ] and the power of His resurrection, and the fellowship of His sufferings, being conformed to His death.

(Philippians 3:10)

The Greek word translated *"know"* in the above verse is *ginosko*, which means "to come to know, recognize, perceive" (NASC, G1097). These definitions indicate "to experience." The above verse refers to having an experience with the person of Christ and the power of His resurrection. This was the apostle Paul's desire, and it should be ours, too, because what we know of Christ determines the faith we can put into effect today. If we don't know Him, we will never be able to demonstrate resurrection power, for only those who have experienced Him can demonstrate it.

The phrase *"That I may know* [Christ]*"* includes having an experience with His resurrection power in every aspect. For example, we must know the power of Christ as dominion (territorial power), anointing (the power to serve), faith (the power to do miracles), rule (the power of God in the realm of authority), perseverance (the power for character transformation), strength (the power for spiritual warfare), prosperity (the power to gain wealth), and so forth.

The outpouring of the Holy Spirit is the continuation of Christ's resurrection.

We can recognize a person who has had an experience with the power of Jesus' resurrection, because that person will exhibit a new perspective—the perspective of God. When you have a revelation of, and an experience with, the power of the resurrection, no one can tell you that there's something God cannot do. So many theologians speak about God but have never had an experience with His power, and this is evident by the limited things they say about God and about themselves. Every time people have a true experience with Jesus and the power of His resurrection, they will be transformed, and their way of thinking will be changed. They will know that anything is possible, because they will have God's outlook.

Every aspect of supernatural power is concentrated in the power of Christ's resurrection. We cannot be satisfied with merely knowing about Jesus. We will be able to carry out the Great Commission and spread God's kingdom throughout the world only when we have experienced Him and the power of His resurrection.

The resurrection life that flows through us is supernatural by nature and origin. Miracles, signs, wonders, and the raising of the dead should be the norm for us.

In light of the above, I need to pose a question: When we understand the power that released Christ's resurrection and understand that nothing is impossible if we have His faith, can believers raise the dead today? Of course they can! This was one of Christ's mandates for His disciples.

And as you go, preach, saying, "The kingdom of heaven is at hand." Heal the sick, cleanse the lepers, raise the dead.... (Matthew 10:7–8)

Mani Efran is a Turkish pastor and prophet. He and several of the leaders whom he is training attended a conference in Turkey where I taught on the supernatural. All the attendees left filled with supernatural faith to pray for the sick. One of the pastors who is under the covering of Pastor Efran's church returned to Iran, where a church member asked if he could pray for his father, who was very ill. This pastor and his wife went to the hospital, but when they arrived at the room, the nurses were disconnecting the machines that had been hooked up to the patient, who had just died. As soon as they were alone with the man, however, they laid hands on his dead body, declaring that God would resurrect him. When nothing happened, they were saddened and went to find the man's family in the waiting room.

They offered their condolences and apologized for arriving too late, but the man's son said, "What are you talking about? My father is not dead!" And he ran to check on his father, who was indeed alive—in a different hospital room. In the meantime, another family was shouting with joy, saying that *their* father had awakened from the dead, asking, "Where is the couple that prayed for me? Bring me the couple. I saw them!"

As it turned out, the desk clerk had directed the pastor and his wife to the wrong room. God had raised the other man from the dead after their prayers! This man said that he'd had a vision of his hospital room, and he'd seen his dead body as he'd watched the couple come into the room and pray for him. He recognized them when he saw them again. He was totally healed and started telling everyone that Jesus had resurrected him! Consequently, he and his entire family received Jesus as Savior. Although the man for whom this couple had prayed was not the person they had originally gone to see, God still did the miracle because of their supernatural boldness. They had prayed for his resurrection, and the power of God had raised him from death!

There are certain aspects concerning the resurrection of the dead that are essential to understand. When I was on a twenty-one day fast, God told me that raising the dead would be a common occurrence in my ministry and in the ministries of the people whom I teach and train. This word has come to pass. When someone reads one of my books or listens to one of my messages, that person is activated to do what I teach and describe, through God's power. In this way, resurrections from the dead have multiplied. Through the years, the Lord has trained and equipped me regarding how to conduct myself in relation to this mandate. As we continue to discuss principles for how to walk in resurrection power, I will give you some important revelations to observe in order to raise the dead.

5. Recognize and Understand God's Sovereignty

God is the Author and Finisher of life, and we need to acknowledge His sovereignty in all aspects of manifesting the supernatural. The sovereignty of God means that He does what He wants, as He wants, and when He wants. Therefore, raising a person from the dead depends totally on His will. Life and death are in His hands; they are out of man's control. We must pray in order to discern His will and receive guidance from the Holy Spirit.

One time, a woman in our church asked me to raise her nineteen-year-old son from the dead. I proceeded to the funeral home, full of faith, believing that God would raise him. When I arrived, the body of the young man was lying in the coffin. He had been dead one day. I didn't know what to do because I had not yet seen anyone resurrected in my ministry. I took the ice-cold hand of the young man and rebuked the spirit of death, but nothing happened. I prayed three more times, and still nothing happened. Then I heard God say, "He is with Me." I didn't want to hear that. I wanted to see the young man rise from the dead. However, I obeyed God and told the man's parents what I had heard from Him. Their response was, "Stop praying. That is enough for us." It was not God's will to raise this young man from the dead, and the parents simply wanted to have the assurance that their son was with Christ. God is sovereign.

6. Receive a Rhema, or a Revealed "Now" Word, from the Holy Spirit

To act with supernatural power in the realm of healing or miracles, we must have a "rhema," or a revealed word from the Holy Spirit for the now. (*Rhema* is a Greek term for "word.") This is why, when the time comes to raise a person from the dead, we need to have a rhema for the specific circumstance in that particular moment. We cannot raise the dead simply by a general confession of promises from the Bible.

Christ defeated death; it is a conquered enemy. However, death still has authority over those who live in disobedience, and this is why I have emphasized the importance of dying to ourselves and living according to Christ's faith. Believers who are full of Christ's resurrection power have dominion over death. Therefore, if we receive a rhema from the Holy Spirit concerning raising someone from the dead, we can rebuke the spirit of death in the name of Jesus and cast it out with authority. Then, we can order the person to return to life. Jesus said, "*I am the resurrection and the life. He who believes in Me, though he may die, he shall live*" (John 11:25).

According to Jewish tradition, it took three days—from the moment of death—for the soul to depart from the vicinity of the body.[7] In Lazarus's resurrection, Jesus may have been acknowledging this tradition by waiting until the fourth day—after the doctor and priest had declared Lazarus dead, and after the body had begun to decompose—to prove the veracity of the miracle of raising him. When Jesus ordered the stone taken away from the tomb, Martha answered, "*Lord, by this time there is a stench, for he has been dead four days*" (John 11:39). There was no question that Lazarus was dead. Standing outside the tomb, Jesus called, "*Lazarus, come forth!*" (verse 43). And Lazarus appeared!

Leticia Palmer is a youth pastor at a church in Mexico that is under our church's spiritual covering. When she and her husband, Pastor Rodrigo, visited King Jesus Ministry for the first time, they were ministering to eighty-three young people. Since that time, there has been a youth

---

7. www.biblegateway.com/resources/commentaries/IVP-NT/John/Jesus-Raises-Lazarus.

explosion in their church, so that they now have more than 4,000. The Palmers are an example of submission and obedience to God, which has caused them to experience His supernatural power in amazing ways. They have seen countless miracles and healings as a result of the impartation of power they received through our ministry.

One such miracle occurred while Pastor Leticia was at the movies with her family. She received a phone call from one of her disciples, who told her that the mother of a twelve-year-old boy from their church was extremely ill; her vital signs were weakening in an alarming way. Because the boy's family lived in a rural town, far from the city, it took a long time for the ambulance to arrive. Pastor Leticia called the young boy and heard him crying, saying that the paramedics had arrived and declared his mother dead. Immediately, two memories came to her mind. The first was of a woman whom she had prayed for two years earlier who had not resurrected from the dead. As a result of this experience, Pastor Leticia had acquired a fear of praying for resurrection. The second memory was of the deliverance from this fear she had received during a session of the Supernatural Fivefold Ministry School sponsored by King Jesus Ministry.

Pastor Leticia then took a bold step of faith and asked the boy to place the phone close to his mother's ear, so that she could pray for her. He did, and she began to rebuke the spirit of death with renewed authority. Within moments, she heard the boy's mother vomiting, and so she continued praying. The paramedics rushed the woman to the hospital to stabilize her. The Spirit of God had delivered her from the spirit of death and brought her back to life! And that isn't all. The testimony fired up the church's youth, and, on the very same day, as some of the young people traveled to the hospital to visit with the twelve-year-old boy, they proclaimed the gospel to their taxi drivers. They witnessed to the woman's family members at the hospital, and they also began to pray for the sick. The woman's entire family, who had witnessed her death and resurrection, gave their lives to Christ. Many souls were saved that day!

A few days later, Pastor Rodrigo preached to the church about stepping out in faith to pray for healings, miracles, and resurrections. Two young girls, ages fourteen and fifteen, took hold of that word. Just a week later, their grandmother suffered a severe heart attack and died, bleeding from her nose and ears. The two girls ran to her, scared but full of the boldness of the Holy Spirit. They got on top of her and prayed, and the grandmother's vital signs returned! She was taken to the hospital, and the doctor could not understand how a ninety-year-old woman could have survived such a severe attack. The Lord had raised her from death by His power! These testimonies are transforming lives, and pastors Rodrigo and Leticia are planting the seed of the supernatural in the youth of their church. The glory of God is moving in their city like never before!

Raising the dead is an amazing miracle and sign. Jesus did it, the apostles did it, I have done it, others whom I have taught and trained have done it, and you can do it, too! Release the power of His resurrection right now!

In the latter days, the resurrection of the dead will be a common manifestation, because believers will understand the power of Christ's resurrection.

In addition to raising people from physical death, God resurrects us in other ways. He can resurrect our visions, dreams, ministries, families, finances, and businesses. He can resurrect our health by doing creative miracles, such as generating new organs. Receive this revelation right now, in the name of Jesus! He is stirring up a new generation of believers who will raise the dead physically, spiritually, psychologically, emotionally, and financially. Are you a member of this new generation? Are you available for God to use you? Do you believe in the power of the resurrection? If you do, I want to guide you in a prayer of surrender to God, so that He can live His life in you and manifest His power through you. Please pray the following out loud:

Lord Jesus, thank You for dying for me, descending into hell, and paying the price for my sins. You received the wrath of God in my place. I give You all honor and glory. Forgive me for living life on my own terms and not allowing You to rule me. From this day forward, I surrender to You, and I ask You to rule over me and to live Your life through me.

You resurrect my life, my vision, my dreams, my health, my home, and my finances. I am healed and free. I receive a creative miracle, right now! Jesus, I adore You because the impossible has become possible through Your resurrection. I am now able to exercise dominion and rule over the enemy in the territory You have given me. Thank You for making me a fellow heir with You of God's blessings.

I acknowledge that the power of the resurrection is available and active through me wherever I go. I can do all things through Christ who strengthens me! Nothing is impossible for me, as nothing is impossible for God. I am an extension of the resurrected Christ on earth in order to advance His kingdom. He lives, and I live according to His life and faith. Amen!

4

The Spiritual Conflict
Between Two Kingdoms

We are living in times of great conflict! Many people are aware of the wars and political unrest that are taking place around the world, but most people overlook the invisible spiritual conflict that takes place daily between the kingdom of light and the kingdom of darkness. Each person on earth, without exception, is aligned with either one kingdom or the other, whether he realizes it or not. There is no neutrality.

One of my spiritual sons, named Peter, is fully engaged in this battle. Here is his testimony.

"When I was fourteen years old, my father died of AIDS, and I started doing drugs every day. I smoked and drank alcohol and got kicked out of schools. By the time I was seventeen, I was diagnosed with schizoaffective disorder and obsessive-compulsive disorder. The doctors said there was no cure for me and that I would be on medication for the rest of my life. I was empty and wanted to die. I also felt trapped. During this time, I believed in God but not in Jesus.

"A friend of mine would always preach to me and invite me to church, and one day I accepted. It was the wildest church environment I had ever seen! I knew something special was happening; I just didn't understand what it was. They made the call to accept Jesus, and although I had my doubts, I felt something pulling me to go up to the altar. I accepted Jesus and got baptized. I felt like a new, changed man. That night, I felt electricity going up and down my body. From that point on, God has been speaking to me and showing me that Jesus is the only way. He delivered me from mental illness, and I got off the medication. My psychiatrist told me that I would last between two weeks and two years without the medication, but no more than that. It has been over nine years since I have been off the medication, and I am still free from depression.

"After I truly committed to the Lord, I would spend hours worshipping Him and evangelizing people. In 2002, I started visiting the church that is now my home church, King Jesus Ministry, and I joined the Evangelism Explosion Ministry. We were all on fire and crazy for souls. I became an evangelistic leader, and, nowadays, we are moving in miracles, signs, and wonders, bringing the supernatural power of God to people in the streets, at colleges and universities, at shopping malls, in restaurants, in hospitals, and more."

Peter and his leaders and disciples are defying the forces of darkness with the supernatural power of God, bringing healings, signs, and wonders, and opening the spiritual eyes of people who are trapped in Satan's kingdom. They are waging warfare, and the kingdom of God is being established by spiritual force!

To truly fathom this conflict between the kingdom of God and the kingdom of Satan, we must have a thorough understanding of how these two kingdoms are diametrically opposed to one another. In this chapter, we will first explore the root of spiritual conflict. Then, we will learn the nature of God's kingdom and how it rules, and contrast it with the kingdom of darkness and how it functions. We will examine in greater depth the reason these two kingdoms are at war and how Satan was thoroughly defeated through the cross. We will conclude by addressing two related battles: the war between the flesh and the Spirit, and the major conflict of the end times.

The Root of Spiritual Conflict

In chapter 2, we saw that rebellion began with Satan's desire to take God's place, leading to his mutinous action of enlisting a third of the angels to wage war with him against their Creator. This constituted the first act of sedition in God's kingdom. Sometime after Satan was cast out of heaven, he tempted Adam and Eve, who believed his lie and denied God's commandment, thereby birthing the sinful nature in themselves and their descendants. The sinful nature—also called the carnal nature—produces perverted, rebellious, deceptive desires that go against the will of God. In this way, lies and deception can be said to be Satan's children. When man allowed sin to manifest within him, he also allowed spiritual death to enter him.

The root of all spiritual conflicts can be summarized in one word: rebellion.

Because of their carnal nature, many human beings continue to rebel against the righteous government of God. They operate under the "world's system," a mind-set and its resultant attitudes and actions that do not acknowledge God and His ways. Sometimes, this mind-set is institutionalized by nations and organizations. Rebellion against God—whether or not it is recognized as such—is the reason most people lack peace. When I minister to the people in my church or preach to people in other nations, I find that their problems and difficulties have three parts, similar to a tree with its roots, trunk, and branches. Most people deal with the symptoms, or "branches," of their situations, but even when they cut off the branches, the situation remains unchanged or is resolved in an incomplete, unsatisfactory way. What they must do is deal with the root of the problem.

For example, addiction is a symptom, or a "branch." Often, the reason people get drunk on alcohol or get high on drugs is to find relief from the pain or guilt they feel over some past event, which has produced low self-esteem, a lack of forgiveness, anger, and more. This is the "trunk" of their problem. But if we go deeper than the trunk, into the "root," we will find that their sins (and/or the sins of their parents or other ancestors, resulting in a generational curse) have blocked their relationship with God, thus sentencing them to their bondage to guilt and pain. When the church uses psychology or psychiatry to minister to people in this condition, it is really dealing with the branch or the trunk of their problems, rather than the root, which is always sin, or rebellion against God.

Rebellion—against God, His laws, and His kingdom of righteousness—is the root of all sin and all that goes wrong in people.

We can find rebels not only in the world but also in the church—I call them "religious" rebels. Many of them choose not to submit to their pastors or leadership—those who are God's delegated authorities over them. Some of these rebels leave their churches to start their own ministries, and they take members of their congregations with them. Later, they find that their own ministries do not grow but rather keep dividing, as people leave to find a different church or to start a new one. Religious rebels don't realize they sowed division when they founded their ministries on the seed of rebellion. The soil of their lives is dry and will never see genuine fruit. *"But the rebellious dwell in a dry land"* (Psalm 68:6).

Many churches today are the result of division, and this is why God's power and presence are absent from them. They are operating under the spirit of Satan, or rebellion. Only when they repent will they be able to see God's fruit manifest.

The kingdom of darkness is in total opposition to God's kingdom and in conflict with the souls of men and women. These two kingdoms will always collide and be in conflict, and we must decide with which kingdom we will align ourselves.

Alex Pineda, a leader in our prayer ministry, was confronted with this very decision. He gave the following testimony of his deliverance from the kingdom of darkness through God's revelation and power.

"Years ago, I used and sold drugs. I could go seven days without sleeping while under the influence of the drugs. I also prostituted myself with men and women. I had gone to court for identity theft, fraud against the Social Security office, and production of pornographic videos. I'd also had to take mental health classes for psychological imbalance.

"Growing up, I had everything, including the constant love of my mother and family, and I lived well, until I started to spend time with the wrong people and got involved in wrongdoing. One thing led to another, until I became corrupted and lost all sense of time. One day, after spending time out on the street with the lowest of the low, I found myself in my room at home, desperate, depressed, and trying to find the solution to my loneliness. It was there that, suddenly, Jesus came and called me by name: 'Alex!' I left my room and asked my father if he had called me, but he said that he had not. I returned to my room, and I heard the voice again, saying, 'Alex, I have given you many opportunities, but you have turned your back on Me. This is your last chance to choose correctly. If you choose right, you will receive the promise.' I answered, 'The only way I can serve You is if You take from me all desire to do what I have done.'

"That night, the power of God delivered me. I am a different person today. I used to have thousands of dollars stashed away that I had obtained illegally, but I burned them. I had drugs and an expensive wardrobe, which were also purchased by illegal means, and I threw them away. I destroyed everything that represented my past. Today, I serve God in my church, in the prayer and intercessory team, praying for people to end their sinful lifestyles. I do warfare against the enemy of our souls and uproot him from the territory that belongs to Jesus."

Simply put, obedience to God and His delegated authority aligns us with the kingdom of God, while disobedience to God aligns us with the kingdom of darkness. Let us now see how each of these kingdoms exercises its rule.

How the Kingdom of God Rules

The objective of God's kingdom is to give eternal life, righteousness, peace, and joy. God's kingdom rules in the following ways.

1. Through "Fatherhood"

The kingdom of God is not just a system of laws and statutes, nor is it merely the association between a sovereign and his subjects. It is the relationship of a Father to His children, and vice versa. God rules by fatherhood. He gives His children identity. He affirms, nourishes, disciplines, and reveals to each one the reason for which he or she was created. Unlike Satan, the Father does not desire to overpower, torture, or destroy people. He loves His children, and He wants to give them eternal life so they can dwell and rule together with Him.

2. Through Revelation, or Revealed Knowledge

When "light" is mentioned in the Bible, it often represents revelation, or revealed knowledge from God. (See, for example, John 1:4–5.) The enemy cannot dominate us in any area in which we both have knowledge *and* put that knowledge into practice, offensively or defensively, in furthering God's kingdom. Satan attacks us in areas in which we lack revelation knowledge, because those are the areas in which we are vulnerable. He also tries to nullify the knowledge we have already gained by creating confusion and causing us to doubt the truth of what God has said, just as he did with Adam and Eve.

It is not just "knowledge" but revealed knowledge from God through which we exercise dominion in the kingdom of God. A person may be educated in several academic fields, but if he doesn't know Jesus and lacks access to God's revelation and wisdom, he is still living in spiritual darkness; therefore, the enemy may exert control over his life. Suppose a surgeon operated on a patient who had contracted lung cancer due to smoking, but once the operation was over, the doctor immediately went outside to smoke a cigarette because he was addicted to nicotine. The doctor is fully aware of how dangerous smoking can be to his health, but he needs the spirit of revelation to help him overcome his habit. He must recognize that he has a spiritual enemy who desires to destroy him, and he must receive the power of the resurrection through Christ, so he can become free of his addiction.

We can reign above natural laws and logic, and we can rule over all the power of the enemy, as we manifest the supernatural through revelation and the power of the resurrection.

3. Through People's Voluntary Obedience and Submission

After we have been freed from the kingdom of darkness, our mind-set must change so that we may learn to live in full obedience to God and according to the righteousness, peace, and joy of His kingdom. Jesus is the best role model on how to live in total obedience to the Father as His child, without reservations. Submission and obedience are voluntary, but if we fail to practice them, we will live according to principles that are contrary to God's kingdom, and rebellion will still be operating in our hearts. The spirit of submission to authority responds to the order of God's kingdom, so that unity may be maintained and the kingdom's purposes fulfilled.

Being under authority is the key to exercising authority.

How the Kingdom of Darkness Rules

We will now examine the structure and rule of the kingdom of darkness.

And you He made alive, who were dead in trespasses and sins, in which you once walked according to the course of this world, according to the **prince of the power of the air***, the spirit who now works in the sons of disobedience.* (Ephesians 2:1–2)

The Greek word translated *"prince"* is *archon*, which means "one who is first in rank or power," "chief," "magistrate," "prince," or "ruler" (STRONG, NASC G758). The word translated "power" is *exousia*, and among its meanings are "authority," "jurisdiction" (STRONG, G1849), and "power to act" (NASC, G1849). From these two Greek words, we can conclude that Satan is a ruling fallen angel; he is the chief of the realm or jurisdiction of the *"air."*

I believe the word *"air"* refers to the atmosphere adjacent to the surface of the earth. When Satan was defeated by Jesus, he had to let go of his dominion of the earth. However, the iniquity of the *"sons of disobedience"*—people who are still disconnected from God and remain under the devil's sway—allows him to retain some measure of rule. Satan's kingdom has access to people's lives directly through their own sin and rebellion. It also has the ability to manipulate and tempt people through the avenue of the earth's atmosphere. Even though the atmosphere is not a tangible territory, we can recognize the influence of Satan's dominion there through transmissions of unhealthy programming, music, and Web content that people distribute over the airwaves through television, radio, and the Internet. The *"air"* is the devil's domain, and it is the means he uses to fill homes throughout the world with pornography, perversion, and anti-God/anti-Christian messages. These types of programs produce a negative atmosphere and contaminate the entire family. The church must take a stand and exercise dominion over the airwaves by broadcasting programs containing God's Word and His principles, in order to dispel this negative atmosphere.

The kingdom of darkness generates chaos and violence; it has nothing good to offer, and, as we have seen, it is founded on deceit. It rules in the following ways:

1. Through People's Spiritual Ignorance

Spiritual ignorance is the absence of spiritual knowledge, or a lack of revelation from God and His Word. The kingdom of darkness dominates its subjects by keeping them unaware of, or blinded to, eternal realities— such as their true spiritual condition, their purpose on earth, and the power of Christ through the cross and the resurrection. A lack of revelation leaves people vulnerable to demonic strongholds in their minds, and this is how the enemy gains the upper hand to enslave them.

For example, people who are in bondage to depression do not realize that their depressed state is often produced by an evil spirit, and that they can be set free. People who are enslaved by pain often ignore the work of Jesus on the cross to heal them—*"by His stripes we are healed"* (Isaiah 53:5)—and the power of forgiveness in healing (see, for example, James 5:15–16). People who have a congenital sickness often aren't aware of the existence of generational curses that come through one's bloodline, or how to break them. Some generational curses can also cause a history of alcoholism, divorce, or abuse in families. In all these examples, Satan enslaves, subdues, and rules over people through their ignorance.

The kingdom of darkness and of "religion" thrives on our tendency to continue in spiritual ignorance.

2. Through People's Disobedience

The prince of the power of the air [is] *the spirit who now works in the sons of disobedience.* (Ephesians 2:2)

As we have seen, people who live in rebellion and disobedience to the kingdom of God are automatically a part of the kingdom of darkness, whether they realize it or not. Satan and his kingdom operate within or dominate everyone who is disobedient to God, regardless of race, intellect, social status, or nationality. People's disobedience is either voluntary or a result of ignorance, such as we discussed above. In the natural world, people sometimes break laws because they are unaware of the existence of those laws. In many of these cases, there are still consequences, even though the consequences may be minor. And, if some of these people are forgiven for breaking the law, it is by grace, because they are still guilty of the violation.

God allows Satan to rule over rebellious people who have been blinded, since their sinful nature or rejection of Him has opened the door to the enemy's influence. However, God wants us, as His ambassadors in the world, to intercede for these people and to break Satan's bondage, thereby releasing them to come under the authority and freedom of His kingdom. Such people usually don't know who controls them, and they are unable to see the light of the gospel. We must ask God to remove the blindfold from their eyes, so they can repent and so the enemy will no longer keep them enslaved.

---

*Any religion that is unable to deal with
a person's rebellion is ineffective.*

---

3. Through Domination and Control

"To dominate" means to rule people in order to make them do what we want, with the help of the spirit of witchcraft or a demonic power that replaces the authority of God and the power of the Holy Spirit. Satan often rules his kingdom through rebellious people who oppress others by manipulation, control, and intimidation; sometimes, they may employ witchcraft, magic, and other occult practices. Satanic domination can even occur in the church, when people try to rule over others without the leading of the Holy Spirit. When Satan is in control, the Spirit of God is not present.

---

*The law of the kingdom of darkness is domination and
control over people. The law of the kingdom of
God is submission freely offered to Him.*

Our Fight Is Not Against People but Against Evil Spiritual Beings That Have No Bodily Form

For our fight is not against any physical enemy.
(Ephesians 6:12 PHILLIPS)

We must understand that the conflict we are involved in as believers is not waged with a physical enemy; it is not against humans beings, even though the enemy can use people by influencing them through demonic spirits that have gained a legal right to operate in or through them. Neither is this conflict fought using material weapons. It is a spiritual war, fought against evil spiritual beings that are invisible and have no bodily form. When we have a revelation of these truths, half the battle has already been won, because Satan likes to disseminate the lie that he doesn't exist; he doesn't want us to know that we have a spiritual enemy. When he can make us think that a spiritual problem or situation we are dealing with is either in our imagination, is psychological, or is the fault of another person, such as a spouse, an in-law, or a boss, then he has prevailed over us. It is time to realize that behind such situations are evil spirits from hell trying to destroy us.

Ignorance of these realities is the reason psychologists and psychiatrists often fail to give accurate diagnoses for many imbalances from which people suffer. They are unaware of the reality of certain situations because they deal with only the mind, not the spirit. They lack revelation of the truth in Jesus Christ that can bring the cure. For example, the most doctors can do to treat an autistic child is to prescribe medication to keep his or her behavior under control; they begin with a low dose but gradually increase it. Unfortunately, by the time that child becomes an adult, he or she may have become dependent on the medication. Autism is a lifelong issue, unless it is healed. God can give believers the discernment and revelation to perceive the spiritual root of various sicknesses, so they can be cured.

Are you struggling with an issue you cannot identify? Perhaps you are dealing with spiritual entities of disease, financial distress, divorce, or strife in the family. Maybe you can tangibly sense the hatred of demons toward you and God. If so, ask the Lord for the discernment to deal with these entities and to cast them out of your life, marriage, and home. Then, watch how they begin to disappear. Let me clarify that evil spiritual entities are not human beings who have died and have returned to torment people. They are not "ghosts." Rather, they are demonic spirits in Satan's service that are not human and never were.

We cannot remain ignorant of the existence of Satan's invisible and wicked kingdom. His kingdom is well structured and undivided because he learned from God that power comes from a coordinated effort—even though he creates his united effort through force and subjugation by his spirits, rather than through true harmony. This "unity" lacks kindness and brotherhood; it is an accord of hate, violence, and destruction.

Results of Jesus' Victory Over Satan at the Cross

The good news of the kingdom of God is that Satan can in no way reverse or invalidate the annihilation he suffered by Jesus' death and resurrection. We must live in the revelation of Christ's victory! The enemy was routed in four main ways: he was (1) defeated, (2) dethroned, (3) disarmed, and (4) destroyed.

1. Satan Was Defeated

[God]…made a bold display and public example of [the principalities and powers], *in triumphing over them in Him and in it [the cross].*

(Colossians 2:15 AMP)

The images of *"bold display," "public example,"* and *"triumphing"* apparently are a reference to Roman military victory processions. When I visited Rome, the guide in our group explained how these concepts were used during the days of Roman Empire. When a Roman general defeated an enemy army, it was considered a great victory because it meant that another city, nation, or territory was added to the empire. When that general returned to Rome, the Senate awarded him a "Triumph" procession. They would place him in a chariot and drive him throughout the streets of Rome. The people would gather on both sides of the road to applaud and celebrate the conqueror.

To demonstrate the greatness of the general's victory, all those whom he had captured were paraded before the crowds, often in chains. Among the prisoners were generals, other officers, and foot soldiers. Our guide said that this is how General Titus celebrated his victory after destroying Jerusalem in A.D. 70. He had all the Jews he had captured chained to his chariot.

Also included in the victory procession were the spoils of war, such as gold and silver, as well as animals for sacrifice. When the celebration ended, the prisoners were executed or sold as slaves. What had taken place was a public exhibition of the enemy's defeat and of the conquered territory.

By means of His death on the cross and His resurrection, Jesus took captive Satan, his principalities, and his strongholds and put them on public display. Satan thought he had finally killed Jesus, but, in reality, Jesus was surrendering His own life for God's purposes. Satan thought the sins of humanity would hold Jesus in hell forever, but Jesus victoriously took back the keys of death and hell, abolishing the enemy's authority and power. Then, when Satan thought nothing worse could happen to him, the Father raised Jesus from the dead. Christ's reappearance among the living, glorified with all authority and power, triumphant before His followers, constituted the public humiliation and exhibition of Satan's defeat. After the resurrection, Jesus' disciples were no longer afraid of the enemy. They continued to follow their Master, and after He sent them His Holy Spirit, they dedicated their lives to enforcing Satan's defeat by making him submit to God and by casting him out of the territories he had gained in various people and places.

> *By way of the cross, Jesus inflicted on Satan a total, permanent, eternal, and irrevocable defeat.*

To give you a more personal application of the truth we have been discussing, imagine Jesus standing in a victory chariot while being driven along the road, with all the enemies He has defeated chained behind Him, and all the citizens of the kingdom applauding from both sides. Where would you be standing? Would you be among those applauding and cheering the Conqueror, or would you be among those captured, chained behind the chariot?

Those whom Christ has redeemed are seated in heavenly places with Him. (See Ephesians 2:6.) By faith, we are on that chariot with Him! That is our place—the place of conquerors. If we take the position in the kingdom government He has given us, then we will release His power and authority over the enemy. I believe this is one of the connotations of "spreading the aroma of the knowledge of Christ." (See 2 Corinthians 2:14.)

Are you living in the victory Jesus has won for you? We must defeat every work of the devil, wherever we might find it. The authority is ours! Remember that we are on the chariot, standing with Jesus, and the enemy and his demons are held captive in chains behind us. Raise your head high, like a true child of God, because Jesus has overpowered the enemy and is now releasing the fragrance of His victory. The only place for Satan, now that Jesus has defeated him, is under our feet. (See Romans 16:20.)

2. Satan Was Dethroned

> *When a strong man, fully armed, guards his own palace, his goods are in peace. But when a stronger than he comes upon him and overcomes him, he takes from him all his armor in which he trusted, and divides his spoils.* (Luke 11:21–22)

Jesus taught the parable of the strong man after He was accused by some religious leaders of casting out demons by the power of "Beelzebub," a term for Satan. (See verse 15.) In this parable, two "men" are mentioned: the *"strong man,"* who represents Satan, and the *"stronger"* man, who represents Jesus Christ. Satan was the ruler of the kingdom of the earth, and he thought he was safe in his *"palace."* Then, Jesus defeated him, removing him from his throne and rulership, and stripping him of his authority and power. The "strong man" had trusted in his ability to strike at God through defeating His Son, but he was overtaken by the Stronger Man. When Jesus was victorious over the enemy, He "divided the spoils" of His triumph with humanity and gave the dominion of the earth back to us.

3. Satan Was Disarmed

> *[God] disarmed the principalities and powers that were ranged against us....* (Colossians 2:15 AMP)

Jesus nailed to the cross every weapon the devil uses to torment people. The enemy is described as *"the accuser of our brethren"* (Revelation 12:10), and one of his main strategies is to fire darts of guilt at us through accusation. People throughout the world live in guilt over past mistakes; even some Christians, after repenting and knowing they have been cleansed by the blood of Jesus, still experience guilt. This is one weapon on which Satan can rely. As long as he can make us feel guilty about something, we will never become skillful spiritual opponents who are capable of confronting him.

Every day, keep in mind that Jesus defeated Satan at the cross and disarmed him of all his weapons. Are you feeling guilty over something you have done or failed to do? Then, by faith, receive the victory that Jesus won for you. To do this, you must assume responsibility for your actions, repent, and confess your sin to God. The blood of Jesus has the power to cleanse you. Stop being a victim of guilt!

When we belong to God's kingdom, we have spiritual weapons to disarm Satan through God's power. These weapons are the Word, supernatural power, prayer, fasting, praise, worship, our testimony, the blood of Jesus, and more, including all the pieces of God's spiritual armor. (See Ephesians 6:14–17.) Every time the devil comes to tempt, accuse, or persecute us, let us use the weapons God has given us and thwart him from making inroads into our lives. Then, we will be *"more than conquerors"* (Romans 8:37).

*The spiritual victory of the Son of God
makes us more than conquerors.*

4. Satan Was Destroyed

…that through death [Jesus] might destroy him who had the power of death, that is, the devil.   (Hebrews 2:14)

Jesus came to earth to destroy all the plans and works of the devil. As we have seen, by His death and resurrection, Jesus broke the power of sickness, sin, demons, poverty, and death. We have the authority to enforce

Christ's victory—to *keep* destroying the devil and his works by delivering people through supernatural revelation and manifestations.

A testimony of a teenager in our ministry is a clear example of how deliverance comes through Jesus' resurrection power and how those who minister the kingdom of light can subdue the kingdom of darkness. Here is her story:

"I was born in a traditional Catholic family, but one that also practiced witchcraft. My parents were divorced when I was only six years old, and I was sent to live with my great-grandfather, who abused me every day. There is a history of incest in my family. My mother was raped by her uncle, and every woman in my family has been abused by family members, but no one ever admitted anything, in order to prevent staining the family's good name.

"The pain of my circumstances caused me to live in rejection, humiliation, and rebelliousness. At fifteen, I lost my virginity and became pregnant. I was so young and felt so lost that I chose to have an abortion. To suppress the depression I felt, I began to attend parties, have sex, be promiscuous, and use heavy drugs—pills, cocaine, ecstasy, angel dust, and others. I hated life when I was sober. My heart was hardened, and I took advantage of anyone who got in my way. I dominated the men in my life and hurt them before they could hurt me.

"Sometime later, I was diagnosed with HPV (human papillomavirus)—an incurable infection that attacks the cells around the neck of the uterus and can cause cancer. The news led me deeper into drugs and alcohol in my futile effort to repress all feeling and emotion. I no longer cared about anything!

"One day, my mother, tired of my rebelliousness, gave me an ultimatum. We had a serious fight, and I left home. I lived in the streets until I came to Florida to live with my father, who was now a Christian and who had spent years praying for me. While living with him, I decided to give God a try, and so I surrendered my heart to Jesus. I knew it had to be then or never, because I knew I would die if I did not. Through King Jesus Ministry, I was led to forgive my great-grandfather. I was delivered from drug addiction and alcoholism; from sexual immorality, fornication, masturbation, and lust; from self-pity, guilt, and suicidal tendencies; from pride, witchcraft, and the occult. While they ministered to me, I felt my ovaries activate and begin to function. I had never experienced such a feeling! I knew then that I was completely free and that God had totally healed me. Every dead cell in me was restored. Everything has changed since that day. I feel alive! Jesus delivered me! I continue to have encounters with the love of the Father every day, and I don't ever want it to end."

Satan Has Still Been Given Three Legal Rights

The cross and the resurrection form the bridge that leads us out of the kingdom of darkness and into the kingdom of light. Now, we are seated in heavenly places in God's kingdom, where He gives us the privilege of ruling together with Him.

[God the Father] *has delivered us from the power of darkness and conveyed us into the kingdom of the Son of His love.* (Colossians 1:13)

Since this is the case, some people wonder why the devil continues to attack believers. The answer is that, until his final defeat at the end of the age, he still has been given the legal right by God to fight against us using three methods: (1) temptation, (2) persecution, and (3) accusation.

+ *Temptation:* Temptation is the first tier of attack. All temptation is based on deception or a lie. The stress that the temptation generates within a person corresponds with his desire. If you desire something that is wrong, the temptation to act on it will strengthen that desire. If you don't have a desire for something, the temptation will have no power over you. However, repeated temptation can increase our desire for something, and the enemy's first plan, such as he carried out against Adam and Eve, is to wear us out by continued temptation.

+ *Persecution:* Persecution is the second level of attack. (See John 15:18–21.) Satan will incite other people to oppress believers for the purpose of stopping them from preaching and demonstrating the kingdom of God. Jesus experienced persecution by many of the religious leaders of His day. Their hatred and opposition of Him grew to such a degree that He was eventually betrayed, captured, and killed. What can we learn from the opposition Jesus experienced? The enemy will attack anyone who dares to carry out God's will; he will try to destroy anyone who wants to establish the kingdom, and he will oppose any Christian activity or movement that leads to glorifying God and delivering people from demonic bondage. Again, he is not willing to surrender the territory he has gained in people's lives, and the instant he feels threatened, he will attack with all the wickedness and power at his disposal.

+ *Accusation:* The highest form of attack is accusation. (See Revelation 12:10.) I believe that, in the end times, the most prominent role of the devil will be that of accuser. As I wrote earlier, he will always accuse believers of sin and try to make them feel guilty. However, this particular form of accusation is a last resort—a reserved weapon—of the enemy to attack the credibility of believers when they become a threat to him and his kingdom. Jesus was unjustly accused by the religious leaders of being a blasphemer, of using the power of the devil, and of committing sedition against the authority of Rome. The leaders used these accusations in their quest to put Him to death. There was no greater threat to Satan than Jesus Christ, and the enemy used rebellious people to hurl accusations against Him in order to eliminate Him.

We are embroiled in an inevitable conflict with the devil. The moment we were born again, we were immediately transferred into the kingdom of light. At that instant, we entered into warfare against the kingdom of darkness. We can no longer be at peace in the kingdom of darkness—or with it. To use the example of citizenship in a nation, when immigrants become citizens of the United States of America or any other country, their allegiance must be to their new country, and, in times of war, their new country's enemies become their enemies. The same happens with believers at the moment of their rebirth. They become full citizens of God's kingdom, and the enemy immediately becomes aware of their new citizenship. When people first come to Christ, they may experience strong satanic opposition that manifests in their families, their friendships, their workplaces, their finances, or their health.

Satan wants to challenge the authority that we believers have been given in Christ, so we must stand on that authority and resist him. We have been delivered from Satan's stronghold and have been translated into the kingdom of light, but the final sentence against the enemy has yet to be carried out. Even though he no longer has dominion over us, he will continue trying to either bring us back into his kingdom or undermine our spiritual effectiveness. But we have the power to overcome him!

For you to be a real danger to the kingdom of darkness, you must be ready to resist satanic attacks. God's kingdom is not about theology or doctrine but about resurrection power that can defeat the enemy. When the power of God rests upon a man or a woman, demons have to flee. We have the power and authority to bring deliverance!

I must give a word of warning: Though Jesus delivered us from the power and dominion of darkness, if we continue to disobey God, or if we decide not to follow Him, we are automatically under the enemy's authority again. We might not realize this fact, because the prince of darkness has blinded us from seeing or knowing Jesus or the truth of the gospel of the kingdom. If this is the case, only God's revelation can remove the blindfold so we can see what is really going on.

When we establish the kingdom of God, therefore, hell will rise up against us. We must learn to protect ourselves from Satan's attacks and also to protect those who are new to the kingdom, because they, too, are being pursued by their prior lord and master. Let us remember that the only authority the devil can have over us is the authority we give him through our disobedience. (See Ephesians 4:27.) If we obey God, the enemy cannot prevail against us. He might have power but not authority (he no longer has that right), and he cannot use this power to defeat us unless we allow it. Because of what Jesus did for us, we can force Satan to submit; we can destroy all of his works!

Since we know that the enemy was completely defeated, dethroned, disarmed, and destroyed through Christ's victory at the cross, let us now focus on a specific way by which Jesus said we can verify that His kingdom has arrived in our midst.

An obedient church will render the devil powerless, but a disobedient one will empower him.

Clear Evidence That the Kingdom Has Arrived

But if I cast out demons by the Spirit of God, surely the kingdom of God has come upon you. (Matthew 12:28)

Jesus declared that the casting out of demons, who are under orders from the kingdom of darkness, is clear evidence that the kingdom of God has arrived and is active!

In the Old Testament, we do not see anyone casting demons out of people. I have read that, in those times, people who were possessed by demonic spirits were kept outside of the city, separated from the rest of the people. They could not be a part of society—similar to the separation and isolation experienced by patients at today's mental institutions. Apparently, that was all that could be done with a demon-possessed person.

I believe that demons could not be cast out during Old Testament times because Satan still had the legal right, given to him by Adam, to rule the earth. Since every person had a sinful nature, or Satan's seed of rebellion, demons had a right to invade people who left themselves open to possession. Satan was the only one who could have exercised the authority to remove a demon from someone, but he never would have done that, because he would have been going against his own purposes. (See Matthew 12:25–26.)

Yet, when Jesus came to earth as the Son of God, He had the power to cast out Satan and his demons, because there was no sin in Him, and He was bringing the kingdom of light into the world. The demons were aware of His identity and mission, and that is why some of them screamed things such as *"Have You come here to torment us before the time?"* (Matthew 8:29) before they vacated people at His word.

Jesus did not come as the son of Joseph, His adoptive earthly father, but with the nature of His heavenly Father. He was holy and without blemish.

Had He come with the Adamic nature, He never could have saved humanity from sin and death, or cast out demons, because He would have been born in sin, like everyone else. But Jesus was sinless, and He came with the authority and the mission to rule over the kingdom of darkness, which includes demons, and He cast out demons everywhere He went—in the streets, in people's houses, and even in the synagogues, as we see in this passage:

> *But Jesus rebuked him, saying, "Be quiet, and come out of him!" And when the unclean spirit had convulsed him and cried out with a loud voice, he came out of him. Then they were all amazed, so that they questioned among themselves, saying, "What is this? What new doctrine is this? For with authority He commands even the unclean spirits, and they obey Him."*　　　　　　　　　　　　　　　　　(Mark 1:25–27)

The synagogue was the meeting place of worship and fellowship for Jews in the first century, similar to our local church today. And we read in Mark 1 that a synagogue was one of the first places where Jesus cast out a demon from someone. While Jesus taught with authority, a demon manifested in one of the people gathered (see verses 21–24), and He rebuked the demon.

The reaction of those present was dramatic. I imagine they thought to themselves, *Even Moses didn't do this*—and Moses had been sent by God as their role model. Elijah, Samuel, David, and Daniel never did anything like it, either, so the people viewed what Jesus had done as a new and startling doctrine. However, this was not just a new doctrine or teaching. It was a sign that the kingdom of God had arrived through the presence of its King, and that the kingdom of darkness was being overthrown from that territory.

The preaching of the kingdom of God with power brings with it the casting out of demons.

> [Jesus said,] *"Behold, I cast out demons and perform cures today and tomorrow, and the third day I shall be perfected."*　　　　(Luke 13:32)

In the above verse, I believe Jesus was saying that until His work on earth was completed, He would heal people and cast out demons. Knowing that His ministry was based on four activities—preaching, teaching, healing, and casting out demons—we can surmise that He may have spent 50 percent of His ministry dedicated to healing the sick and casting out demons. Today, the church seems satisfied with just teaching and preaching, and when believers heal people or deliver them from demons, they are sometimes accused of false practices. On the contrary, they are simply doing the same things that Christ did! Jesus said that deliverance is the *"children's bread."* (See, for example, Matthew 15:21–28.)

Jesus declared that the casting out of demons is clear evidence that the kingdom of God has arrived at a place.

Whenever Jesus cast out a demon, it indicated four vital principles in relation to the kingdom:

+ The kingdom of God will arrive at a specific place, here and now.

+ The kingdom of God will come into a specific situation, here and now.

+ The kingdom of God is far more powerful than the kingdom of darkness.

+ Satan is totally defeated.

This incident in the synagogue, in which a demon manifested itself at the same time Jesus publicly taught about the kingdom, exposed the conflict between the two invisible and spiritual kingdoms. When the light arrived, the darkness was revealed—and then defeated. The superiority of the kingdom of God was confirmed by the demonic spirit's submission to Jesus' authority. Jesus wants us to use the same authority today to deliver people from demonic possession and oppression, as we can see from the following testimony.

During one of my ministry trips, I met Pastor Ellie Davidian, formerly a devout Shiite Muslim from Iran. She had been wonderfully saved through a dream in which Jesus introduced Himself to her. She and her husband started a ministry with a passion to reach the Muslim community. Her congregation consists of Muslims who have emigrated from Iran and who have been saved and delivered. When she began to watch my TV program, she immediately identified with my teaching about visions and revelations, and the supernatural power of God took her ministry to the next level.

Several weeks after Pastor Ellie received my teachings on supernatural authority, a woman named Suzanne, who was listening to Pastor Ellie's radio program in Iran, was radically saved. A couple of weeks later, Suzanne visited her aunt, with whom lived one of Suzanne's cousins named Elizabeth, who had been violently demon-possessed for the past thirty years. Elizabeth had lost her own mother to breast cancer when she was five years old, and her two sisters had died of breast cancer, also, so her aunt had raised her.

People could hardly get near Elizabeth because she was so aggressive. For example, when someone tried to feed her an orange, she would snatch it out of the person's hand, screaming, and bite into it immediately without even peeling it. Her aunt testified that Elizabeth would tear apart all her own clothing, bedding, and pillows. She could not stand to wear a single piece of clothing, so she would cover herself only with blankets. She also had been urinating on herself for the past twenty-five years, so that the smell penetrated the walls. When Suzanne visited her aunt, she found her cousin with a chain fastened around her stomach; the chain was attached to a hole in the wall, to keep her from harming others. The atmosphere there was charged with spiritual opposition.

Suzanne was able to contact Pastor Ellie via cell phone, and, through it, Pastor Ellie preached to Elizabeth, who began screaming. Pastor Ellie commanded the demons—spirits of fear and suicide—to leave her, in the name of Jesus. Suddenly, Elizabeth stopped screaming. Pastor Ellie then told Suzanne, "You have the authority, in the name of Jesus, to continue praying." So, Suzanne began to pray, sing, and worship God, and Elizabeth calmed down.

After this, for the first time in thirty years, the ropes and chains were removed from Elizabeth, and she began to behave normally. That night, she showered for the first time in two-and-a-half decades. She ate her dinner calmly like everyone else, and she slept on a bed with her clothes on. The aunt felt such relief and thankfulness to Jesus over the deliverance of her niece that she cried and confessed Jesus as her Savior! Pastor Ellie had discovered that she had authority through Jesus to cast out demons from people who are possessed, and she began to manifest Jesus' power in her territory!

Jesus brought to light the reality of the total opposition between the kingdom of God and the kingdom of Satan by casting out demons. There was collision and conflict, until the greater kingdom prevailed. We cannot see these two kingdoms with our natural eyes, but we can see the physical manifestation of their existence.

How many church activities today represent a genuine threat to the kingdom of darkness? I would say, in general, very few. The ministries that do present a threat to the enemy are under great persecution. They are even undergoing judgment and accusation by their own peers. We must be careful not to become the devil's allies, accusing our own brothers and sisters in Christ of error when they manifest the kingdom by casting out demons and performing other supernatural demonstrations.

---

*Casting out demons is a manifestation of
the dominion and rule of God's kingdom.*

Receiving and Ministering Deliverance from Satanic Oppression

If you have allowed Satan to prevail over you, it's time to equip yourself with the weapons of deliverance that Jesus provided. And, if someone you know is being oppressed by the devil, you need to understand how to bring deliverance through the kingdom of light. Be aware that even though you are a Christian and cannot be physically possessed by demons, you can still be influenced by them; there may be areas in your life that are being held captive by Satan due to unforgiveness or generational curses. Deliverance is something that one must practice regularly.

I have been ministering for over two decades, and I have learned to first lead people to carry out certain conditions for their deliverance. I believe that repentance represents about 95 percent of the work, and the other 5 percent consists in casting out the demons. If these conditions are not observed, the demons will usually not leave; or, if they do leave, they will return, and the deliverance will be lost. I don't want this to happen to you. I want you to be free and to keep your deliverance.

Below is a list of conditions that will help you to be free of all demonic oppression operating in your mind, will, and emotions. To receive deliverance—and to stay free—you must:

+ Have a personal revelation of Jesus as Lord and Savior.

+ Humble yourself before God (those who refuse to humble themselves should not continue with the deliverance).

+ Confess all sins of commission and omission.

+ Repent wholeheartedly.

+ Choose to forgive everyone who has offended you.

+ Desperately desire your deliverance from the enemy's oppression.

+ Break any pacts you have made with the occult through witchcraft, Santeria, or any other false religion or sect.

+ Believe, confess, and receive, by faith, the divine exchange that took place at the cross of Christ.

+ Exhale, so that every evil spirit can leave your body.

Deliverance will not come if you are passive and do nothing, or if you just cite Scripture. It will come when you take action and rebuke the demons.

You may use the following prayer as a guide. It will keep you from forgetting any important aspects of deliverance. Remember that as you pray this prayer, you must exhale, as an act of faith, so that every evil spirit will leave you.

Dear Lord, I believe that You are the Son of God and that You died on the cross for my sins; that You were raised from the dead so I could be forgiven and receive eternal life. Right now, I take hold of Your work and renounce all religious self-righteousness and any other sense of pride that does not come from You. I ask for Your mercy and grace, knowing that I have nothing to boast about. I wholeheartedly repent of and confess all the sins I have committed, as well as everything I should have done but failed to do. I choose to end my sinful lifestyle so that I may have new life in You. Of my own free will, I make a decision to follow You. I forgive everyone who has hurt me and has wished me harm. I renounce and let go of all unforgiveness, bitterness, hatred, and resentment. I specifically forgive [mention the names of those who have hurt you], and I ask for Your supernatural grace to forgive them.

I renounce every pact I have made with the occult, including witchcraft, divination, and false doctrines or religions. I also commit myself to destroying every object in my home or office that is associated with the occult and idolatry.

Lord Jesus, thank You for taking my curse on the cross so I could receive Your blessing. I am redeemed and free in Your name. I stand with You against Satan and his demons. I renounce the curses I have seen in operation in my life [mention all the generational curses you may have identified: sickness, depression, alcoholism, adultery, suicide, premature death, and anything else]. Now, I receive Your blessings. I resist the devil and submit to You. I order every demon that has control over my life, health, finances, and family to leave, right now! I cast them out, now, in the name of Jesus. I am free!

The Conflict Between the Flesh and the Spirit

Satan and his demons are not the only enemies we must contend with. We have another "enemy" that fights against us: the "flesh," or the carnal nature. In the previous chapter, we talked about dying to the carnal nature in order to manifest the resurrection life of Jesus. Satan will use the flesh in his attempts to defeat us, because the carnal nature is the area in which temptation takes place. However, the flesh is not the same thing as the devil, so we have to deal with it differently than we deal with him. Learning to overcome the flesh is a vital part of our spiritual defense. I have witnessed a number of cases in which people who have been delivered from the bondage of Satan or received healing have relapsed and experienced the return of oppression or physical symptoms, because they have given a foothold to the devil by yielding to the flesh.

Throughout the New Testament, the Word teaches that there is a conflict between the flesh and the spirit. In fact, this is often the first conflict we encounter when we are born again and enter God's kingdom. It is also the first conflict we must learn to deal with effectively. We have to learn to crucify the flesh and live according to the Spirit while we are in this world. Many believers have sinned because they opened a door to Satan by living in the flesh, which led to their falling prey to additional temptation and spiritual vulnerability, and their eventual downfall.

Once, when I ministered God's supernatural power in Chile, I met a young man named Marcelo who'd had a considerable struggle with the fleshly nature. He had been gay and had spent ten years practicing all types of perversions. He had been known as the "neighborhood homosexual" and had been the victim of mocking, rejection, and discrimination. As hard as he tried, he was unable to let go of that lifestyle, and his day-to-day existence was a torment.

While watching television one day, Marcelo found my program, *Time for Change*, and the message he heard deeply touched his heart. It immediately led him to repentance and gave him the faith that change was possible. He felt true love and peace fill his whole being, such as he had never experienced before that time. When I asked those watching on television to pray with me, he fell to his knees and set his hands on the television set, begging God to deliver him. While the Holy Spirit ministered to him, images of his sinful past went through his mind, and as the power of God delivered him, he was filled with holy fear. Crying, he repeated after me the prayer of salvation and accepted Jesus as his Lord and Savior, and he felt something like a current of fire burn within him.

Marcelo reported, "Months later, many things have changed. I made a covenant with God to serve Him by proclaiming the truth of the kingdom.

My sin was forgiven. My shame and dishonor have left. It was hard, but today, I am willing to share what God did in me." And his mother testified, "Now, he is in a healthy relationship with a good girl; he's the complete opposite of what he used to be." Sin had dominated Marcelo, but the power of God delivered him when he, of his own free will, surrendered to God.

Understanding the Fleshly Nature

And those who are Christ's have crucified the flesh with its passions and desires.   (Galatians 5:24)

Earlier, we saw that we humans are tripartite beings: we are spirit, we have a soul, and we inhabit a physical body. (See 1 Thessalonians 5:23.) When we accept Jesus, our spirit is born again, but our soul is merely "rescued"—it is now capable of being renewed, but it is not yet fully transformed. From the moment of our salvation, we must continually work on the transformation of our souls.

The carnal nature is the combination of our ungodly passions, perverted emotions, bad thoughts, stubbornness, and evil desires. Paul wrote that the works of the flesh are "*adultery, fornication, uncleanness, lewdness, idolatry, sorcery, hatred, contentions, jealousies, outbursts of wrath, selfish ambitions, dissensions, heresies, envy, murders, drunkenness, revelries, and the like*" (Galatians 5:19–21). The flesh often manifests when the soul and body act independently of the Holy Spirit. If we truly belong to Jesus Christ, God expects us to crucify the flesh, with the power He has given us through His Spirit.

The flesh is anything that is void of the control and influence of the Holy Spirit.

Many believers today seem to be trying to "cast out" the flesh and "crucify" the devil. They have it backward. Jesus defeated the devil and sin at the cross, but it is our responsibility to crucify the flesh; no one else can do this for us. It is important to maintain a balance because many people blame the devil for everything bad that happens to them. Some people see demons behind every tree when, in reality, they have given Satan a foothold through their fleshly nature. On the other hand, there are people who do not believe in spiritual warfare, so they blame the flesh for everything that happens; they fail to discern that Satan is the true culprit behind some of their problems. We must come to understand the difference between the flesh and the devil.

When we crucify the flesh, we submit to the lordship of Jesus Christ and no longer live a sinful lifestyle. We live by the faith of the Son of God. After we learn to live in this way, if we still fail to experience spiritual victory, we must suspect Satan and his demons as the cause of our problem and rebuke them. When we order demons to leave, they will not obey us unless we have first crucified our flesh in the area from which we want to expel them—regardless of whether we are expelling them from ourselves or another person. Surrendering to the desires of our flesh nullifies our authority, and it also makes us vulnerable to Satan's temptation.

We crucify the flesh, but we cast out demons.

How to Crucify the Flesh

If anyone desires to come after Me, let him deny himself, and take up his cross, and follow Me. (Matthew 16:24)

Let us look more closely at the process of crucifying the flesh. We crucify the flesh when we choose not to satisfy our ungodly desires and passions; this must be something that we freely decide to do. If Jesus had acted according to His flesh, He never would have gone to the cross or maintained His holiness. Jesus experienced fatigue, pain, sadness, hunger, and everything else you and I experience. Though He was tempted, he never sinned. (See Hebrews 4:15.) The flesh is defeated when we determine to apply the cross of Jesus to our souls by denying the carnal self.

For whoever desires to save his life will lose it, but whoever loses his life for My sake will find it. (Matthew 16:25)

The soul is composed of the mind, the will, and the emotions. When we live for the soul, we are directed by it rather than by the Spirit. The will says, "I want." The emotions say, "I feel." And the mind says, "I think." If we allow

our souls to control us, then we are living according to the flesh, whose motivation is to satisfy the ego. The apostle Paul instructed us, "*Walk in the Spirit,
and you shall not fulfill the lust of the flesh. For the flesh lusts against the Spirit,
and the Spirit against the flesh; and these are contrary to one another, so that you
do not do the things that you wish*" (Galatians 5:16–17). Living to satisfy the
"flesh" or "self" is disobedience, and it attracts demons to attack us. The cross
is the only safe place for us to be! Again, we are each responsible for crucifying our attitudes, motives, desires, and lifestyle birthed in the "self."

A husband and wife named Joel and Cheryl had to make the decision
to surrender to God; otherwise, their marriage would have ended. "We
hated each other," Cheryl said. Only nine months into their marriage, Joel
had relapsed into a drug addiction that Cheryl never knew he'd had. He
came from a long line of users and abusers, and he had started drinking
and smoking marijuana at a very early age. "It was common to see my un-
cles drunk and unable to finish watching a football game with me because
they were passed out somewhere," Joel revealed. His aunt had died at the
age of seventy-six while she was passed out due to alcohol abuse.

Joel's life had also been marred by a spirit of rejection. His father re-
sented him. The man to whom he looked for love and approval was cold
and ambivalent toward him, though also violent. So Joel had dived into his
addictions even more to mask the pain he felt inside. After he and Cheryl
married, he would be absent for days at a time. Cheryl became bewildered,
distraught, and angry. She suspected that drugs and alcohol were the cause
of his absences. When she became pregnant, her husband still was not
around to give his family the emotional or financial support they deserved.

Finally, Joel acknowledged that his wife was the best thing that had
ever happened to him, and he didn't want to lose her, so he tried to change.
His recovery was long and hard, and it included several failed attempts at
rehabilitation. Even after spending three months in a rehab facility, he fell
into drug use again. During this period in their lives, he squandered almost
$100,000, while his wife was left with little to pay their bills. They were
broke in every way possible.

Life was unbearable for Joel and Cheryl, so they decided to seek God and
started attending King Jesus Ministry. They wanted to turn their lives around

and stop the madness and constant pain in their hearts. One day, I taught on God's plan for the family. Cheryl recalled, "Apostle's teaching was so powerful that it taught me to love Joel God's way." They understood that they needed inner healing, so they decided to attend a deliverance retreat. "There, our lives changed! Our marriage changed!" exclaimed Joel. For Cheryl, the breakthrough came when she decided to give up her bitterness. "If I were to receive the blessings, I had no choice but to let go of the hatred and resentment that I had carried around for years." God came in and healed her broken heart. Meanwhile, Joel was delivered from his addictions. He decided to give up his old life, surrender to God, and do what he had to do as a husband and father. Joel and Cheryl renewed their wedding vows in a special ceremony for married couples at our church, and now they live in freedom and love due to Jesus' resurrection power, because they decided to crucify their flesh.

The Conflict of the End Times: A Battle of Powers

I must briefly mention one other essential aspect of the clash between the kingdom of God and the kingdom of Satan. In these end times, we will see this battle escalate exponentially.

> *And because lawlessness ["iniquity" KJV] will abound, the love of many will grow cold.* (Matthew 24:12)

Jesus warned us that iniquity would multiply in the end times. It is my opinion that the last days before Christ's return will unfold with the manifestation of opposing supernatural powers, rather than by a collision of theories, philosophies, or doctrines. Christians must demonstrate that the kingdom of God is greater than the power of witches, warlocks, satanists, and all the power of the enemy, because what we have is not merely theology, doctrines, principles, concepts, rites, ceremonies, and so on. What we have is a kingdom of glorious power!

A Prayer of Commitment

Let us finish with a prayer of commitment to God. We must be ready to deal effectively with the spiritual conflicts we have been discussing in this chapter. They are already occurring and will continue to increase as the end approaches. The conflict between the kingdom of light and the kingdom of darkness demands that all Christians live in obedience to God and in the fullness of His revelations. The conflict between the flesh and the spirit requires us to crucify the carnal self and its uncontrolled passions and desires and to live by grace in the Spirit in order to keep Satan from infiltrating our lives. Last, the end-time conflict—which will demonstrate once and for all the superiority of God's kingdom over Satan's kingdom—will demand that Christians manifest the supernatural and creative power of God by preaching, teaching, healing the sick, casting out demons, and raising the dead, just as Jesus, the Son of God, did before us. It will require that we call others to repentance and proclaim that the kingdom of God has arrived so that signs, miracles, and wonders will manifest to support our message. Are you willing to go and demonstrate God's power? Make this commitment to the Lord by praying the following out loud:

Jesus Christ, You are Lord. You are God's Son and the only way to the Father. You died for my sins and were raised from the dead on the third day. You purchased me with Your blood and transferred me from the kingdom of darkness into Your glorious kingdom of light. You freed me from slavery to Satan and enabled me to be reborn as a child of God. Now I recommit myself to You. I am willing to crucify my flesh and stand in the authority You gave me. I place myself at Your disposal. Do with me as You wish. Send me wherever You want me to go. From this day forward, You are my Lord, and I, of my own free will, submit to Your kingdom. Everything I do will be in obedience to Your Word and Your kingdom. I will no longer rule myself. Thank You for accepting this covenant of commitment. I know that I am not worthy, but Your blood makes me worthy. I am accepted. I am Your child! Anoint me with power to go and expand Your kingdom and to do warfare against the kingdom of darkness and destroy the works of the devil. Wherever I go, I will proclaim and demonstrate the gospel of Your kingdom to those who have yet to hear it and see it. Here I am, Lord—send me!

5

The Gospel of the Kingdom
Proclaimed in the Now

What message did Jesus preach as He went about His ministry on earth? He preached *"the gospel **of the kingdom**"*; in accordance, He healed *"all kinds of sickness and all kinds of disease among the people"* (Matthew 4:23).

The Greek word translated *"gospel"* is *euaggelion*, which means "a good message" (STRONG, G2098), or "good tidings" (NASC, G2098). It is the good news! Jesus brought the good news, but it was specific news. It was the good news of the kingdom. If we leave out the kingdom, we are not proclaiming the same gospel that Jesus announced. That gospel includes the message of His resurrection—not just that He resurrected 2000 years ago but that the power of His resurrection is still active today.

The gospel of the kingdom is what Jesus is doing through individual believers, and through churches and ministries, in the now. Most people have heard what religion says, but they have not heard what the gospel of the kingdom says. As Paul wrote, this gospel is the power of God for salvation—in all its manifestations of redemption, healing, and deliverance.

> For I am not ashamed of the gospel of Christ, for it is the power of God to salvation for everyone who believes.　　　　(Romans 1:16)

The Gospels are the life of Jesus demonstrated in the flesh, and the epistles are the life of Jesus demonstrated by the Spirit.

The true gospel of the kingdom is changing lives in every realm of society, because it is a living and creative gospel. Denise Scanziani is a young lawyer who "had it all" yet could not fill the void she felt inside her until she encountered the kingdom of God in the living Christ. Here is her testimony.

"By the world's standards, I had made it. I had achieved all my goals. I was a successful attorney with my own practice, I had enough money and the perfect family, but something was still missing. I had not planned on feeling an unmistakable emptiness from which I could not escape. I felt disoriented and could not understand why I was so often sad, depressed, and fearful, in need of something more and not knowing what it was. While looking for answers, I decided to run for judge, partly in search of that elusive feeling of fulfillment, and partly to escape the ever-present question ringing in my mind: *Is this all there is to life?*

"As part of my campaign for judge, I visited King Jesus Ministry, where I came face-to-face with a fundamental truth—Jesus Christ. He was the answer that forever changed my life! He spoke to me through the message, and I felt something that started as a tickle in my belly, pierced my heart, and sprang forth as tears from my eyes! That very day, Jesus melted my heart as I gave it to Him. I began my own personal relationship with Him, as I felt His presence for the very first time in my life. I realized I had been created with a special purpose that did not include sadness, fear, or emptiness. Jesus Christ filled that void inside of me! He has given me purpose and a fulfilling, richly satisfying life.

"In the end, I lost the election, and yet the victory was mine! Where there once was sadness, worry, and fear, there is now joy and peace. Where there once was lack and emptiness, there is now abundance, confidence, and the knowledge of my identity as a daughter of God. I now know that He is in control!"

The gospel of the kingdom changed Denise's life in an instant, giving her a genuine experience with the resurrected Christ!

The power of God does not rest in a personality but in the Truth, which is the Word of God.

The Kingdom Gospel Versus Other Gospels

Many religions have their own "gospels," and they announce good things. However, they lack supernatural power to deal with people's sin and rebelliousness and to transform their lives. They lack the power to heal a sickness or to deliver someone from mental or emotional oppression. They are substitutes for the true gospel.

Even in much of the church, parts of the gospel message have been diluted or abridged into various human versions that lack power. In some cases, these human versions are even anti-power. The message of the gospel of the kingdom is not being presented as it was by Jesus and the early church. These significant elements have been left out: a call to wholehearted repentance and the manifestation of God's presence by healing, signs, wonders, the casting out of demons, and the raising of the dead.

As a result, the church has become accustomed to hearing an incomplete gospel. The apostle Paul warned believers of the danger of preaching and following other gospels instead of the gospel of the kingdom:

If anyone preaches any other gospel to you than what you have received, let him be accursed. (Galatians 1:9)

This danger of preaching and following a false or incomplete gospel continues to exist. God wants to restore the true gospel in the church, so that the good news can be preached to the world as it ought to be. Let us look more closely at various kinds of "gospels" with which the gospel of the kingdom has been replaced in the church, so that we can return to the genuine gospel.

1. The Historical Gospel

Many Christians of various denominations are fixed in a historical, traditional gospel that lacks the presence and power of God. They believe in a God of history but not in a God who is with us today—a God whose name is in the present tense: "*I AM WHO I AM*" (Exodus 3:14). For example, they believe in the God who parted the Red Sea and delivered His people from bondage in Egypt. They believe in the God who listened to Joshua and stopped the sun, who confirmed His name by making fire descend from heaven to consume Elijah's sacrifice, and who did many other wonders, as recorded in the

Bible. However, they don't believe God will act today. They believe that Jesus walked the earth over 2,000 years ago, healing all kinds of sicknesses, delivering people from demon possession, forgiving sins, raising the dead, and much more, but they don't believe that He will do the same today.

There are some people who do believe that God still does these things today, but they have no idea how to bring the power of Jesus' resurrection in the here and now to enact His works, because they lack revelation. If we can't bring Jesus to the here and now, then His death, resurrection, and ascension to the throne at the Father's right hand in heaven have no meaning or purpose for our present circumstances.

2. The "Future" Gospel

The mentality of much of the modern church is to present a gospel that simply proclaims forgiveness of sin so that a person can go to heaven when he dies. Although that is certainly part of the good news, it is not the whole gospel of the kingdom. It says nothing of reigning with Christ on earth now with dominion authority and power.

Other believers reflect a different aspect of the future gospel. They believe that God can bring healing and deliverance to people on earth. Nonetheless, since their mind-set is always that God "will" do these things, they never receive or minister them. For example, they may say, "I believe that God will heal, deliver, prosper, and bring revival at some point." In other words, it will happen later, at an unspecified time in the future. Yet God is the God of the now. It is true that He acts according to His sovereignty. However, these believers keep waiting for something that God has already promised and that Jesus has already provided through His death and resurrection.

3. The Social Gospel

While the "future" gospel focuses on heaven, the social gospel centers exclusively on the earth; its advocates seek to relieve societal problems, such as hunger, poverty, and injustice. Addressing people's physical needs and concerns is central to kingdom living, because God wants us to love others as He loves us. (See, for example, Micah 6:8; Matthew 25:31–46.) I believe in and practice these things. For example, our ministry is involved with helping orphans and feeding the poor. However, proponents of the social gospel often downplay or ignore the spiritual element of a relationship with God the

Father through Jesus His Son. They do not seek or rely on God's supernatural power, through which people can be healed physically, emotionally, and mentally, and through which they have access to God's abundant provision, power, and strength. Therefore, they do not present the complete gospel.

4. The Gospel of Conformity

This human "gospel" leaves people in a spiritually stagnant condition, unable to move forward, retaining their sin and never regaining their dominion. It neither deals with the root of rebellion nor challenges people to change, so that they are left in sickness, scarcity, and oppression. A gospel that doesn't produce change is contrary to the kingdom message of repentance that Jesus preached, and it fails to bring about the transformation that Paul urged believers to actively seek. (See Romans 12:2.) When the true gospel of the kingdom is proclaimed, it produces repentance, and people are transformed by the power of the Holy Spirit.

5. The Motivational Gospel

This as a "self-help" gospel in which God's Word is spoken without power; the cross and the resurrection of Jesus are not proclaimed, and the supernatural is absent. It is a gospel adapted to what people want to hear, and it fails to confront them with the destructiveness of their sin, in an effort to avoid offending them. Its main purpose is for people to walk away feeling satisfied with themselves and encouraged to reach their personal goals. While it is good to have goals and to accomplish them, Jesus came to announce much more than that! (See Matthew 6:33.) The gospel of the kingdom lovingly but firmly confronts us with our iniquity and challenges us to live in holiness through the resurrection life of Jesus and the power of the Holy Spirit. It is not an egocentric message that leaves us comfortable in our sinful nature.

A subcategory of the motivational gospel is the "prosperity" gospel. Please understand that God promises prosperity, and He wants to give us His provision and abundance. (See, for example, Philippians 4:19.) Yet some believers go to an extreme so that all they think about are money and material goods. They become consumed with prosperity while neglecting other indispensable aspects of their relationship with God, such as holiness, prayer, and serving others. On the other hand, some Christians criticize any teaching on prosperity. Many of them often struggle financially while rejecting the very provision God wants to give them. We must maintain a balance by keeping our focus on the kingdom of God, in all of its facets.

The main feature distinguishing the gospel of the kingdom from all other "gospels" is supernatural evidence of God's presence and power.

To summarize, churches and ministries that don't preach the gospel of the kingdom produce a complacent Christianity. Many of them present a "friendly" gospel, one that is aimed at placating the conscience. They make no room for the supernatural, and they do not believe that all things are possible with God. This is precisely why we do not often see the manifestations of God's power in the church.

Pastor Nicky van der Westhuizen, the son of a great South African evangelist, was living according to an incomplete gospel. The ministry in which he had been trained operated with few elements of the supernatural, and, upon the death of his father, a religious spirit became the foundation of his church. "We really lost the power of creative miracles," he said.

Then, he watched one of my television broadcasts, during which I pointed at the camera and made this statement: "There is a pastor watching now. You used to operate in the supernatural but have lost the power. God is restoring that right now! And your name is Pastor Nicky." The statement shook him profoundly. He recalls falling out of his chair onto the floor, sobbing, as he knew unmistakably that God was talking to him.

Pastor Nicky then attended a meeting where I ministered to him, and he fell to the floor under the weight of the Holy Spirit. "I felt the power of God so immensely, and Jesus pouring new oil upon me," he said. When he recounted his experience to me at dinner, I began to prophesy over him: "You have quenched the Holy Spirit in your church by putting time limits and programs on it. You need to repent, and the power of God will return."

He did repent, and everything changed in his congregation. The people now walk in the supernatural power of God! Attendance has grown 50 percent in no time, because they preach the gospel of the kingdom in the now, with visible evidences. Pastor Nicky explained, "We began to see and document creative miracles, cancers healed, deaf ears opened, blind eyes seeing, people debt free in twenty-four hours, businessmen and women prospering."

He also had a very personal case with his son. "My youngest son's left foot started to become very weak, causing him much pain, due to a disease of the nervous system. We took him to doctors, but they could not do anything except tell us they would make him a splint that would pull his leg straight. I was very disturbed and cried so much before the Lord, for I was praying for the sick and seeing creative miracles but was not able to help my own son. After I attended a service in South Africa at which Apostle Maldonado ministered, I was able to talk to the apostle about this. He then said, 'The Lord told me that He would heal a twelve-year-old boy of a club foot today.' And he anointed a towel with oil and said that my son must wear it for three days. We did this, full of faith in God. By the second day, the pain had already left, and by the third day, the foot was completely straightened! Now we have the splint as a testimony, because God healed him while they were still making it. To God be all the glory!"

Pastor Nicky had to make a hard transition, but he now preaches and manifests the true gospel with unquestionable evidence that Jesus Christ lives and that His power is as real as ever.

The gospel is the supernatural invasion of the kingdom of God! It is the good news that God wants to bring His kingdom rule to each person. Those who repent and submit to His kingship will find salvation, righteousness, peace, joy, health, eternal life, and whatever else they need. They will be restored to the original dominion that was given to Adam and receive the supernatural power of God. Other gospels don't announce or offer these things!

Are you living the gospel of the here and now, or are you following the historical gospel, the future gospel, the social gospel, the conformity gospel, or the motivational gospel? You must decide to either be left behind in one of these substitute gospels or accept the challenge of the gospel of the kingdom.

If you are living according to a substitute gospel, how can you make the transition to the true gospel? God's Word challenges us to establish ourselves *in the present truth* (2 Peter 1:12). Living the gospel of the here and now can be achieved only if we receive revelation for today.

How to Manifest the Kingdom Through Revelation in the Now

In the New Testament, the word *"revelation"* is translated from the Greek word *apokalupsis*. It means "disclosure" and has connotations of "appearing," "coming," "lighten," "manifestation," "be revealed," and "revelation" (STRONG, G602); it also means "an uncovering" (NASC, G602). The verb form, *apokalupto*, signifies "to disclose," "to reveal" (STRONG, G601), or "to uncover" (NASC, G601).

An important element of divine revelation is what I define as "a fragment of the knowledge of God that comes into our spirit in an instant, without the need for prior research or investigation, according to God's will and timing." A revelation, or a fragment of God's knowledge that is given to us, is something that was previously unknown to us. It always brings new knowledge or insight to light or manifests something fresh. If it is not new or fresh to us, it is not revelation. Everything that is revealed can be considered new, even if it has already come to pass. Something that is not new to you can be new to me, and vice versa. Revelation elevates, stimulates, activates, and accelerates our spirit; it is an impelling force that drives us forward, inducing spiritual motion that leads us to seize the truth and apply it to our lives or to the lives of others.

A doctrine doesn't move our spirit—revelation does.

We cannot proclaim the gospel of the here and now without present revelation. The kingdom gospel we announce must be aligned with what God is revealing today, not just with what He has revealed in the past. Most revivals and movements of God have ended because fresh revelation ceased. We have an enemy who is working to steal from us and destroy us. (See John 10:10.) We cannot defeat him with a historical gospel, or with any other substitute gospel, because none of them has revelation for the now. Without a "now" revelation, there is no real dwelling place for God among His people. There is a place only for His "visitation"—a sovereign and spontaneous movement that is not connected to a rhema, which is a revealed word from the Holy Spirit for the now about how to bring His presence into our midst.

The nature of the new is that it must be revealed.

When a revival ends, people often continue to operate in the initial revelation. This causes their "gospel" message to become a human version and mere religion; it turns dry and mechanical, lacking the move of the Holy Spirit—essentially, it becomes a historical gospel. When revelation stops flowing in a church, there is nothing new or fresh to receive, and there is no direction or vision. (See, for example, 1 Samuel 3:1.) Many ministers today are practicing their faith according to spiritual knowledge and wisdom that others received years ago, and they wonder why it doesn't work now the way it did then. People are hungry for God's revelation for today. This is why the Lord has raised up apostolic and prophetic ministries to bring fresh revelation of His Word in the present. (See Ephesians 4:11.)

Every move of God began with a divine revelation.

Revelation Is to Be Acted Upon

A person doesn't have to be "super-spiritual" to receive revelation, which is also called "revealed knowledge." At the beginning of human history, revealed knowledge operated in Adam, and it enabled him to rule over Eden and all created things. Similarly, each revelation we receive is to be acted upon in accordance with our calling and anointing.

Some revelation is given for the manifestation of a healing or deliverance. Other revelation enables us to have a deeper encounter with God. What we must realize is that spiritual revelation from God cannot manifest in the physical world without the assistance of a human being, because that is how God designed it to work. God is attracted by a spiritual "movement," or desire, within a person; He does not respond to those who are spiritually stagnant or complacent. God wants to hear us speak His "language," and His language is revelation and faith. For example, the woman in the New Testament who suffered from the continual flow of blood moved into the crowd of people surrounding Jesus, seeking Him in faith, even though she was risking public rebuke. And Jesus made her whole. (See Mark 5:25–34.) Likewise, the centurion whose servant was paralyzed received a revelation of Jesus' authority and power, and he acted on it in faith. The result was that he received the healing he desired for his servant. (See Matthew 8:5–13.)

What is not yet revealed remains in the realm of the impossible.
Revelation removes the impossible.

If you have an "impossibility" in your life, similar to the woman with the flow of blood and the centurion whose servant was dying, remember that a revelation from God is sufficient to address your problem, crisis, or circumstance. A rhema from God can make your impossibility a possibility.

Our Personal Gospel

Now to Him who is able to establish you according to my gospel and the preaching of Jesus Christ, according to the revelation of the mystery kept secret since the world began but now has been made manifest....
(Romans 16:25)

The concept of "mystery" is often associated with something mystical or superstitious. God's mysteries are altogether different. A mystery of God is essentially a part of His knowledge or purposes that has not yet been revealed to humanity through revelation. God's mysteries are unfolded to those who hunger for Him and have the fear of the Lord. (See, for example, Psalm 25:14.) When God reveals a spiritual mystery, it is a demonstration of His will and purpose for the here and now. He allows us to understand and apply this mystery in our natural realm. Moreover, God may choose to reveal mysteries related not only to spiritual knowledge but also to natural knowledge, such as science, engineering, art, or any other area of life. In His sovereignty, He may bring fresh revelation into any realm.

Everything of which you have a spiritual revelation will make you a shareholder in heaven's "stock market." In other words, you become the "owner" of that portion of God's knowledge. God revealed to Paul the mystery of the gospel (see Galatians 1:11–12), which had been hidden *"since the world began"* (Romans 16:25) and *"from ages and from generations"* (Colossians 1:26).

It is important to clarify that when the apostle Paul spoke of *"my gospel,"* he was not referring to a different gospel but the true gospel of the kingdom founded in the Scriptures. I believe he called it "his" gospel because he took hold of the truth that had been revealed to him. Preachers must lead people to seize the truth, live it, and practice it. Of course, we must first experience it. It was Paul's gospel because he testified of his experiences with Jesus and the Word, thanks to the revelation of the gospel of the kingdom.

Everything of which you have a spiritual revelation will make you a shareholder in heaven's "stock market."

When we receive Jesus into our hearts, and He begins to heal our bodies, transform our minds, restore our families, and bring us peace, joy, and righteousness, He has truly been revealed to us. "Our" gospel of the kingdom is our personal experience of what God has done and is doing in our lives. No one can share our gospel like we can; no one can say what God is doing in us, day by day, the way we can, because we live it firsthand. In this sense, every Christian must write his own gospel. Everyone has something to share about what God is doing in his life! If we stop sharing our personal experiences, then what we share will inevitably be someone else's gospel, and people will be able to tell the difference. If we testify of what God is doing today, then we are living the gospel of the here and now, rather than a historical gospel.

A personal gospel is also an expression of a "generational" gospel. Just as every believer must have a personal revelation of the truth of the gospel of the kingdom, each succeeding generation must experience the gospel firsthand. We must realize, however, that owning the truth of the gospel for today will require that we pay a price, which will include sacrifice, time, and death to self, and which could also include rejection, persecution, defamation, and much more.

Each time God reveals a truth, we are activated to obey it and "own" it.

In our ministry, we are experiencing an evangelistic explosion through our young people who have received revelation and who testify of the "now" gospel with unquestionable supernatural signs. About a year ago, a church leader and mentor named Orlando made the decision to go to the next level in his faith, after reading my book *How to Walk in the Supernatural Power of God.* He was led to spearhead a hospital ministry with a group of disciples—to visit patients, pray for the sick, and bring salvation to the lost. They began to see healings, miracles, and salvations.

For example, Steven Clark and his friend were the innocent bystanders of a drive-by shooting at a gas station. When the paramedics arrived, the two young men were in such bad shape that it seemed they would not survive long enough to make it to the hospital. Sadly, Steven's friend died, but Steven survived, even though he had more bullets in his body than his friend had.

Orlando and a disciple named Adam met Steven at the ICU when he was unable to move or speak. They prayed for him and his family, all of whom received Jesus as their Savior. A week later, the doctors said that because of fluid buildup in his lungs, Steven would need surgery, or he could die. The young evangelists took an anointed cloth that I had prayed over and placed it on Steven's chest; two days later, his mother called Orlando to say that the doctors were releasing Steven from the ICU—they were astounded and could not understand why he no longer needed surgery and was out of danger! Today, Steven is completely healed, and he participates in hospital outreaches, testifying that the healing power of God is real.

In another example, a teenage boy named Joseph was involved in a terrible accident in which he was ejected from a car. He sustained multiple broken bones and experienced swelling, as well as bleeding in the brain; eventually, he went into a coma. The doctors said his chances of survival were slim, and if he did survive, he would be a vegetable. As Joseph lay lifeless on his bed, a member of Orlando's team named Juan prayed over him, declaring the supernatural power of God. A week later, Joseph was awake and speaking! He also received Christ as his personal Savior!

But the team's victories did not come without obstacles. They had to overcome opposition from nurses and security officers. However, after a while, God gave them favor and grace with the hospital personnel. The team grew exponentially and has seen over forty souls won for the Lord in a single night.

To preach is to proclaim the truth of God's Word. To testify is to share personal knowledge as a result of experiencing His Word and power.

Stewards of God's Revelation

And I will give you the keys of the kingdom of heaven, and whatever you bind on earth will be bound in heaven, and whatever you loose on earth will be loosed in heaven. (Matthew 16:19)

The word "*keys*" represents both authority and revelation. In the natural world, a steward is one who has charge over the keys of a household and knows which key opens which door. When we receive revelation in any area, we have the key to close or open, or to bind or loose, on earth what has already been closed or opened in heaven. Accordingly, we are given the knowledge to apply or to manifest the "how" of the resolution to a situation that has been revealed. We cannot bind or loose anything of which we lack revelation.

Whenever we receive a revelation or manifestation of God's power, we become its caretaker, or steward. The greater the revelation, the greater our responsibility to protect it.

And you shall know the truth, and the truth shall make you free. (John 8:32)

Revealed knowledge causes us to "own" truth, and when we own the truth of the gospel, it liberates us. We are not discussing just any truth but *the* Truth, Jesus Christ (see John 14:6), the truth that sets us free (see John 8:31–32). The truth in Jesus Christ is the highest level of reality. It operates beyond human reason, and it cannot be known by the mind, only by revelation.

The level of revelation that a "steward" of God's mysteries has attained is measured by how that steward affects and alters the spiritual atmosphere around him.

Preaching the Gospel of the Kingdom with Supernatural Evidence in the Now

Now as [Jesus] sat on the Mount of Olives, the disciples came to Him privately, saying, "Tell us, when will these things be? And what will be the sign of Your coming, and of the end of the age?" (Matthew 24:3)

In this verse, the disciples asked Jesus three questions, which He answered very specifically. Among other things, He stated that the sign of His return and the end of the world will be the preaching of the gospel of the kingdom to every nation:

And this gospel of the kingdom will be preached in all the world as a witness to all the nations, and then the end will come.

(Matthew 24:14)

The preaching of the gospel to all the world, which will bring about the end of the age and the coming of Christ, is the church's responsibility. The initiative does not belong to political, military, or scientific leaders. However, in the two thousand years since Christ lived on earth, many in the church have not fulfilled this responsibility. I believe that God is raising up a new generation of people today who are full of passion for Him and His gospel. He has placed them in a movement of glory that has accelerated them to win a multitude of souls to salvation, such as has never been seen before in history. This generation is preaching the gospel of the kingdom with miracles, signs, wonders, the casting out of demons, and the raising of the dead.

The gospel must be preached, announced, or proclaimed, which means it must be public and active. In addition, it is not simply to be taught. To teach is to explain or to expand on a subject. But people must not only learn about the gospel of the kingdom; they must also experience it, and the Holy Spirit alone can reveal the gospel, or make it known, to them.

Where there is no supernatural proof or evidence, there is no kingdom, only abstract theology.

Note that Jesus said the gospel of the kingdom would continue to be preached *"as a witness."* In other words, it is evidence. It provides supernatural confirmation that results in real transformation in people's lives. Jesus healed every type of illness and affliction—mental, emotional, spiritual, and physical. He healed everyone who came to Him for healing, and He cast out demons from those who were possessed. This was the evidence that the kingdom of God had arrived, a fact that Jesus affirmed to John the Baptist. After John was imprisoned, he sent two of his disciples to ask Jesus if He was really the Messiah. (See Matthew 11:2–3.) This is the response Jesus sent back:

> *Go and tell John the things which you hear and see: The blind see and the lame walk; the lepers are cleansed and the deaf hear; the dead are raised up and the poor have the gospel preached to them.*
>
> (Matthew 11:4–5)

To supply evidence that He was indeed the Messiah, Jesus did not discuss the Old Testament prophecies that predicted His coming. He did not list His genealogy to show that He was humanly descended from King David. He did not try to convince John of His divine character. He simply referred to the supernatural fruit that the kingdom of God had produced. If Jesus had been a false Messiah, the combination of these supernatural signs would not have been manifest in His ministry, because it was written in the Scriptures that these signs would accompany the Messiah, the Son of God, who was sent to redeem humanity. (See, for example, Isaiah 29:18; 35:4–6; 61:1–2.) The signs made Him credible.

God never authorized the church to preach a gospel of mere words. He empowered it to preach with supernatural evidence.

In the church today, we have settled for mental knowledge about God, and we no longer experience the demonstration of His power on a regular basis. The church has not been producing what it has been preaching. It has not been demonstrating what it teaches. It lacks revelation because it does not seek the kingdom of God with the passion to see it manifested.

Are you proclaiming the gospel of the kingdom? Do you consider supernatural demonstrations to be isolated events, or a lifestyle? Can you testify of what God is doing here and now? Is your ministry producing supernatural evidence that proves Jesus is alive today? Are the sick being healed in your church? Are souls being saved? Are people being delivered of mental and emotional affliction and oppression? If you are not seeing the power of God doing through you what it did through Jesus, then you are preaching an incomplete or substitute gospel.

Our faith cannot be founded on the wisdom of men; it must be founded on God's power alone. (See 1 Corinthians 2:4.) God is doing great miracles, signs, and wonders around the world, as evidence that Jesus lives and that the gospel of the kingdom has arrived. Some of the signs are difficult to understand or explain, but this should not cause us to worry, if we know how to discern the true from the false. True signs from God are not ends in themselves; rather, they always point to a higher truth—Jesus Christ and the power of His resurrection. (See 1 John 4:1–3.)

It is foolish to worship signs, but it is more foolish to ignore them.

When we seek God, we must do so knowing that He is supernatural. If we think we understand and know how to explain everything that God is doing in and through us, then He is probably no longer involved. Even in the natural realm, our minds can manage to understand only a small part of our world and how it functions. How much more is this the case when we are dealing with the supernatural! There will always be elements of the unknown that challenge our reason, and this is precisely why God has given each of us a measure of faith. (See Romans 12:3.) Every day, we must believe for the impossible, and we will experience joy as we see impossibilities bow down before God and become possibilities in our physical world.

Everything we have been discussing up to now in this chapter has been for the purpose of emphasizing that the gospel of the kingdom should manifest in tangible proof and demonstrations of miracles, healings, transformations of the heart, and the like. When a person receives the revelation of the gospel of the kingdom, evidence will be produced. The blind will see, the deaf will hear, the depressed will be joyful, the oppressed will experience peace, and those in torment will be delivered.

In our ministry, we have seen manifestations of the gospel of the kingdom occur countless times in countries around the world. Hundreds of thousands of testimonies of God's supernatural power back up our ministry, because we preach the complete gospel. For example, we held a meeting in Argentina at which thousands were saved. At the same meeting, I began to pray for certain sicknesses that the Lord had revealed to me through prayer, and I included infirmities of the mind. Among those attending that meeting were a young boy named Samuel Soto and his parents. Samuel had been born with gastroesophageal reflux disease, which affected one of his lungs. He had also suffered from pulmonary disease, fever, and convulsions, which had left him with serious neurological problems. As he grew, his parents noticed that he did not respond to stimuli, and it was hard for him to speak. At school, he had a difficult time learning. The neurologist diagnosed him with developmental delay, expedited a handicap certificate, and started treating him with medication.

During the meeting in Argentina, when I declared healing for infirmities of the mind, Samuel's parents appropriated the word. At that moment, Samuel felt the power of God and said, "It's burning me! Here, Mommy, it's burning me!" He was touching the left side of his forehead. His mother moved his hair out of the way and saw a scar with what appeared to be two stitches. The amazing part was that he'd never had surgery! His mother then began to test his intelligence, and, to her surprise, he responded correctly to everything she asked, without difficulty. Later, when Samuel's pediatrician saw the scar, he said, "Right here, where you see the stitches, is where the development of intelligence takes place." The parents consulted a neurologist, who declared Samuel healed and then discharged him. God had cured him!

Samuel's parents have his medical records, as well as his previous school tests and homework, as evidence of his former developmental delay and incapacity. Now, he attends school like any other child of normal intelligence. While he used to receive grades of zero or F, he now receives As and Bs. His handwriting is legible, and he is able to draw and do everything that a healthy child his age is expected to do. The emotion his mother exhibited when sharing their testimony revealed how difficult this situation had been for the family, but it also demonstrated the greatness of the miracle. Medical science could not heal this impossible condition, but the Holy Spirit of God "operated" on Samuel and restored him to full health!

The Gospel of the Kingdom Transforms Lives and Agitates the World

The gospel of the kingdom contains great power. Our message is simple: There is a King who has all authority and power. He is seated on His throne in heaven, and His kingdom is in the process of coming to earth. His name is Jesus. He has come to redeem us from sin, cure the sick, deliver the captives, heal the brokenhearted, and bring prosperity to the poor. We must let everyone know that the kingdom is among us, here and now!

The gospel of the kingdom is simple, practical, and powerful.

People who are entrenched in the world and its mind-set are not afraid of religion. However, they are intimidated by supernatural power from God that exposes their rebellion and sin. As in the New Testament, when the church truly begins to preach the gospel of the kingdom of God, opposition—stirred up by the kingdom of darkness—will be immediate. Civil and religious authorities will come against us. If we are not suffering some oppression, then we probably have not caused the devil enough damage. First-century religious leaders said about Peter and John, "*These who have turned the world upside down have come here too....And these are all acting contrary to the decrees of Caesar, saying there is another king; Jesus*" (Acts 17:6–7).

The first Christians were always in trouble with the authorities for preaching about Jesus and doing what He did. Proclaiming the gospel of the kingdom both transforms lives and agitates the world! The gospel will bring freedom and joy to those who believe, and it will cause consternation and fear to those who refuse to believe. When Jesus was born, and the wise men came to worship Him, King Herod of Judea felt threatened because he thought he would lose his kingdom and authority. So, he ordered the murder of every boy in the region who was two years old or younger, but God protected His Son from Herod's wrath. (See Matthew 2:1–3, 12–16.) Also, as I wrote earlier, during His ministry, Jesus suffered persecution from hard-hearted and stubborn religious leaders, who finally turned Him over to the Romans authorities to be killed (see Matthew 26:3–4), although this was all used by God in His plan for our redemption.

The Power of the Kingdom Comes from the King's Word

In the New Testament, we find many examples of men of God who preached the gospel of the kingdom, starting with Jesus. Each of the four Gospels emphasizes a different aspect of Jesus, and the book of Matthew reveals Jesus as the King who fulfilled the messianic prophecies of the Old Testament. Appropriately, Matthew contains the first New Testament reference to Jesus preaching the gospel of the kingdom. (See Matthew 4:23.)

In Ecclesiastes, we read,

Where the word of a king is, there is power; and who may say to him, "What are you doing?" (Ecclesiastes 8:4)

King Jesus does not need to answer to anyone; His supernatural presence and manifestations speak for themselves. The gospel of the kingdom has power because its message comes from the King Himself, who does not speak empty words, as men are prone to do; His words are full of authority and power. When we proclaim them, He confirms them with supernatural evidence by the Holy Spirit—the same Spirit who worked alongside Him during His ministry on earth. The words of the kingdom of God come from a King who surrendered Himself to save humanity—who died and was raised on the third day, defeating sin, death, hell, and the devil—and who now rules from His throne in heaven with power and glory.

*Without a "now" word from the King, there will be no power,
even if the words we speak are biblical.*

When He was still on earth, Jesus sent out His twelve apostles to preach the gospel of the kingdom under His anointing (see Matthew 10:5–8); later, He sent out seventy disciples to various towns to prepare the people for His forthcoming visits, in which He proclaimed the kingdom of God (see Luke 10:1). After Jesus' resurrection and ascension to heaven, Peter, Philip, and the rest of the apostles proclaimed the good news. (See, for example, Acts 2:14–41; 8:4–12.) Then, the apostle Paul had an encounter with the risen Christ, became converted, and was taught the gospel by revelation of God. Although Paul was eager to help the poor, he did not say, "I fed the poor and the widows, and I clothed the orphans, and this is how I fully preached the gospel." Instead, he said that Christ had worked through him *"in word and deed…in mighty signs and wonders, by the power of the Spirit of God,"* and that was how he had *"fully preached the gospel of Christ."* (See Romans 15:18–19.) Every apostle to whom Jesus had entrusted the gospel when He ascended to heaven preached the message of the kingdom in word and deed. (See Hebrews 2:3–4.)

The church must continue the pattern established by the men and women who first proclaimed the gospel of the kingdom. (See Mark 16:15–18.) If you won't even talk to your neighbor about Jesus, then there is no need for supernatural signs to manifest. If you want to go to church and just sing songs, then the signs will not follow you.

*The gospel of the kingdom can never be separated from saving,
healing, and casting out demons.*

Principles of Our Kingdom Commission

Go therefore and make disciples of all the nations, baptizing them in the name of the Father and of the Son and of the Holy Spirit.

(Matthew 28:19)

The message of the gospel has not changed; it is still the same, and it will continue to be the same until Jesus returns. Some people might say that the mandate in the above verse was just for those who were alive in Jesus' time. However, Jesus' next statement proves that the gospel is a multigenerational message: *"I am with you always, even to the end of the age"* (Matthew 28:20). Jesus was aware that none of the apostles or other believers of the early church would live long enough to see the end of the age. He knew that you and I and multitudes of other people would be born into this world and be commissioned with the same mandate that they were.

The end of the world cannot come until every human being on earth has heard the gospel of the kingdom.

We don't know when Jesus will return; it could be five, ten, fifty, or one hundred years from now; only the Father knows. (See Matthew 24:36.) What we do know is that our mission is to gather the harvest of souls by preaching the gospel of the kingdom to every person in every tribe, race, and culture on every continent. We are to make disciples in every nation, until His return—every other purpose is secondary. This is a simple concept to understand. The problem of the church is its rebelliousness against obeying it. The heart of the Lord has always been to reach every person, to the ends of the earth. That is His burden. With this in mind, let us explore three essential principles of our kingdom commission.

1. We Are Empowered to Go and Proclaim the Gospel of the Kingdom Now

It was as the apostles went about preaching that the Lord confirmed His Word through supernatural signs. (See Mark 16:20.) If we do not go out and preach God's Word, then He has nothing to confirm. We must assume our responsibility as a church!

And as you go, preach, saying, "The kingdom of heaven is at hand."
(Matthew 10:7)

Sin is increasing in the world because believers have no idea of their true calling from God. They are involved in doing good works and enjoying fellowship with one another, but these are not the primary mandate of the church. As long as we fail to understand who we are and what our responsibility is, we will not be able to carry out our mission. The church is not a social club or a funeral home; it is not a charitable organization, a political group, or a foundation for social outreach; it is not an extension of a government or business. It was brought into being for the purpose of exercising dominion and bringing the kingdom of heaven to earth. God loves the world—you and me, as well as everyone else on earth, from our neighbors to the people who live in other countries—everyone! (See John 3:16.) The church is not merely to inhabit the world but to win it. We are to love what God loves—people— and hate what He hates—sin. We have been given authority and power to make Satan yield to God's ever-increasing kingdom in this world.

Supernatural signs and evidence are guaranteed to those who "go."

Many Christians say, "Be wary of the people in the world; don't associate with them." With this mentality, we would need to separate ourselves from everyone whom we are called to bring into the kingdom! (See 1 Corinthians 5:9–10.) It is impossible to carry out our mission if we don't go where people can be found. Of course, as we go, we are not to enter into friendship with the world system. (See James 4:4.) We are not to adopt its mind-set and ways; rather, we are to be the light that will guide people to Jesus.

We are not called to become like the people of the world but to guide them to Jesus, so they can become like Him.

2. The Harvest Is Ready Now

Lift up your eyes and look at the fields, for they are already white for harvest! (John 4:35)

The harvest has been ready since Jesus began His ministry on earth. In the above verse, He was essentially declaring, "Stop saying that the harvest is not ready and that people are not ready to be saved!" Your spouse, your children, and your other family members are ready. Jesus made the above statement about the harvest more than two thousand years ago, but the church has yet to believe it! Our harvest is ready and mature, but it has to be gathered. When fruit becomes overripe, it starts to decompose and smell bad. The jails are full of murderers and thieves because the church did not gather them in time. They are overripe, and now they "smell bad." This doesn't mean that they cannot still be rescued, but it does mean that we shouldn't wait for Satan to destroy people before we consider going to them with the gospel of the kingdom.

> *The harvest truly is plentiful, but the laborers are few. Therefore pray the Lord of the harvest to send out laborers into His harvest.*
> (Matthew 9:37–38)

Jesus has a problem with the workers, not the harvest. The harvest is ready, but more people are needed to work in the fields. In addition, even though the harvest is ripe, the workers are still green and immature and do not know much about gathering crops. The answer is not more prayer for souls to come into the church but prayer for God to send workers who are established in His authority and power out into the fields where the people are.

God is the Lord of the harvest. He sowed and watered the seed and ripened the crops. Our only job is to gather the harvest. God doesn't want anyone to perish but for all to repent and be saved. (See 2 Peter 3:9.) People around the world, of all backgrounds—presidents, prime ministers, senators, businesspeople, actors, singers, teachers, police officers, doctors, scientists, religious leaders; the young, the old, the rich, and the poor—are crying out, "We need God's help!" Yet most believers are doing nothing about it. There are churches all over the United States, and in many nations around the world, but the majority of them are not being the light of the world and the salt of the earth. (See Matthew 5:13–14.)

God's greatest passion is to see everyone in the world—now more than seven billion people—saved, filled with the Holy Spirit, and living holy lives.

3. We Are to Go and Evangelize Our Own Ethnos

God has a global mentality. The word *"nations"* in Matthew 28:19 is translated from the Greek word *ethnos*, from which the English word *ethnic* is derived. *Ethnos* means "a race (as of the same habit), i.e., tribe," with the implication of "nation" or "people" (STRONG, G1484).

People who belong to a particular ethnic group generally speak the same language and have the same beliefs, ways of thinking, values, and traditions, among other shared characteristics. One key to developing a nation is culture—people coming together who have common standards, customs, and practices. Within nations, there are also subgroups of people, based on their interests, needs, and/or vocations. Each one of these subgroups can be considered an ethnos, as well.

Let us look at twelve ethnos subgroups that are found in many nations and cultures, keeping in mind that the list isn't all-inclusive, and that some of the areas overlap. Each ethnos has its own mind-set and "language." We must identify in which ethnos we participate, so that, together, as the church, we can bring the gospel to all the ethnos of the world. We must start out where we are, in our "Jerusalem and Judea," and expand from there. (See Acts 1:8.)

+ *Politics and Government:* This ethnos centers on the development and administration of a country and its laws and policies. In addition, many governments have departments that represent and administer various ethnos in the country. For example, they may have departments of education, defense, health, social welfare, trade, labor, and finance. People of this mind-set are geared toward government; administration; political campaigns; voters; the economy; local, national, and global political events; and so on. The "language" of their ethnos—what they talk about, and the vocabulary they use—reflects these areas. Those in the politics and government ethnos also fall under additional subcategories, depending on their philosophies and inclinations. In the United States, these subcategories can be identified by political party—such as Democrat, Republican, or Libertarian—or by political persuasion—such as liberal, conservative, and moderate, as well as left-wing and right-wing variations. People in this ethnos are presidents, prime ministers, governors, senators, mayors, councilmen, legislative assistants, political consultants, and political "junkies," to name a few.

- *Religion:* Religion may generally be defined as a nation's belief system relating to ultimate reality and the meaning of life. In some countries, multiple religions are practiced, and each one has specific beliefs, patterns of behavior, activities, liturgies, and so forth. The "language" of religion includes the concepts of God (or gods), life, sin, death, the afterlife, sacred writings, theology, and so on. Each religious ethnos is composed of religious leaders and their followers, devotees, or believers. We should realize that a distinct approach is needed when proclaiming the gospel of the kingdom to people of different religious ethnos, such as Roman Catholics, Jehovah's Witnesses, Buddhists, and Muslims.

- *The Media:* The media ethnos includes those who work in radio, television, the Internet (Web-based programs), other electronic communications, and print—such as books, newspapers, and magazines. They are news reporters, public speakers, actors, producers, camerapersons, lighting technicians, publishers, editors, writers, and many others. The media ethnos (as are all ethnos) is almost a world in itself, with its own concepts, activities, and "dialects," including such terms as cinematography, graphic design, computer animation, production, HDTV, streaming, and many more.

- *Business:* The business ethnos is made up of men and women who dedicate themselves to selling and buying tangible and intangible goods or providing services; they are involved in small, midsize, or large companies, which may be privately owned or have their shares traded on the stock market. They are businesspeople, salespeople, administrators, customs agents, and importers and exporters, to name only a few. Many of them are constantly thinking about how they can establish a business, secure credit for a new enterprise, or perform transactions. The language they speak is filled with terms such as business plans, statistics, marketing strategies, products, services, quotas, supply and demand, and financial statements.

+ *Education:* The education ethnos is composed of those who teach ideas and information; those who make discoveries, do research, and advance the pursuit of knowledge; and those who study ideas and information and perform their own research and analysis, often with the goal of preparing for a vocation or job. They are teachers, professors, researchers, philosophers, and students, and their language is filled with knowledge, learning theories, training methods, educational psychology, outcomes, textbooks, and tests, as well as dialects related to their particular fields, such as literature, engineering, or social work. Some of these dialects overlap with their vocational counterparts in the outside world.

+ *Science:* Science involves the study and use of the physical world, and includes the fields of biology, chemistry, physics, astronomy, paleontology, geology, ecology, and more. People in the science ethnos fulfill roles such as scientists, researchers, lab technicians, teachers, environmentalists, and product developers. They generally share a common language, mind-set, and belief system, using such terms as experiments, testing, analyses, theories, exploration, and more. Many scientists believe only what they can prove in a laboratory or by logic and the physical senses.

+ *Technology:* This ethnos is populated by people who explore new possibilities, make products more user-friendly, and change the way people live. It comprises engineers, computer scientists, technicians, research and development managers, and manufacturers, to name just a few. Depending on their area of expertise, they speak a language that includes words such as inventions, electronics, robotics, valves, appliances, food processing, data, fabrics, plastics, paint, and much more.

+ *Medicine:* The medicine ethnos includes medical personnel of diverse specialties, such as cardiology, physiology, dermatology, podiatry, emergency medicine, and much more. People in this ethnos fulfill such roles as doctors, nurses, technicians, therapists, nutritionists, and researchers. They, too, have their own mind-set and dialects, which center on patients, procedures, diseases, injury, diagnoses, medicines, surgery, treatments, and cures.

+ *Economics:* This ethnos includes those who study and/or participate in national and global financial structures, trends, and policies; banking; the stock market; economic development; and many other areas. They function in such roles as economists, professors, market analysts, entrepreneurs, CEOs, brokers, and financial planners. Their mind-set and language reflect such concepts as statistics, assets, equity, productivity, mergers, stocks and bonds, yields, loans, debt, standards of living, and growth.

+ *Sports:* The sports ethnos is made up of people in both the amateur and professional realms who engage in physical activity and exercise, and/or who excel in physical ability demonstrated through various athletic events and team sports, such as football, basketball, baseball, softball, tennis, swimming, and track and field. They may be players, coaches, owners, managers, trainers, referees, sportscasters, sports therapists, or spectators. Each sport has a distinct set of goals and rules, which their own dialect centers on, although almost all sports require physical discipline and focus, and these elements unite the members of this ethnos.

+ *Entertainment and the Arts:* This ethnos includes those who are involved in theater, film, television, radio, the Internet, music, publishing, art, and many other endeavors involving creativity and communication. They are actors, directors, musicians, writers, painters, sculptors, graphic artists, computer animators, special effects technicians, photographers, dancers, and more. Their dialects include such terms as audiences, ratings, performances, 3-D technology, CGI, best sellers, Web content, designs, scripts, musical scores, color theory, and many more. People in the arts seem to have a special sensitivity. By and large, the artist lives in his own world, seeking the freedom to create and rejecting anything that limits or ties him down.

+ *Law and Justice:* The law and justice ethnos is concerned with such concepts as constitutions, laws, rights, liabilities, contracts, and law enforcement. It is generally made up of an integrated community of lawyers, district attorneys, judges, jurors, police officers, social workers, prison wardens, and more. People who take part in this ethnos have a mind-set and language that focus on legal interpretation, regulations, policies, plaintiffs, defendants, litigation, crimes, arrests, sentencing, rehabilitation, and more. In the ideal scenario, this ethnos seeks to maintain a stable society by eliminating wrongdoing and promoting justice.

The most effective way to win the world for Christ is to first testify of Him within your ethnos, while manifesting God's supernatural power.

Since each ethnos and sub-ethnos has its own mind-set and language or dialects, a believer who participates in a particular ethnos will usually have a better opportunity to communicate the kingdom to people of that ethnos than he would to those of other ones. For instance, a scientist will be the most effective individual to speak to other scientists about the kingdom. Scientists don't go around saying, "Praise God," and most doctors don't enter their offices or hospitals saying, "You must be saved, hallelujah!" If a Christian tried to speak to them in this way, he would likely be rejected, simply because of the language he used. However, a scientist or doctor who is saved and filled with the Holy Spirit, and who also knows the language of the scientific or medical community, can bring the gospel of the kingdom to that ethnos.

Let me give you another example. I have seen young people who use rap music to win souls. Many Christians might not comprehend or appreciate rap, but those who speak the language of rap music understand them. These young artists are communicating the kingdom to people of the same ethnos. Likewise, when a gang member is saved and transformed by the power of Christ, he may return to his former ethnos to witness to other gang members who will listen to him because he knows their mind-set, language, codes, pacts, and the like. Again, this is how we begin to spread the kingdom of God—each person going to his own ethnos. The doctor evangelizes his fellow doctor, the scientist evangelizes the lab technician, the teacher evangelizes the student, and so forth. The following testimony is an example from the sports ethnos of a baseball player who was brought to the Lord by the testimony of a fellow player.

Octavio Fernandez was born in the Dominican Republic and was a Major League Baseball player for eighteen years. He says, "My achievements include four times as an American League Gold Glove Winner, a World Series Championship, and five times as an All Star. Although I was brought up by godly parents, I would say they were also very religious. My brothers and I could not engage in activities such as sports or going to the movies, because everything was 'sinful.' I wanted to serve Christ, but I also wanted to enjoy my teenage years, especially playing sports. So, I prayed that God would bless me with a baseball career, and I promised Him I would in turn bless His people and my parents. I became a star at an early age and wanted to enjoy life. Meanwhile, my parents were constantly praying for me. Despite all the success, to my surprise, my heart was empty. In time, I injured my hand severely and had to stop playing. That was devastating to me! The Lord touched one of my teammates to preach to me. But my hand healed, and I returned to the game, did very well, and put God on hold. Everyone, except for my manager, was amazed at how well I was playing. That hurt my feelings, because I wanted his approval, also. There was a void in my heart, and baseball was not my main passion anymore. I needed something real, something better.

"Then, my friend took me to the baseball chapel, where I gave my heart to Jesus. I do not know how to explain it, but I felt that a heavy burden had been lifted from my soul, and I immediately wanted to share the joy I was feeling inside of me. The hatred, hard feelings, resentment, bitterness, and more began to go away. I am so thankful to my teammate. God used him to get to me. Before, I'd always wanted to be perfect in every game; if I did not perform up to that standard, I would get mad at myself, and people misunderstood me. Afterward, I became more tolerant of myself. The biggest transformation took place after I joined King Jesus Ministry. My marriage and family relationships were in 'intensive care,' and the enemy was about to destroy us completely! So, I cried out to God for help, praying early in the morning, as our spiritual fathers teach us. I can definitely say that inner healing has taken place and restoration has begun in every aspect of our lives. Family, ministry, friendship…all has been restored! Today, trivial things don't bother me anymore. My confidence level, founded in my new identity, is much higher than before! Now I can say I am a new creation in Christ Jesus!"

This is a wonderful example of a believer reaching out to someone in his own ethnos with the gospel of the kingdom. Yet this is not all the church is called to do. I believe that in these last days, evangelism will be accelerated by God's supernatural power, so that believers will be able to cross from one ethnos to another and reach even more people for Christ. For instance, when I witness to a high school student in an informal setting, I don't evangelize the same way I would during a service at my church. We must change our approach if we want to reach people who inhabit a different ethnos from our own. Jesus is our best role model for accomplishing this purpose. He interacted with people of various social strata and backgrounds, such as religious leaders, tax collectors, prostitutes, doctors, businesspeople, and Roman centurions. He brought the visible and tangible demonstration of God's power to the rich and the poor; to Jews and Gentiles; to men, women, young people, and children.

Believers in the twenty-first century must be trained to cross over into any ethnos—from sports to the media, from science to business, and so forth. Likewise, they must be able to talk to people of various races and nationalities. Today's leaders need to train the church to be versatile, to let go of their limitations, and to extend outward in the Spirit. (See Isaiah 54:2–3.) I believe the church must become multiracial and multicultural, bringing together different ethnos. The kingdom of God is not about a specific race, nationality, or culture. It includes all races, tribes, nations, and ethnicities.

A few years ago, the Lord led me to transition King Jesus Ministry from a Hispanic church—which we had been for over a decade—to a multicultural one. In the beginning, there was much opposition from a few of the Hispanic families who felt uncomfortable with the change and who seemed to believe that the kingdom was made solely for Hispanics. But we obeyed God and opened an English service and made other services bilingual. In only a short time, attendance at the English service grew to thousands of people; the change also opened doors for us in English-speaking nations worldwide. We began to televise our services throughout the United States and to broadcast on various television and radio stations across the globe. Now, we even reach Africa, Russia, and Europe, thanks to God's initiative. My mind-set had to change from a local mentality to a mentality of kingdom expansion, so that I could cross over from one eth-nos to another—from Hispanic to multicultural. Today, over sixty nations are represented in our church.

Evangelization in the twenty-first century demands that Christians be able to cross over from one ethnos to another through the supernatural.

Are you willing to make yourself available to take the gospel of the kingdom everywhere you go? We need to permeate the world with the proclamation of the good news, and with God's supernatural manifesta-tions, through the various ethnos. The gospel must be preached to every nation with signs and wonders, because only supernatural power can reach the entire world. God seeks and calls committed and passionate workers who will take His kingdom message into their own ethnos—and beyond. He is raising up a new generation, filled with the power of the Holy Spirit, who have the fire and passion to reach souls. Are you a part of this new gen-eration? Will you go in God's name? Will you begin right now to proclaim the gospel and testify of what He has done for you?

God is calling you to decide, right now! You don't have to wait for your pastor to lay hands on you, anoint you, and send you out as a missionary before you can testify of Jesus. You can begin today. You can testify of Jesus in your everyday life—while you are working at the office, eating at a restaurant, attending a sporting event, shopping at the mall, sitting in a theater, or enjoying a vacation—everywhere you go. And I declare that His power comes upon you now to activate you and give you a passion for souls, so you can bring them to salvation and deliverance.

God has commissioned you to be light and salt to people in your own ethnos and other ethnos. The challenge is here and now. The harvest is ready, but the workers are few. Decide to go out in the supernatural power of the kingdom of God! The Lord will confirm His gospel with signs, mir-acles, and wonders. Amen!

6

The Restoration of the Supernatural in the Church

The church was birthed in the supernatural, through Jesus' resurrection and the power of the Holy Spirit. Miracles, signs, and wonders verified and established the church's doctrine. Christians in the New Testament lived a supernatural lifestyle, and the power of the kingdom caused the early church to multiply. Today, the church seems to have lost its life and power, but God has begun to restore the supernatural to individual believers, churches, and ministries who have opened their hearts to receive it. His desire is to fill His entire church with His presence and power.

In my book *The Glory of God*, I included the testimony of an amazing creative miracle, something that is impossible by human logic, and I want to report that the miracle continues to manifest. Matías Rodríguez of Argentina suffered from achondroplasia, a genetic condition that stunts growth. Affecting one out of every 25,000 children, it is the most common type of dwarfism. While the length of the vertebrae is normal, the arms and legs are short, and there are other irregularities.

When I first met Matías, at a healing service in Argentina, he was twenty-one years old, but his height was that of a ten-year-old boy. He had visited several doctors, but they had all concluded that there was no cure. Due to his condition, he had grown up with low self-esteem and a sense of guilt that made him bitter. He felt that he was a burden to his parents.

Matías sought relief in alcohol and drugs but thankfully avoided becoming addicted. He also left school to escape the rejection and mocking of his classmates. In time, he underwent surgery to correct the curvature in his legs, which threatened to leave him an invalid, but the results were not good. Matías's forearms also had limited mobility and caused him much pain.

The day I ministered in the healing service that Matías attended, I declared creative miracles. When I asked people to testify, he came forward. He said that God's fire had touched him, and he could now move his arms. That young man couldn't stop crying. I wanted to know what sickness he had. When he told me, my heart was filled with compassion. With the guidance of the Holy Spirit, I declared that within twenty-four hours, his body would grow so much that his clothes would no longer fit him. He fell to the floor under the power of God, and the Holy Spirit ministered to him.

After I arrived home, Matías's pastor—who is also a doctor—reported to me that the young man was growing! In the first twenty-four hours, he had grown a little over two centimeters (about three quarters of an inch). Forty-eight hours later, he had grown three more centimeters (a little more than an inch); seventy-two hours later, three additional centimeters. He grew until his clothing no longer fit him properly. In three days, he grew a total of eight centimeters (a little more than three inches)!

As he became taller due to the accelerated growth in his bones, tendons, and muscles, he experienced intense "growing pains." A year later, I saw him again, and he was still growing! He is now thirteen centimeters (more than five inches) taller than when I first ministered to him. This is a creative miracle, impossible to anyone except God.

Understanding the Supernatural

The gospel of the kingdom is supernatural because it brings heaven to earth, just as it did for Matías. If we are to proclaim this gospel in its fullness, as we discussed in the previous chapter, we need a better understanding of the supernatural, so we may recognize and walk in it.

1. The Supernatural Is the Nature of God Himself

God is a supernatural God, and He cannot be described outside of this context. Let us review some of His qualities.

+ *God is Spirit.* As we saw in chapter 2, God is an invisible, eternal Being, with supernatural abilities and attributes that are infinitely superior to the natural world.

> *God is Spirit, and those who worship Him must worship in spirit and truth.* (John 4:24)

God is not a material being; He doesn't have a tangible body or physical needs. He is Spirit, and He exists and moves in the spiritual realm. This is why our worship of Him must be in spirit and truth—supernatural and sincere. It must come from the heart. God should be sought after and adored as a supernatural God. If we approach Him in any other way, we will not receive much from Him.

The supernatural, or spiritual, is the form in which God exists.

+ *God has life in Himself.* He doesn't depend on the natural realm of time, space, and matter in order to live, nor does He need anyone or anything else to sustain Him. He is self-existent, meaning He has life in and of Himself, and He is the Creator of all things. As we have noted, God revealed Himself to Moses as *"I AM WHO I AM"* (Exodus 3:14). He lives in the eternal "now."

Although we are made in God's image, we are not the same as God; we depend on Him for our lives and existence.

+ *God is almighty.* "Holy, holy, holy, Lord God Almighty, who was and is and is to come!" (Revelation 4:8). The Greek word translated as *"Almighty"* is *pantokrator*, which means "the all-ruling, that is, God as absolute and universal sovereign" (STRONG, G3841), "almighty" (NASC, G3841), or "ruler of all" (VINE, G3841). God's might and power are matchless.

+ ***God is not a man.*** Some believers treat God the Father as if He has the same mind-set and finite abilities as fallen human beings. Consequently, they try to gain His attention through natural means, but we cannot approach God according to how we function in the natural realm. When we do so, we set boundaries around who we think He is and what we believe He is able to do. *"God is not a man"* (Numbers 23:19). To separate God from the supernatural is to attempt to "naturalize" Him, but this is impossible. Given His supernatural nature, such an approach to Him is inappropriate; it fails to acknowledge His essence and will, and it dishonors Him. God doesn't think or act as people do, with their limitations and weaknesses! For example, God is able to make everlasting promises because He will always keep them; in contrast, human beings, even with the best of intentions, lack the ability to be faithful to their promises at all times.

2. The Supernatural Is the Nature of God's Kingdom

Just as God cannot be described outside the context of the supernatural, the same is true of His kingdom. *Supernatural* is derived from the prefix *super-*, which means "over" or "above," and the noun *nature*. Therefore, to live in the supernatural means to live above, beyond, or outside of the natural realm. Although the word *supernatural* doesn't appear in the Bible, the concept is demonstrated throughout the Scriptures in the miracles, signs, and wonders that God enacted, which reflect who He is and what He is able to do. Biblical terms and phrases such as "spiritual," "kingdom of heaven," "kingdom of God," "not of this world," "omnipresent," and "omnipotent" all refer to our supernatural God and His supernatural realm.

3. The Supernatural Is Normal for God

From God's perspective, the supernatural is normal life. From Genesis to Revelation, the God-inspired Scriptures consistently show Him to be supernatural—creating matter out of "nothing" and superseding the natural laws of earth. We must realize that God wants the natural to become elementary to us and the supernatural to become our norm, too, as we become mature kingdom citizens.

The supernatural is the impact and influence of the spiritual world on the physical creation, and its interaction with the same.

4. The Supernatural Rules Over the Natural

The supernatural is not just above or beyond the natural world, but it actively rules over it. God is Lord over both the spiritual and physical dimensions. He created the visible world to be ruled by the invisible realm. Therefore, we should not be amazed when He does something supernatural on earth today, such as healings, miracles, signs, wonders, the casting out of demons, and the raising of the dead. All these demonstrations of His presence and power reflect His rule in our natural world.

5. The Supernatural Is Reality, Not Magic or Superstition

Some people think God's supernatural power is an expression of mysticism, superstition, magic tricks, optical illusions, deceit, or something else false or unreal. But the divine supernatural is not magic or trickery. It is the deepest reality we can know, and it is a kingdom, with conditions and established laws that must be obeyed. For example, the supernatural will not work in our lives if we seek healing but harbor unforgiveness at the same time. (See, for example, Matthew 6:14–15.)

The supernatural is truth revealed in the physical dimension. If the truth is removed, God is, in essence, also removed, leaving only an illusion.

6. The Supernatural Is Without Limitation

We recognize and establish limitations in the natural realm, but we can't do that in the eternal realm, because eternity is infinite. Therefore, we have to remove any limitations we have tried to place on God. A miracle is a supernatural intervention of God that takes place in the natural realm and defies natural laws, destroys mental paradigms, and supersedes the dominion of human reason.

A woman in our church, Ivis Vilato, discovered the unlimited nature of God's supernatural power when she was pregnant with twins. Six months into her pregnancy, the doctor discovered that the female twin had an abnormal chromosome count, and he diagnosed her with mosaic Turner syndrome, a genetic condition that occurs in one out of every 2,000 births. The normal number of chromosomes in a human being is forty-six, two of which define the sex. Females normally have two X chromosomes, but in the case of the female twin, one of those was missing, and she had other abnormalities. Mosaic Turner syndrome causes physical deformities and other problems.

Ivis's doctor advised her to abort the baby. The news shocked her, and she started crying. Instead of aborting, she chose to keep the baby and declared that her twins would be born healthy. Sad and crying, she went to a church service, where the youth pastor prayed for her and declared healing over the baby. Immediately, Ivis felt the sadness and worry leave. In faith, she went back to the doctor and told him that her baby was healed and fine. He was skeptical, so when the twins were born, he had the female tested for the syndrome, and, to his surprise, her chromosome count was normal! She had been supernaturally healed of the disorder and was completely healthy, to the glory of God. The doctors could not believe that such a tremendous miracle had occurred. Ivis thanks the Lord and is in constant joy about her baby's health. It was not reasonable or logical for her daughter to be born healthy, but the supernatural power of God broke through the natural world and created the missing chromosome.

Each one of God's miracles is a contradiction of natural facts, reason, logic, and time.

7. The Supernatural Will Increasingly Manifest on the Earth

The kingdom of Satan is inflicting thick darkness on the world today. It is exerting such pressure on believers that God's supernatural kingdom will become visible more frequently in response to this assault. We will see angels, visions, blood, fire, and smoke. (See, for example, Acts 2:19–20.) Supernatural manifestations of miracles, signs, and wonders will become commonplace. We cannot be afraid of these demonstrations of God's power! In the Bible, every time God manifested in a supernatural way to one of His servants, His first words were, "Don't be afraid" (see, for example, Luke 1:29–30), because when our reason encounters something it cannot explain, we become fearful. God tells us not to be afraid, and He gives us peace, so that we will know it is He who is manifesting, and that nothing bad is going to happen to us. God wants to demonstrate His presence and power in your life visibly, just as He promised.

> *He who has My commandments and keeps them, it is he who loves Me. And he who loves Me will be loved by My Father, and I will love him and manifest Myself to him.* (John 14:21)

Opposition to the Supernatural

"Adversary" is one of many names by which the devil is known. (See 1 Peter 5:8.) He opposes God and His purposes in both direct and subtle ways. Over the past two thousand years, one of his tactics has been to attack and tempt the church so that it will remove the supernatural and reduce itself to a natural institution. Let us look at two forces through which Satan has pursued this purpose: the spirit of antichrist and a mind-set of human reason and logic.

1. The Spirit of Antichrist

> *As you have heard that the Antichrist is coming, even now many antichrists have come, by which we know that it is the last hour.* (1 John 2:18)

The above verse mentions that the Antichrist will come in the end times. The Antichrist is a figure who will oppose the true God and pass himself off to the people of the world as the one whom they should believe in and worship. But the verse also says that *"many antichrists"* will manifest. This is a reference to the *"spirit of the Antichrist"* (1 John 4:3) operating through people. In 1 John 2:20, the spirit of antichrist is contrasted with the anointing from God: *"But you have an anointing from the Holy One, and you know all things."*

The devil's plan has always been to reduce the church to the natural.

The Greek word for "Christ" is *Christos*, which means "anointed"; it designates the Messiah (STRONG, G5547). The prefix *anti-* in *antichrist* means "against." The enemy's ultimate goal is to replace the true Christ for a false one in people's lives. If he is unable to enter the church through the front door, then he will bring forth people with an antichrist spirit or substitutes for Christ through the back door. The true Christ is the Anointed One who has the supernatural power of the Holy Spirit. (See Luke 4:18–19.) Similarly, "the anointing" is a term we use to refer to the power a believer receives from God. We cannot separate Christ from the anointing, or power, He received from God; if He had lacked this anointing, He would have been a false Messiah.

From the time the Holy Spirit was poured out on Jesus' followers at Pentecost, the early believers recognized and manifested the supernatural in the church. It was normal for them. What is it like for us today? In some Christian circles, denominations, and ministries, anyone may speak openly of religion, philosophy, psychology, psychiatry, and even politics. However, if someone speaks of Christ—the Anointed One with supernatural power to heal the sick, baptize with the Holy Spirit, and cast out demons—the other people in these circles, denominations, and ministries become upset and worried! They want to believe that those who practice the supernatural are a kind of cult or sect. Why? Sometimes, they simply seek to justify their own lack of power. Other times, they are afraid. Often, their minds have been trained to think in only natural contexts, which I will describe in more detail below. Sadly, they are under the influence of the spirit of antichrist, which is anti-anointing and anti-power.

When the supernatural is absent, it is replaced by a manifestation of the spirit of antichrist.

When we supplant Christ, the Anointed One, what we have left is a system of principles, moral laws, ideas, and traditions. These lead to impotent and dead religion.

Having a form of godliness but denying its power. And from such people turn away! (2 Timothy 3:5)

The Greek word translated "*form*" is *morphosis*, which means "formation" and indicates "appearance" (STRONG, G3446). It comes from the verb *morphoo*, meaning "to fashion" (STRONG, G3445). To have a "form of godliness," therefore, means to assume the appearance of being religious. This depiction describes a great number of people within the church today. Many believers are like models or copies of the real thing, because they lack God's power. We must identify the spirit of antichrist and remove it from our lives and ministries so that we can live and minister as Jesus did.

Religion is a form or appearance of godliness, without power.

---

2. The Greek Mind-set

The history of the Greek mind-set—and its offshoots—in undermining faith and a belief in the supernatural is a broad topic, so I will give only a general overview here, highlighting some key consequences. Generally, by the Greek mind-set, I refer to one based solely on human reason and logic, one that excludes faith and the supernatural. We have seen that miracles, signs, and wonders were a part of the church since its inception. Although the spirit of antichrist has always sought to pull people away from the supernatural, a shift occurred in the church as people's faith in God and the supernatural began to be eroded by the cultural influence of the Greek mentality and as the church became more institutionalized.

As the centuries passed, the separation between faith and reason became more significant. The rise of secular humanism caused people to shift the center of their world from God to humanity. Secular humanism is a collection of philosophical ideas that elevate man and the mind of man to the highest position of esteem. Slowly, reason overtook faith, while faith was given second place or completely ignored. During the Modern Age, the belief was promoted that any type of religious commitment was an obstacle to objectivity. This idea took hold particularly in the universities, and religious neutrality was endorsed or encouraged. A major development occurred at the University of Berlin, when theology became a separate field within the historical and sociological branches of study. Theology turned into an academic discipline with its own rules of research, which were trapped in the Greek model for interpreting the world through data, logic, theory, and scientific methods alone. It did not include a practical experience of faith or supernatural evidence or revelation from God, and it did not encourage a personal relationship with Him.

In the nineteenth century, liberal Christianity attempted to eliminate from the Bible anything having to do with the supernatural or miraculous, such as the virgin birth of Jesus, the resurrection, the casting out of demons, angels, miracles, signs, and wonders. It argued that belief in the supernatural was an old-fashioned idea, an archaic myth, that could not be accepted by a modern, educated society. Many people began to think that belief in the Bible and the supernatural was anti-intellectual and naive.

Restoring the supernatural to the contemporary church has been difficult because intellectualism and reason are highly regarded by many people. The Greek mind-set pervades the educational system in Western countries; it forms the foundation for learning in most public and private schools and secular and Christian universities, as well as Bible institutes and churches.

In saying this, I am not diminishing the importance of intellectual education, which has its place in the natural realm. I am pro-intellect. I believe that if we submit our mind, reason, and logic to the Spirit, God can make them creative and powerful. I am a studious man. I have both a master's degree and a doctorate in theology. I am pro-education. I encourage young people to attend college and professional schools. I even support several students financially, so they can graduate. What I am saying is that, due to the way most of us have been educated, we tend to think miracles cannot take place, because they seem "illogical" or "unreasonable."

The Greek mentality can take people only so far and can be misleading. For example, many doctors who are trained according to medical science based on evidence believe that if something cannot be proven scientifically, it is not valid. Imagine demonstrating the possibility of a miracle in a laboratory! Lawyers trained in the Socratic method analyze everything according to logic. If something doesn't align with the evidence, it is considered inadmissible and then rejected. They are taught to doubt anything that cannot be proven or explained by logical analysis. Imagine trying to explain the forgiveness of sin to a lawyer! This is why it is so difficult for people who have been trained in this manner to believe in the supernatural.

The Greek mind-set is also why so many people in the church are satisfied with rhetoric; they don't expect to see anything supernatural manifest in a church service, and some don't even consider it important to practice what is preached. Their minds are focused on theory alone, or they are closed-minded to believe only what seems logical from a natural standpoint. Yet theology without a personal experience or divine encounter is worthless—it is mere religion, not the gospel of the kingdom that arrives with supernatural power. We can know the theology of salvation and still be lost for eternity, because salvation comes through a personal encounter with Jesus Christ. When humanism and reason take over people's minds, they reject the supernatural, and they abandon God.

In Western countries, education trains us in what is and is not supposed to be possible for us, as well as what to think and how to reason in various situations. Education explains why certain entities and concepts are real and valid, based on scientific research or philosophical thought. Reason has certain parameters, beyond which everything else is labeled "impossible." But the demonstration of the supernatural can break through that mind-set! A miracle invades the dominion of human reason. The fact that the supernatural realm supersedes reason is no grounds to reject it. While some people will dismiss a supernatural manifestation when they witness it, others will come to acknowledge that there is more to life than what can be known by the physical senses.

Education trains our reason in what is possible and impossible.

Replacements or Substitutes for the Supernatural

Through the centuries, the supernatural has been attacked by various forms of the spirit of antichrist. It has been dismissed by substitutes for spiritual reality that endeavor to replace God's presence and power in our lives, families, schools, churches, cities, and nations.

Since the topic of substitutes for the supernatural is thoroughly covered in my book *How to Walk in the Supernatural Power of God*, I will summarize just a few significant ways in which the supernatural has been displaced, adding some new revelation. We must recognize these substitutes if we are to restore the supernatural to the church and enable it to fulfill its kingdom mandate.

The problem in the church today is not a lack of people having a personal experience with God but the practice of the absence of His presence.

---

1. Reason Has Supplanted Faith

As we noted above, the Greek mind-set has encouraged people to replace faith with reason and logic. I believe the phrase *"by faith we understand"* in Hebrews 11:3 indicates that we must first believe in order to understand God's purposes and ways. God has called us to do what is impossible according to logic and our own abilities, because it can be accomplished through His supernatural power. If the influence of your education is stronger than your revelation, then it will be very difficult for you to live by faith.

Again, I am not against learning. I support people who want to study and prepare for a vocation or career, but I also understand that *"the carnal mind is enmity against God"* (Romans 8:7). It denies everything it cannot understand or explain, or has not experienced. On the other hand, the renewed mind can become a powerful weapon capable of moving in the supernatural because it operates with God's perspective. If you have yet to experience a breakthrough in a difficult situation, it may be because you have been trying to make sense of what God has told you concerning His promises. That is not faith; therefore, the breakthrough has not taken place. God empowers your faith to eliminate any reason you might have not to believe. If you are still trying to make complete sense of things, then you will likely come up with facts and logic for why you cannot receive a supernatural answer from God.

If you think God has called you to do something that makes sense to your reason, then perhaps it is not what God wants you to do, because then you would not need Him to accomplish it.

Other than God's supernatural power, how do we explain the case of Daniel, who was thrown into a den of hungry lions but walked away without a scratch? (See Daniel 6:16–23.) How do we explain three young men being thrown into a fiery furnace and not being burned up? (See Daniel 3:15–27.) If you attempt to do what God tells you to do, while at the same time trying to make sense of it, you will block God's purposes, because He works through your faith, not your reason.

The impossible is founded on reason and established by logic.

2. Counseling Has Replaced Deliverance

In the book of Acts, very little is mentioned about counseling, but much is mentioned about the casting out of demons. (See, for example, Acts 16:16–18.) Counseling can help people to move in the right direction for their lives, enable them to talk about situations and put them in perspective, correct some harmful behavior, and impart wisdom and knowledge that can be applied to specific circumstances. Counseling is useful—I practice it myself. However, when someone is oppressed or possessed by a demonic spirit, that person doesn't need counseling but deliverance. The demon must first be cast out so the person can follow the counseling advice.

I believe many Christian leaders are counseling people who are in need of deliverance. The enemy will use a situation of oppression or possession not only to torment people but also to wear down a counselor spiritually, due to the amount of hours he spends working with someone who is demon possessed. Because the counselor is unable to discern the operation of a demonic spirit, he ends up "counseling" a demon and wasting his time, as well as the time of the person he is trying to help.

3. Charisma Has Replaced the Anointing

Many times, people are drawn to the personal charisma of a pastor, evangelist, or other spiritual leader, mistaking his charisma for God's anointing. How can we tell the difference between mere personal magnetism and anointing? By the fruit that is produced. If no one receives salvation, healing, or deliverance, and if people's hearts are not transformed and drawn closer to God, the only thing the minister has accomplished is perhaps to lead the people to an emotional high, which is worthless for bringing about true change and transformation. Sometimes, even when miracles are present, a leader may rely too much on his own charisma or may try to take credit for himself, so the fruit of his life must also be evaluated over time. What is not of the Spirit is of the flesh. (See, for example, John 3:6.)

4. Entertainment Has Replaced Worship

Many people attend Christian concerts and worship services for entertainment purposes alone. In such cases, their flesh or emotions may be stimulated, but they never really worship God in spirit and truth. I believe concerts are great, as long as their purpose is to exalt God and bring His presence to heal, deliver, and save people. Sadly, many singers minister with their talents alone and not with the anointing. I believe that when they do this, it is similar to what the Bible calls offering *"profane ["strange"* kJv] *fire"* (Leviticus 10:1) before the Lord.

5. An Extreme Message of Grace Has Replaced the Fear of the Lord

But by the grace of God I am what I am, and His grace toward me was not in vain; but I labored more abundantly than they all, yet not I, but the grace of God which was with me. (1 Corinthians 15:10)

We are saved by the grace of God. All that we are, have, and experience is by His grace. However, some people have taken the message of grace to the extreme, teaching that because Jesus has completed His work, there is nothing left for us to do; we can behave in whatever way we want, and it won't matter. Some even claim that prayer is no longer needed and that fasting is not necessary for seeking God. While it is true that Jesus did a complete work at the cross, we must still appropriate His work through faith. And *"faith without works is dead"* (James 2:20).

Even though Jesus was the Son of God, He prayed and fasted to keep Himself on the cutting edge of what the Father was doing and saying. If He had to pray and fast, what makes us think we don't need to? Prayer and fasting don't buy God's favor, but they are vital in preparing us to receive it. The fear, or reverence, of the Lord, which we receive by grace, makes us sensitive to His presence and hungry for more of His power, leading us to seek Him to a greater extent. If we truly reverence the Lord, we will not settle for an isolated event of experiencing His presence and power; we will always want more.

6. Executives and Administrators Have Replaced Apostles and Prophets

And God has appointed these in the church: first apostles, second prophets, third teachers, after that miracles, then gifts of healings, helps, administrations, varieties of tongues.   (1 Corinthians 12:28)

Jesus established a pattern for the church, or an order to be followed, in relation to its leadership. First, He appointed apostles; second, prophets; third, teachers. Those who work miracles come after these three offices. Yet the church has generally altered this established order. When we eliminate any of the first three, then *"after that miracles"* probably will not take place. This helps to explain the absence of miracles in the church. In many cases, the ministries that pave the way for the supernatural have been replaced by executives and administrators who lack spiritual discernment and a kingdom mentality. The ministries of apostle and prophet bring forth the supernatural, including the anointing that delivers breakthroughs; spiritual vision; and an impartation of the knowledge of God's fatherhood, which gives people a sense of personal identity. They bring order, cause change and transformation, and release power to the body of Christ.

The voices most often heard on Christian television are those of pastors, teachers, and evangelists. While this is a very good thing, rarely, if ever, are the voices of the apostles and prophets heard. One spiritual office is not better than the other, but we need to follow the order that has been established by God if the church is to function as He intended.

7. The Church Has Replaced Israel

Some Christians think that because the church is the new, spiritual Israel, the physical nation of Israel is no longer an essential part of God's purposes. They base this belief on passages such as Ephesians 2:14–16, in which Paul discussed the fact that believers of both Jewish and Gentile descent have been made *"one new man from the two"* (verse 15) in Christ. However, I believe this perspective has caused many in the church to disregard the continual importance of the nation of Israel in God's plan for the world. On the Mount of Transfiguration, the appearance of Moses and Elijah with Jesus (see, for example, Matthew 17:1–5) was an announcement depicting Moses as the representative of the former glory, which is Israel, along with Elijah as the representative of the latter glory, which is the church. Therefore, it is a great mistake to say the church has completely replaced the nation of Israel. If we ignore or reject the fact that God's blessing on Israel continues, we may end up without God's supernatural power and with dead or dying churches, because God told Abraham, *"I will bless those who bless you, and I will curse him who curses you; and in you all the families of the earth shall be blessed"* (Genesis 12:3).

The modern church is satisfied with substitutes rather than seeking true supernatural power.

The early believers stayed on their knees in prayer until they received a spiritual breakthrough. (See, for example, Acts 4:23–31.) We must recover this approach and seek God as they did. Do you prefer the artificial—something that resembles and sounds like God—or the supernatural—the true and living God Himself? Are you satisfied with what the spirit of antichrist offers, or do you want real power? The persecution suffered by the early church forced believers to seek God and His supernatural power. Because they continually sought Him, signs and wonders were continually evident. (See, for example, Acts 5:17–19; 8:36–40; 12:6–11.) If you already move in the supernatural, God will sometimes allow persecution to come into your life to keep you on your knees and living by the supernatural.

The Restoration of the Supernatural

God is restoring *"all things"* to the church, including the supernatural, in preparation for the second coming of Jesus.

> *Repent therefore and be converted, that your sins may be blotted out, so that times of refreshing may come from the presence of the Lord, and that He may send Jesus Christ, who was preached to you before, whom heaven must receive until the times of restoration of all things, which God has spoken by the mouth of all His holy prophets since the world began.* (Acts 3:19–21)

The restoration of all things was declared by God's prophets; this refers to the climax of the end times and the purpose of our redemption. We are beginning to see this restoration manifest today with our own eyes. Let us examine a few key words from the above passage that will help us to enter into God's restoration plans.

1. "Repent"

In chapter 1, we talked about the necessity of repentance for entering the kingdom of God. We also noted that repentance is something we must engage in continually as we renew our hearts and minds according to God's Word. To repent means to stop being rebellious and to change one's mind-set and direction in life. Every time we depart from God's path, the essential, unavoidable condition for returning to Him is repentance.

Times of refreshing cannot arrive without true repentance.

---

2. "Refreshing"

Spiritual refreshing comes through the Holy Spirit and manifests as revivals, the outpouring of the Spirit, the supernatural fire of God, the *shekinah* (the visible manifestation of God's glory), joy, laughter, and other spiritual phenomena. When they receive refreshing, however, many believers consider it an end in itself; they enjoy it, but they do not share the power and presence of God they have experienced. For example, they do not minister to other people what they have received from His anointing and glory.

Yet spiritual refreshing is a step toward the final objective—extending the kingdom of God in the world and bringing the message of salvation to every person on earth.

3. *"Restoration"*

The prefix *re-* in *restore* means "back" or "again." We find the same prefix in other verbs in the Bible, including *"reconcile"* and *"renew."* To restore something means to return it to its original purpose or state of being—to make it as it was in the beginning. Every cycle must be completed before a new one can begin, so that the new is determined by what has already been accomplished. When all of God's purposes for the salvation of the world have been completed, Christ will leave heaven and return bodily to earth as King, at which point this earthly cycle we are currently living in will come to an end and the new heavens and earth will come into being.

God moves in cycles, times, and seasons.
The restoration of all things will close this earthly cycle.

Likewise, the church of Christ must return to God's original plan through restoration, because there are many ways in which we have become "artificial" and have wandered from His purposes. I have witnessed the restoration of some spiritual truths in the church, such as ministerial gifts; the presence and power of the Holy Spirit; the fatherhood of God; the reinstatement of the woman in the family, professional, and ministerial areas; praise and worship; the kingdom of God; faith; prosperity; grace; and the supernatural.

Isaiah prophesized, *"Behold, I will do a new thing"* (Isaiah 43:19). Although God isn't doing anything new with the plan of redemption, because it has already been finished in Christ, He is working to restore everything to its original design. However, there are other areas in which He is doing new things. For example, He is always revealing something new about Himself to His people. No one can fully know Him. There are many aspects of God that have not yet been seen by any generation. Let us receive the new revelation He has for us, even as we cooperate with Him in the restoration of all things.

It is often hard to accept that there is something beyond what we have experienced.

Why We Need the Supernatural

Most human beings—including many believers—desire to live independently of God's presence and supernatural power. This is not a new development. For over two thousand years, much of the church has essentially looked for methods, systems, and formulas through which it could avoid depending on the Holy Spirit, believing that it doesn't really need God's power. People think they can function according to their own strength—which was Adam's original sin—even while doing God's work. As we have seen, when the supernatural is absent from the church, all we have left is an institution, a form or appearance of godliness, that lacks power. Many people have come to rely on various substitutions for God, such as wealth, medicine, insurance, and self-help groups, so they no longer believe they need His supernatural power, nor do they seek it. When people do seek the supernatural, it is only after they have exhausted all other avenues. Some people have to hit bottom and eat dust before they will return to God. I have seen people in Africa and South America receive miracles faster than people in the United States or other developed countries because God was their one and only option.

People will not seek the power of God as long as they still have other options to try.

This was the case for a child who lives in an impoverished area of Argentina, near where our ministry held a conference. He had a need that only God could answer. At the final event of the conference, while I was ministering, this child and his mother came forward to testify. He had been born with unusually large ears, and he had suffered greatly at school from the mocking comments made by his peers, who would call him "big ears." His mother said that while I declared healing, she placed her hands on his ears and began to pray for him. To God's glory, when she looked at his ears, she noticed that they were smaller! When I asked the child what he had experienced, he said, "Warmth." The boy was overwhelmed by the miracle God had done for him. He was happy because no one in school would make fun of his ears again. His mother was emotional and could not stop looking at his smaller ears and thanking God for this miracle. Perhaps, if this young man's family had lived in the United States, doctors could have performed plastic surgery to correct his physical abnormality, but the geographical location and financial condition of his family gave them only one option—to depend on a miracle from God.

People who have turned the gospel into mere religion fail to see the need for the supernatural in their daily lives. Let us therefore explore several reasons why we must have God's supernatural power, besides the fact that the church is not the church of Jesus Christ without it!

1. The Supernatural Proves God's Existence by Manifesting Evidence

God's existence doesn't belong to the realm of common sense but to the realm of the spirit. However, when the supernatural manifests on earth, it impacts people's natural senses, giving evidence, or proof, that He is real. For most people, only the natural is real. To them, anything else is fantasy or science fiction. Yet the spirit realm is the true reality, and anything is possible with God. He is raising up a generation that will challenge the natural order of things. This will not be an uprising or revolution against civil authorities; rather, it will be an uprising against the strongholds of Satan, the *"prince of the power of the air"* (Ephesians 2:2). God and His kingdom will manifest as never before.

Anything that is eternal and true is found in the spiritual realm.

2. The Supernatural Reveals God in the Now

Mere religion, in all its forms, cannot bring God into the now, and it cannot draw people closer to Him in their daily lives. It lacks practical solutions for people's afflictions. But when the supernatural manifests, people experience a power that declares God lives here and now (see Hebrews 13:8), and He can instantly meet their needs for healing, deliverance, miracles, a prophetic word, and more. The supernatural proves that God is close—not far away—and that He understands each situation and has a solution for it.

3. The Supernatural Establishes Spiritual Order and the Flow of God's Life in Us

When sin entered humanity, it destroyed the constant flow of God's life in us, thus affecting our spirit, soul, and body. For example, sickness interrupts the cycle and order of health in our bodies. Though we inherited spiritual and physical death through Adam, we have been given resurrection life in Christ. This means that if we are in continual communion with Him, His life flows in us, and the supernatural becomes our norm once again.

I pray at home almost every day, for a certain period of time. Sometimes, however, when I travel, or if I have to change my schedule, I may not be able to have an extended time of prayer on a given day. When this occurs, it is hard for me to reconnect with God the next day. The enemy will always try to break the rhythm of our communion with God and our relationship with Him in every area of our lives. Yet when we diligently seek God and move once more in the supernatural, it reestablishes us in the divine order, and His life begins to flow in us again. In addition, if doubt or fear finds room in our hearts, and our life of faith is interrupted, we will not see miracles. But when the supernatural power of God comes through a revelation from Him, it restores our faith to give us the victory.

Faith and fear cannot flow out of our heart at the same time because fear blocks faith, while faith dispels fear.

---

4. The Supernatural Brings Acceleration

"Behold, the days are coming," says the LORD, "when the plowman shall overtake the reaper, and the treader of grapes him who sows seed."

(Amos 9:13)

The supernatural accelerates the natural, while the natural is often a deceleration of the supernatural. Every time the supernatural stops operating in our lives, we lose our spiritual momentum and become stagnant. In other words, we conform to, or settle for, the natural dimension. The result is that instead of our controlling our circumstances, our circumstances control us. But when the power of God flows in and through us, blessings and provision accelerate in every area; the growth in our personal lives, ministries, homes, and businesses is no longer restricted by natural laws or the limitations of time. If we operate according to the supernatural, the "seed" will grow the instant we plant it, and one season will overtake another in our lives as spiritual acceleration occurs.

The early church grew from 120 believers to thousands in only a short time (see Acts 4:4; 5:14) because the apostles ministered in the supernatural power of the Holy Spirit. Likewise, I have seen our church, our daughter churches, and other churches around the world grow exponentially when they've followed God's pattern, which is to receive His revealed word and supernatural power. God is bringing acceleration and growth so that what would normally take years will take months or even less time.

When a believer becomes spiritually stagnant,
it is because the supernatural has stopped flowing through him.

5. The Supernatural Overcomes the Impossible

With men it is impossible, but not with God; for with God all things are possible. (Mark 10:27)

Many church projects and programs don't allow for the activity of the supernatural, but an infusion of God's presence and power is indispensable to accomplish His vision. Without it, the impossible cannot be carried out. God gave us His power in order to conquer impossibilities!

Not long ago, one of the doctors in our congregation, Dr. Gamal, was experiencing a difficult financial situation because his wife had just lost her job, and he and his wife had also recently had a new baby. Even though they were in a financial crunch, he took a step of faith and decided to accompany me on a mission trip to South America, where we held a conference on the supernatural. He paid all of his expenses with much effort, but he trusted in God's provision. During the trip, we witnessed amazing miracles, but Dr. Gamal was especially impacted when he saw that money began to supernaturally appear in people's wallets and purses. This was a manifestation of the outpouring of the Holy Spirit for supernatural provision.

Dr. Gamal then stood in agreement with his wife, who was watching the conference from Miami via our ministry's Web site, and together they began to declare that if this type of miracle was taking place there, it could also happen to them. The week Dr. Gamal returned to Miami, he asked his wife to bring him all the savings they had, because some bills needed to be paid. As she went to get the money box, he was in the living room, praying, "Lord, You promised that I would live in abundance!" When his wife opened the small box that contained their savings, she was astonished to see the amount of cash it contained. She took out the bills and began to count them, and, as she kept counting, she gave a shout that filled the house. When she returned to the living room with the box and the money in hand, she asked her husband how much cash had been left after he'd taken out the money needed for the trip. After he told her it was $1,200, she said, "There is $11,200!" This was a difference of $10,000, which the Lord had supernaturally supplied. Dr. Gamal recalled, "We both jumped for joy, praising God for such a spectacular miracle." For him and his family, the sacrifice of investing in the mission trip, using everything they had and depending totally on God, was worth it. The manifest presence of God produced a miracle in their finances!

What is your impossibility? Is it finances, health, or a family relationship? Believe that the supernatural invades your situation right now! Your life may be barren, but as soon as the supernatural is restored, you will begin to produce fruit. I declare acceleration over your life, home, ministry, and business. If you think according to human possibilities, you will never go farther than the natural. You will remain in your comfort zone, where nothing changes for the better. I challenge you to believe for the impossible, right now!

When the supernatural is present, spiritual fruit is not only possible but inevitable.

6. The Supernatural Enables Us to Live Victoriously in Our Times

We are living in fearful times—perhaps unprecedented ones—and it will be very difficult for us to survive them and to live victoriously without the supernatural. We must decide whether we will conduct ourselves according to the world's way or God's way. The world's way is to rely on self-effort, human philosophy, the desires of the flesh, the occult, and other substitutes for the supernatural. God's way is for us to die to self and allow the power of Jesus' resurrection to flow through us.

In terms of our health, the time is coming when we will face medical impossibilities, and our only option will be supernatural healing. Regarding our safety, there will be so many crimes, thefts, and murders being committed that only the protection of the Almighty will preserve us. Concerning the economy, the world's system is collapsing, and no one feels secure anymore. Today, we may have a job; tomorrow, we may be let go. Today, we may have a thriving business; tomorrow, we may be facing bankruptcy. Only God's miraculous provision can provide a stable income and wealth.

How to Flow in the Supernatural

The church has deviated so far from the design Christ gave the early church that many believers no longer know where to begin in order to recover God's supernatural power in their lives, ministries, and nations. Let us look at a few essential requirements for flowing in God's kingdom power.

1. Experience a Breakthrough in the Natural Realm

Without a breakthrough in the natural realm, we will never walk in the supernatural. A breakthrough occurs when we receive a revelation from God or when we witness or experience a visible demonstration of His kingdom and power. *"For we walk by faith, not by sight"* (2 Corinthians 5:7). If we continue to live according to human reason, we will not be able to experience such manifestations in our lives. We need to follow the three keys we looked at earlier for entering into God's plan of renewal—repentance, refreshing, and restoration. Then, we can ask God to pour out His Spirit in our lives and give us breakthroughs.

2. Expect the Supernatural

So he gave them his attention, expecting to receive something from them.
(Acts 3:5)

As we have noted, most Christians today don't attend church expecting to see the supernatural. When it does manifest, they often consider it an unusual occurrence that won't be repeated. Do we attend church only to hear a message, or can we expect to see the power of God saving souls, healing the sick, and delivering the oppressed? Most people would not go to work every day if they didn't expect to be paid. They wouldn't go to a restaurant if they didn't expect to be served food and drink. Why, then, do we attend church without any anticipation that God will manifest His presence and power? If the supernatural doesn't manifest, there is a problem in the church!

3. Respond to the Supernatural

God doesn't show up where He is merely tolerated but where He is celebrated. Many people in the church aren't responding to God's Word or presence because they attend services with a spectator's mentality, hoping to be entertained. Yet each time God manifests or reveals a part of His knowledge or wisdom, it is our responsibility to respond to Him. Otherwise, the blessing He desires to bestow will be returned to heaven. I have been in meetings in which God has revealed a certain physical condition to me that He desires to heal. Sometimes in these cases, when I call people to come forward for healing, even though many come, only one receives a miracle. It may be that the others did not respond with faith to appropriate what God had revealed. We must release our faith in His presence to capture the supernatural.

4. Continually Seek God Through Prayer and Fasting

Many believers no longer actively pursue communion with God; their prayers have become monotonous, lifeless, and ineffectual because they lack revelation and power, which come from seeking God and being one with Him in the Spirit. I minister the supernatural in healing and deliverance as the result of prayer, fasting, and spiritual union with God. As Jesus told His disciples after He delivered a boy from demon possession, *"This kind does not go out except by prayer and fasting"* (Matthew 17:21). Only regular communion with God can produce tangible evidence of His power. We must initiate the manifestation of the supernatural by humbling ourselves through fasting and entering into true intimacy with our heavenly Father. This is how Jesus lived and ministered. (See, for example, Matthew 14:23.)

5. Receive Progressive Revelation

Common sense or logic does not enable us to walk in the supernatural, but only revelation *"established in the present truth"* (2 Peter 1:12). Without continual, progressive revelation from God, we cannot function in the spiritual realm or manifest His kingdom on earth, because His kingdom is supernatural in every way—it is a supernatural realm ruled by a supernatural King. Progressive revelation from God takes us *"from glory to glory"*: *"But we all, with unveiled face, beholding as in a mirror the glory of the Lord,* **are being transformed** *into the same image* **from glory to glory***, just as by the Spirit of the Lord"* (2 Corinthians 3:18).

The supernatural offends religious people because it operates beyond human reason.

Living a Supernatural Lifestyle

Jesus pioneered the restoration of the supernatural on earth. He manifested God's eternal power as He took dominion over nature, sin, and death. He walked on water, rebuked storms, turned water into wine, healed the sick, raised the dead, and did other miracles, signs, and wonders. Now we, the members of His body, are the pioneers who must continue His supernatural ministry on earth.

Most assuredly, I say to you, he who believes in Me, the works that I do he will do also; and greater works than these he will do, because I go to My Father. (John 14:12)

Where Jesus' ministry on earth ended, the church's life and ministry began.

There is a miracle recorded in each chapter of the book of Acts; miracles were the norm during New Testament times! As we have seen, the church has gradually regressed from a supernatural lifestyle, although there have been brief periods of resurgence. Many congregations claim that the supernatural is not for today. While they believe that God worked miracles in the past, they do not believe that He works miracles in the present, so their faith has turned into religion. Intellectualism and humanism have led people to replace the supernatural with naturalist theologies. Today, only a relatively small number of believers operate in supernatural power. When people see a demonstration of the supernatural, many of them criticize it, judge it, and reject it.

People often criticize what they cannot produce.

If the church doesn't return to its origins, the supernatural will be lost, along with its essence and purpose. People will consider Jesus Christ a mere myth or legend. Yet God is raising up men and women who are able to demonstrate His supernatural kingdom here and now, especially among those who believe that miracles are for today and have the faith to receive them. Do you want to be counted among them? It is natural for us to have an appetite for the supernatural because human beings were created to live and walk in the power of God. We must redirect our Christian lives and seize the supernatural by bringing the reality of the kingdom of God into our world today.

This is what happened to María Teresa, a gynecologist from Cuba who came from a Catholic background, attended church, sang in the choir, engaged in other church activities, and was committed to her beliefs. When she was young, she went to Spain to study, but she found that the Catholic Church was even more religious there than in Cuba. Tired of not seeing any changes in her life, she began to search intensely for true power. Here is the rest of her story, in her own words.

"I began practicing diverse philosophies, such as Esoteric and Hermetic philosophies, and other religions, even seeking Egyptian gods, and reading as much as I could on these subjects. I graduated as a doctor in Spain and then went to live in Miami. There, for over fifteen years, I looked into spiritualism, Santeria, and New Age. Although I had Christian friends, they never spoke to me about Jesus. I used to think their religion was the same as the Catholic Church, except for the fact that the priests could not get married.

"In time, I felt even more empty, frustrated, disappointed, deceived, and mocked, and I had no hope of ever finding God. In each facet I explored, I would go deep because I wanted to discover the truth, but I never found it. The only thing I found were bad caricatures of the same things, and many lies disguised as truth. Desperate, and not knowing where to look, I locked myself in my room one day and cried, pacing from side to side and yelling, 'Lord Jesus, show me the truth, because I no longer know where to look for it!' Instantly, I felt peace, and it seemed as if something was beginning to unveil within me. After that experience, a friend led me to accept Jesus as my Lord and Savior. From that moment forward, the Lord has given me revelation, and my life has begun to change little by little. My testimony and the changes that I have experienced have been instrumental in leading my husband to accept Jesus, also. Today, I am free of all bondage, and I am happy, full of life, and enjoying abundance of peace. I found the truth!"

It was only when María cried out to the one true God that she received the answer she had been looking for. Nothing else she had tried was able to fill the void in her heart or give her purpose in life.

God is drawing people away from superstition and mysticism and introducing them to His supernatural power. He is taking them out of traditions, religion, old patterns, rigid structures, and many other substitutions for His genuine presence and power. Are you tired of substitutions? Do you want something new and fresh from God?

The church of Christ is the only legal entity that can operate in God's supernatural power on earth.

Each of us must make the decision to walk according to God's supernatural kingdom. To sum up, we must take the following steps: (1) Recognize

God Almighty as a supernatural Being who surpasses reason and the natural world. (2) Renounce the influences exerted by the spirit of antichrist and the culture's overemphasis on the Greek mind-set. (3) Repent of having allowed substitutes for the supernatural to reign in our lives, families, and ministries. (4) Acknowledge our need for the supernatural and ask God to fill us with His presence and power. (5) Commit to walk in the supernatural—not as an isolated event but as a lifestyle.

When believers take these steps, then, together, as the church, we can proclaim the gospel of the kingdom, heal the sick, deliver the captives, raise the dead, and manifest the various gifts of the Holy Spirit, thereby demonstrating the real and living Christ to the world.

Take time to seek God and the revelation of His Holy Spirit so you can demonstrate that Jesus lives today. Go and save souls! Heal the sick! Cast out demons! Raise the dead! Take the kingdom of God everywhere!

7

A Dominion of Kings and Priests

As citizens of God's kingdom, we are not just residents of His realm—we are kings and priests under the authority of Christ, our King and High Priest. (See Revelation 1:5–6; 5:9–10.) Our twofold role delineates our God-given dominion on earth.

It has always been God's intention to make His people capable of developing a close and intimate relationship with Him while carrying out their purpose as His chosen instruments to expand His kingdom on earth. Let us discover how God wants us to fulfill the two ministries of king and priest in the here and now. We will begin by exploring the connection between covenant and kingdom—between our relationship with God and our manifestation of His presence and power on the earth.

The Covenant-Kingdom Connection

The connection between God's covenants with His people and their role in His kingdom is a thread that can be seen in both the Old and New Testaments. God told the Israelites,

> *Now therefore, if you will indeed obey My voice and keep My covenant, then you shall be a special treasure to Me above all people; for all the earth is Mine. And you shall be to Me **a kingdom of priests** and a holy nation.* (Exodus 19:5–6)

The nation of Israel under Moses was a forerunner of the church with its roles of king and priest. God told the Israelites they were to be a *"kingdom of priests"* as they blessed the world. His main goal when He redeemed them from slavery in Egypt and brought them to Mount Sinai was to make a covenant with them, present them to Himself, and establish an everlasting relationship with them. To fulfill God's purpose, they needed to meet two conditions: (1) obey His voice, and (2) keep His covenant.

These conditions still distinguish a true child of God today. The key for us is that, while the Israelites were never able to uphold their part of the covenant, Christ has enabled us to fulfill the new covenant with God. (See Hebrews 9:13–15.) Through His sacrifice on the cross and resurrection, we receive the Holy Spirit to live within us, so we can love God, obey Him, and serve Him. The covenant with our heavenly Father that Jesus provided is similar to the earlier covenant of sacrifice that God made with Abraham, because that covenant was one that was fulfilled only by God, unilaterally, though it required Abraham's faith. (See Genesis 15.) Human beings could never hold up their end of a covenant with God in their own strength and effort.

The most important requirement in any
covenant is the commitment of sacrifice.

In the New Testament, we read,

To [Christ Jesus] *who loved us and washed us from our sins in His own blood, and* **has made us kings and priests** *to His God and Father....*   (Revelation 1:5–6)

God never develops a permanent, personal relationship with anyone unless it is through a covenant of commitment. *"Gather My saints together to Me, those who have made a covenant with Me by sacrifice"* (Psalm 50:5). All parties involved in the covenant must observe the conditions of the promise and be loyal to it and to each other. The same is true in all areas of life. For example, we cannot develop healthy family or ministry relationships without a commitment between those involved. This is why God requires obedience to the covenant, which can be summarized in one word: *loyalty*. We must keep in mind that it is only through Christ's atonement and grace that we are able to remain in right standing with God. (See, for example, 1 Thessalonians 5:23–24.)

Without a covenant of commitment, it is impossible to have a permanent, biblical relationship with God.

Picture our covenant with God like a cross: The vertical post indicates our relationship with Him, and the horizontal one our relationship with our fellow believers and other people. If the vertical relationship is broken, the horizontal relationship is affected, and vice versa. Thus, when our relationship with our neighbor is damaged, our relationship with God also suffers injury. (See, for example, Matthew 5:22–24.)

When God liberated the Israelites from slavery, He presented them with a very special threefold offer to make them a treasure, a kingdom of priests, and a holy nation. The parts of this offer are inseparable—one cannot exist without the others. However, over the years, Israel was interested in the covenant more for the Promised Land and the blessings God offered than it was in God Himself. Unfortunately, the same is true for much of the church today. Moreover, we find it hard to rid ourselves of a "slavery" mentality, just as the Israelites did. It is our destiny to live as kings and priests. Instead, many believers live like slaves—to sickness, depression, fear, rejection, sin, alcohol, drugs, illicit sex, pornography, food, and so on. They are kings in theory but slaves in practice. We must renew our minds to understand our kingship and priesthood, and surrender to God through a covenant of commitment, in order to receive our full inheritance in Him and experience His kingdom life. Do you want to live as a king and a priest under Christ, or do you want to live as a slave under the condemnation and accusation of the enemy?

Believers have only two options: to live like slaves or to live as kings and priests.

Christ redeemed us to make us a kingdom of kings and priests.

And the LORD *will make you the head and not the tail; you shall be above only, and not be beneath, if you heed the commandments of the* LORD *your God....* (Deuteronomy 28:13)

The difference between being the head or the tail is that the head decides, initiates, and gives direction, while the tail simply follows or is hauled along. Where are you now—ahead of your circumstances or behind them? Do you make your own decisions under God's guidance, or are you simply following or being dragged along by the will of other people? There is no middle ground!

The result of being kings and priests—of being the head and not the tail—is that we "gather" people to God. *"He who does not gather with Me scatters abroad"* (Matthew 12:30). There is a world just waiting for us to go and demonstrate that our supreme King and High Priest, Jesus Christ, lives today and that we are kings and priests in God's kingdom. Many people realize that their material possessions are not ultimately satisfying, and they know that their lives aren't working. They are waiting for us to show them practical solutions and to manifest the power and authority we have in Christ to rule over the works of the devil; to show that the gospel of the kingdom is not mere theology, theory, or words, but that God's power can save people, heal their afflictions, and deliver them from bondage.

We are God's representatives, called to bring heaven to earth wherever we go and in the midst of any situation we might be experiencing. I have a spiritual son, now living in France, who endured a situation that was distressing to him and his family, but this did not stop him from manifesting the power of God. His response to his circumstances showed that the declarations of faith he spoke were not mere words. About five years ago, he and his wife were mentors in our Miami church. One day, they received word from U.S. Citizenship and Immigration Services that they had to leave the country voluntarily, or they would be deported. They had built a life here, but they had to leave because they were not U.S. citizens. They moved to France with sorrow in their hearts. There, they started a ministry from the ground up, but their faith and spiritual training were intact. They established a House of Peace and began to manifest the power of God in their new country. Today, José Murillo and his wife, Rosa Maria, pastor a growing church in the city of Toulouse.

"We went to France and began to do what you do," Pastor José told me. Rosa Maria was a member of the choir at our ministry. Now, she trains the worship team at their church and opens the church building for Morning Prayer at 5:00 a.m. Pastor José testified, "The sick are being healed, and money has begun to appear miraculously in bank accounts. A young man planning to commit suicide by throwing himself in front of a train on Christmas Eve had an encounter with the supernatural God when he met the youth of our church at an evangelistic outing. They spoke words of knowledge to him. He felt the supernatural power of God and gave his life to Christ. The next day, he was in church giving his testimony."

The leader of the evangelistic team is an Asian-French man who grew up in Buddhism and lived according to that religion until he was invited to a service where he was touched by the Holy Spirit and transformed. Now, every Saturday, he goes with the youth to malls, bars, and even Catholic churches to impact the people of France with Jesus' love.

Another member of their congregation testified that she came to a service at their church when she was pregnant and very depressed. The father of her baby had abandoned her, and, to make matters worse, she was told that her child was not going to survive because of a problem in the umbilical cord that was preventing the baby from receiving nourishment. She received Jesus and began to intercede, evangelize, and pray. At her next checkup, tests revealed that the baby was growing, and, a few months later, the child was born healthy!

The Murillo family was able to take the training they had received at our ministry, along with their passion for God, and allow Him to work everything in their situation for good. (See Romans 8:28.) Because of this family's faithfulness, and despite their circumstances, hundreds of people in France are being reached for the kingdom of God! They rose above their situation, and the Lord has been glorified in their lives through His supernatural power.

Let us now explore our two main roles in the kingdom. We begin with the office of priest, because we cannot be kings until we have understood our priestly calling and have entered into it. The two roles are always interconnected.

If you have not fulfilled your responsibilities as a priest,
you will not be able to exercise your functions as a king.

Who Is a Priest?

You...are being built up...a holy priesthood, to offer up spiritual sacrifices acceptable to God through Jesus Christ. (1 Peter 2:5)

Our culture's idea of the priesthood is that it is a special calling for only a chosen few. Most of us think of a priest as a man who wears a black robe and a white collar and who is beyond the reach of the common person. He is not allowed to marry and must dedicate his life totally to God's service, and this lifestyle sets him apart from the rest of the people.

Since this image of a priest is so ingrained in us through our traditions, it is difficult for many believers to envision themselves as priests. Therefore, we must set aside our traditional ideas about priests and return to what the Bible says. To be a priest, we don't need ordination or special clothing; we don't need to become recluses and avoid all contact with the secular world. The New Testament concept of a priest is someone who presents spiritual sacrifices to God. The work of Jesus Christ is for everyone who believes in Him and who confesses Him as Lord and Savior of his life. The priesthood of all believers is included in this work. We are priests of almighty God, able to offer spiritual sacrifices to Him, thanks to the work of His Son.

It is important to recognize that there are priests in the kingdom of darkness, also—witches, sorcerers, wizards, and so forth—who sacrifice animals (and sometimes humans) to gain power from Satan so they can dominate and control people and situations. Some people who are in the position to rule over others seek such "priests" in order to gain power. They lend themselves to these practices that offend God. As priests and kings in God's kingdom, we are engaged in a war against the evil spiritual entities that are behind these satanic priests and that strive to gain dominion over all earthly territories.

The Priestly Ministry of Christ

You [Jesus Christ] *are a priest forever according to the order of Melchizedek.* (Hebrews 5:6)

Melchizedek comes from the Hebrew name *Malkiy-Tsedeq,* which means "king of right" (STRONG, G3198, H4442), or king of "rightness," or "righteousness" (NASC, H6664). In the Old Testament, Melchizedek was *"king of Salem"* and *"priest of God Most High"* to whom Abraham gave a tithe of everything he had. (See Genesis 14:18–19.)

Melchizedek was a type, or foreshadower, of Jesus Christ, the righteous King who is also our High Priest. The two offices, which had operated together in Melchizedek, were separated in Israel under the law of Moses: the kingship was given to the tribe of Judah, and the priesthood was bestowed on the tribe of Levi. In those days, the king of Israel was not allowed to offer sacrifices or to burn incense on the altar of the temple; these jobs were performed solely by the designated priests, although other spiritual leaders, such as Samuel, sometimes offered sacrifices, as well. Those who did not observe this rule were punished. For example, it was the reason Saul lost his kingdom (see 1 Samuel 13:7–14) and Uzziah got leprosy (see 2 Chronicles 26:16–21).

In Jesus Christ, the kingship and priesthood were united once again. Jesus served as King and Priest on earth, and He was highly exalted by God the Father as King of kings and Lord of lords after His resurrection and ascension. On the basis of His priesthood, Jesus offered bread and wine during the Last Supper with His disciples as a symbol of His body, which would be presented to God as a living sacrifice. (See, for example, Matthew 26:26–29.) He offered prayers, intercession, and Himself (see Hebrews 5:7; 9:14) to His heavenly Father by means of the Holy Spirit, constituting Himself both as the Priest who ministered the sacrifice and the Sacrifice itself. After making atonement for us, He entered the Holy of Holies in heaven on our behalf and as our predecessor (see Hebrews 6:19–20), so that we can now enter God's presence, also. As we are called to be like Him in the world, we are priests and kings who extend His realm on earth.

"Consider the Apostle and High Priest of our confession, Christ Jesus" (Hebrews 3:1). In this verse, we see two of the Lord's titles: Apostle—one sent by God to carry out a specific mission; and High Priest—one who is the mediator between God and man. Jesus has been our High Priest for more than two thousand years—and He continues to be our High Priest today. He is High Priest "*forever*" (Hebrews 5:6). His work continues in force because no one can approach, communicate with, or bring offerings to God without the mediation of a High Priest. Therefore, we depend totally on Christ. (See Hebrews 7:24–25; 8:6.)

The Role of Priest in God's Kingdom in the Now

For every high priest taken from among men is appointed for men in things pertaining to God, that he may offer both gifts and sacrifices for sins.   (Hebrews 5:1)

As we have seen, both the Old and New Testaments describe a priest as one who offers sacrifices. Believers who rule and exercise dominion on earth have learned to serve as priests of almighty God. This sacred ministry operates in God's presence—the heavenly Holy of Holies—where His throne is located.

The following are some specific responsibilities to which we are called as priests in God's kingdom:

1. Present Our Bodies as Living Sacrifices to God

I beseech you therefore, brethren, by the mercies of God, that you present your bodies a living sacrifice, holy, acceptable to God, which is your reasonable service.   (Romans 12:1)

A living sacrifice is different from the sacrifices of slain animals that were offered on the altar of the tabernacle or temple in the Old Testament. Furthermore, this sacrifice is our "*reasonable service*," given of our own free will and made possible by God. It is something we ourselves are able to give.

Since Jesus' sacrifice was complete when He offered His body on the cross, and since He already did the work of redemption, reconciliation, and restoration, the only thing left for us to do is to offer our bodies as a living sacrifice to God. The altar on which we sacrifice is not an object; rather, it is our heart—and the sacrifice is ourselves.

Presenting our bodies to God is a simple and practical act; there is nothing mystical about it. It means that from this day forward, we will no longer follow what the old nature or "self" wants, feels, or thinks. Rather, we will surrender our body to God's service. We will no longer offer our bodies to drugs, illicit sex, or selfish carnal pleasures, but we will live for eternal purposes in carrying out God's good and perfect will. This sacrifice will never be given in vain! As we offer ourselves to Him and are transformed by the renewing of our minds, we will *"...prove what is that good and acceptable and perfect will of God"* (Romans 12:2). This means that one of the benefits of presenting our bodies to the Lord and having our minds renewed is that He will carry out His will in our lives.

We follow the pattern of Jesus, our forerunner, when we offer ourselves to God as living sacrifices, holy and acceptable to Him. One day, I had just arrived home from a trip to Central America, where I had ministered all week. I was truly exhausted. However, I understand the principle of sacrifice, so I decided to present my body as a living sacrifice to God, and I went directly to our church to minister at a service. Suddenly, I heard God's voice saying, "Numbers 23:19." I took the microphone and briefly preached this word: "Because *'God is not a man'....'*" This phrase was enough to release the most impressive miracles. The Holy Spirit began to give me names of people whom I did not know, along with their health conditions. I called them forward, and they were instantly healed. The supernatural power of God was continuous and intense. It released a wave of healing.

Among those healed, Gloria Sánchez is especially memorable to me. She was from Colombia, where she had been a champion in track and field in the events of high jump and long jump. However, the toll of the demanding physical exercise she had been involved in through the years had damaged her knee menisci, and they had been removed. This had caused injury to her kneecaps and other bones in her knees, and she'd had to undergo additional surgery. Later, she was told that her only option would be to have titanium knee implants, but she'd refused. She'd had to retire from track and field, which made her feel extremely frustrated. It was hard for her to bend her knees or to kneel, but the worst part was the pain she continuously experienced.

When Gloria came forward at the service, the fire of God fell and covered her body. Suddenly, she began to run, jump, and bend her knees without pain or impediment. The power of God created new menisci and restored her ligaments, kneecaps, and other bones! The doctors examined her and confirmed the restoration of her knees. This was a visible and tangible miracle! The church exploded in celebration of God.

Here are some additional testimonies from that service. A twenty-three-year-old man named Juan López had undergone surgery for a torn meniscus and damaged ligaments. He was unable to run, and it was often hard for him even to walk. His health condition caused him to feel depressed. But the fire of God descended over him, creating a new meniscus and ligaments. He ran all around the altar, rejoicing over his healing. In addition, Abedel Metellus, a basketball player, also received total healing of the same problem by the power of God.

Later, another wave of miracles manifested in those who were deaf. I made the call, and several people ran to the altar. Marializ Sosa had not been able to hear since infancy following a severe ear infection. The dose of antibiotics given her by the doctors had been so strong that it had caused deterioration in both ears. As I ministered, she felt a fire embrace her entire body and heat fill her ears. Instantly, she began to hear. This miracle had great impact! With her healing, other people who had the same problem were also healed. Twenty-nine-year-old Carolina González had lost the hearing in her left ear when she was a child due to medical negligence. When she was seven, she'd undergone surgery, but her hearing did not improve. During the time of ministry, she felt fire and an electric charge that entered her hands and arms and went up to her left ear. Immediately, she began to hear! What science had been unable to do in years, the power of God had made possible in an instant.

Another manifestation of healing occurred in a twenty-eight-year-old woman named Nayda Mercado who'd had uterine cancer. She had been tested every three months, and every test had come back positive. The treatments were not working, so she decided to surrender everything to the Lord. When I made the altar call, she came forward and received the impartation. She said she felt fire travel through her. Days later, she went to her doctor for a checkup, and the tests were negative. All the cancerous cells were gone, and she was completely free of the disease!

If I had not surrendered my body as a living sacrifice to God that day, those miracles would not have manifested. Every time we surrender our bodies as living sacrifices, He is glorified through us.

The fire of God always falls where there is sacrifice.

2. Offer Sacrifices of Praise and Worship

Therefore by Him let us continually offer the sacrifice of praise to God, that is, the fruit of our lips, giving thanks to His name.

(Hebrews 13:15)

To praise God at all times and in every place, regardless of our circumstances or how we are feeling, is one of the most important sacrifices a believer can offer. It will keep the devil far from us, and, by our sacrifice, we will affirm God and His works. Why must we praise Him at all times, giving thanks to His name and to all that it represents? Because He is completely worthy of receiving our honor and worship. When we do not offer Him sacrifices of praise, we neglect to carry out our role as faithful priests in His kingdom.

If we worship God according to our feelings,
we have not learned to praise Him.

3. Do Good and Share with Others

But do not forget to do good and to share, for with such sacrifices God is well pleased. (Hebrews 13:16)

It is often a sacrifice to share with others what we have. However, afterward, we can prove that doing so brings great blessings to our lives.

When benefitting other people becomes costly or inconvenient, or when it takes us out of our comfort zone, it is a sign that we are presenting our bodies as living sacrifices to God.

I have come to understand that sacrifice is one of the characteristics of the apostolic ministry. The people close to me know of the many sacrifices my family and I have offered. They know the blood, sweat, and tears that have been shed. These sacrifices are given in prayer, in money, in time, and in physical exertion. Many people might want the apostolic crown of glory but not the sacrifice, because it is costly. The times when I preach while physically exhausted usually produce the greatest miracles, salvations, and deliverances. Sadly, rather than paying the price or sacrificing anything, much of today's generation usually seeks instant gratification and power. Yet God honors our sacrifice!

The anointing and power that I minister are released in the areas in which I have surrendered to God and His will—where I have died to self and crucified my flesh. Are we willing to forgo eating so others can eat? To forgo sleep so others can sleep? To sacrifice our comfort and convenience so others can be saved, set free, and healed? Serving others and sharing what we have with them are essential functions of a kingdom priest.

God will empower us in the areas in which we surrender to Him.

4. Present Physical Gifts and Offerings to God

The high priest under the law of Moses presented both gifts and sacrifices to God on behalf of the people. (See Hebrews 5:1.) The people themselves—those who were called to be a kingdom of priests—were required to provide these gifts and sacrifices from their own possessions. Similarly, Jesus, as our High Priest, receives our tithes and offerings and presents them to God. (See Hebrews 7:8.) I know many Christian leaders who don't tithe or give offerings from their income and possessions. They have neglected their priestly responsibilities, and, as a result, the ministry of their priesthood is malfunctioning. How can God bless a church if the head priest is a thief? (See Malachi 3:8.) The same principle can be applied to the realm of the family or business.

Every priest is called by God to offer gifts and sacrifices.

Monetary offerings presented by believers are sacrifices of worship to God. This is why the collection of tithes and offerings in church should not be taken lightly or treated like just another announcement. It must be done with reverence. I believe that God is raising up a new generation of priests who will worship Him with their offerings. I never attend a service without bringing an offering because I understand the power of this principle. Consequently, God has prospered me, my family, my spiritual sons and daughters, and my ministry.

There will always be lack where God is not
honored with tithes and offerings.

5. **Offer Prayer and Intercession**

Therefore [Jesus] is also able to save to the uttermost those who come to God through Him, since He always lives to make intercession for them. (Hebrews 7:25)

Christ's present ministry in heaven is to make intercession on our behalf. He offered prayers, intercession, and Himself on earth, and now He lives to mediate for us. Since we are the extension of His ministry on earth, we also should prioritize prayers and intercession on behalf of other people. There are countless plans and purposes of God that cannot be carried out until we birth them through prayer. Therefore, we must align our prayers with Christ's prayers. For what is Jesus interceding before the Father in the now? What are His prayer priorities? I believe they are for the expansion of His kingdom on earth, the salvation of souls, and the manifestation of God's children, among other things. What an honor and privilege to be a part of His ministry!

Intercession was Jesus' earthly sacrifice while He was in the world,
and it is His heavenly sacrifice today.

A woman in our church named Rosario was about seven months pregnant when she went for a routine examination and was told by her doctor that there was not enough amniotic fluid to keep her baby alive and that the baby showed signs of abnormality. Worried, the doctor gave her the option of returning home, although there was a risk that both she and the baby might die, or that she would go into premature labor and need to be rushed to the emergency room. After undergoing several more tests, Rosario was scheduled for a cesarean section the following day.

When the baby was born, he was very small, and his health was fragile. The worst part was that his intestines were outside of his body, and the doctors had to perform emergency surgery. Rosario immediately called Rosa López, a woman in our church whom she knew moved in the power of God for miracles. Crying, she asked for prayer for her newborn son. Without hesitating, Rosa began to intercede for the baby, declaring life and not death. Even as the women prayed together, the doctors faced a crisis—the baby died during surgery. All his vital signs disappeared. They did everything possible to save him, but there was nothing more they could do. Suddenly, without explanation, before the eyes of the surprised doctors, the baby's vital signs once again showed up on the monitors, and he became agitated. Intercessory prayer had activated the power of the resurrection and brought Rosario's son back to life! The doctors placed him in an incubator and said it might take six to eight months for him to recover; however, twenty days later, he was fully healthy and in his mother's arms! Today, Rosario testifies of the miracle that took place in her son because of the faithful prayer of an intercessor. She cannot contain her tears each time she is reminded that her baby might have been dead or sick and incapacitated today, but now he is totally healthy because of the power of God.

Intercessors rule on earth from the spirit realm.

I ask the Holy Spirit to enlighten the eyes of your understanding so you can comprehend your ministry as a priest; so you can commit, right now, to present your body as a living sacrifice as you give God praise, tithes, and offerings, and as you intercede for and serve others. I ask Him to give you the grace to carry out the responsibilities of your priesthood acceptably before God.

We will now turn to our role as kings. I believe that the only people who qualify to be kings in God's kingdom are those who are also priests. We cannot be kings until we carry out our priestly responsibilities. If we don't do this, it will be a great obstacle to us when we attempt to rule.

Who Is a King?

Once again, we must set aside our historical and cultural ideas of a king to discover the kind of kings we are to be in God's realm. One traditional image of a king is someone who lives in a grand palace on a hill high above a town or city. Another image is a refined, proud, inaccessible person seated on a throne with a crown on his head and a scepter in his hand, surrounded by many servants.

Based on these characteristics, many people would conclude that they could never qualify for the position of king. They would look at their job in the warehouse, the fields, the office, and so forth, and immediately conclude they were ineligible. Even most people who consider themselves intellectuals or who have amassed wealth could not visualize themselves as kings. The thought would probably never even enter their minds. Yet we must realize that the above descriptions of a king are human concepts. God's kingdom breaks these mental paradigms and brings us back to His original plan, in which every one of His people is a king and a priest, created to take dominion over his assigned territory with the authority and power God delegated to him to extend His reign on earth.

The territory of our allotted "kingdom," or sphere of influence, might be our family, our business, or our ministry. We will discuss functioning in our specific territories in more detail in chapter 10. Yet, regardless of the size of our territories, we are kings over them, and we need to "extend our rods" and begin to rule.

*A king rules and exercises dominion with power
and authority over a certain territory.*

The Role of King in God's Kingdom in the Now

Remember that "authority" is the legal right to exercise power and "power" is the ability to do something. In the case of our role as kings in God's kingdom, we have the legal authority to act on earth as God acts in heaven and to carry out His will through the power of the Holy Spirit. Let us explore the meaning and parameters of our kingly role.

1. Rule with the Rod of Authority

The LORD said to my Lord, "Sit at My right hand, till I make Your enemies Your footstool." (Psalm 110:1)

In chapter 3, we learned the difference between the priesthood of Christ and the Levitical priesthood under Moses. Christ sat down at the right hand of the Father because His work was completely done. It was sufficient to redeem humanity—past, present, and future—from every sin—past, present, and future. His sacrifice was eternal, and the victory He achieved was irrevocable. In contrast, the Levitical priesthood never "sat down," because their job was never done—they had to offer sacrifices on behalf of the people day after day, and year after year. One sacrifice was never enough to expiate the continuous sins of the people.

The LORD shall send the rod of Your strength out of Zion. Rule in the midst of Your enemies! Your people shall be volunteers in the day of Your power. (Psalm 110:2–3)

In biblical times, a rod was "a sign of authority, hence a scepter."[8] The rod is representative of a king's authority—in the case of the above verse, the authority of King Jesus. After He resurrected, ascended, and sat on His throne, He gave us authority to use His "rod" over the nations and to expand His kingdom, carrying out the purpose and plans of the Father. (See, for example, Matthew 28:18–20.)

The rod is the emblem of a king's authority.

8. *The Zondervan Pictorial Bible Dictionary*, Merrill C. Tenney, gen. ed. (Grand Rapids, MI: Zondervan Publishing House, 1967), "Rod," 726.

In the Old Testament, God substantiated the authority of Aaron's rod. Aaron was the first high priest, and I believe his rod was emblematic of Christ's rule. The Israelite camp was in rebellion against the leadership of Moses and Aaron, and one way God dealt with the problem was with a supernatural sign. He had the leader of each tribe of Israel write his name on his own rod. From among the twelve rods belonging to the tribes, Aaron's rod was the only one that budded, blossomed, and produced ripe almonds by God's supernatural power. (See Numbers 17:1–10.) Aaron was confirmed to be the high priest and carrier of divine authority. I believe the flowering and fruit were symbolic of Jesus' resurrection. We rule according to the name of Jesus, or according to His rod of authority.

The authority is in the name written on the rod, but it has no use until it is exercised.

Jesus is on His throne, reigning with authority by the Holy Spirit through the church. Our calling is to be corulers and coleaders with Christ, as we dwell in Him in the heavenly places. (See, for example, Ephesians 2:6.) It is the church's responsibility to rule over Satan and to make his kingdom subject to God's purposes, so His will can be done on earth as it is in heaven. As we enforce the purposes of God and the laws of the kingdom in the world, our role is similar to that of police officers who enforce the law under the authority of the civil government. We "arrest" the forces that rise up against the righteousness and peace of the kingdom of God. For example, when we pray for a sick person, and that person is healed, we are enforcing God's will and rule in regard to healing.

I challenge you as a kingdom ruler to start using the rod of authority you have been given by God. When we receive the revelation by the Holy Spirit that our rod carries the name of Jesus, we will begin to exercise our spiritual authority over the nations. As representatives of God on earth, we can demonstrate His authority with miracles, signs, wonders, and the casting out of demons—but, again, not until we first exercise our priestly responsibilities.

Exercise your rod of authority in your own environment. Take authority over sickness in your body, lack in your finances, depression in your soul, and every attack of Satan. Remember that you are anointed and that God has given you the authority to do these things. Use the rod right now! It has the power to deliver you, your spouse, your natural and spiritual children, and your ministry.

Jesus has all power and authority,
but demonstrating His power and authority belongs to us.

---

2. Rule Through Prayer

Ruling through prayer is one way in which the roles of king and priest overlap. Ultimately, this world is not ruled by presidents, prime ministers, dictators, senators, congressmen, mayors, and so forth. These leaders rule in the natural, but true power in the spirit realm is activated by those who know how to pray in order to establish the kingdom of God and cause His will to be done in their nations. We will be unable to rule through prayer until we understand and carry out the following conditions:

+ *Our prayers must be based on Scripture.* God's will is written in His Word. When we pray according to His own Word, He hears us. (See 1 John 5:14.)

+ *Our prayers must correspond to the rhema of God, or His word revealed in the here and now.* The Greek word *logos* is often used to refer to the written Word of God, which is the "constitution" of His kingdom, while the Greek word *rhema* is often applied to a word from Him revealed in the here and now. As we have discussed, a rhema is given by the Holy Spirit for a specific moment and situation. It might or might not be given verbatim from the Scriptures, but it never contradicts God's written Word; rather, the Bible supports it, and supernatural manifestations will provide the evidence of this.

+ *Our prayers must be empowered by the Holy Spirit.* Over the centuries, the church has committed the great sin of ignoring the Holy Spirit. As I discussed previously, we have dishonored and disrespected Him by trying to replace Him with other methods for accomplishing our goals. The church has searched for "safe" human systems in order to avoid depending on God's Spirit, but this is impossible! We need His guidance, direction, and power. (See, for example, Romans 8:26.) Moreover, God's Word and the Holy Spirit always work together. The Holy Spirit will empower our prayers only when they align with the Word. For this reason, it is important for us to know what the Bible says.

We now turn to two examples from the Scriptures that show how God's people have exercised rule through prayer. In the Old Testament, we read how the prophet Elijah went before Ahab, the king of Israel, to announce God's judgment because of the nation's idolatry and other wickedness. (See 1 Kings 17:1.) The New Testament refers to this circumstance in James 5:17–18, affirming that Elijah was a man with a nature just like ours. He prayed that no rain would fall on Israel for three-and-a-half years, and his prayer was heard. The rain stopped, and a drought ensued.

The dominion of this man of God over nature was impressive. Rain is beyond human control; it depends on weather patterns and, ultimately, on God's sovereignty. What was Elijah's secret to making this decree come to pass? He knew how to apply the truth of Scripture and how to hear God's voice. The pronouncement of the drought, including the length of its duration, was not Elijah's idea. God had revealed it to him through a rhema for that specific situation. Furthermore, I believe Elijah knew of God's warning recorded in Deuteronomy 11:16–17. Before the Israelites entered the Promised Land, Moses had told them not to follow false gods because, if they did, God would close the heavens, stopping the rain and causing a drought.

Elijah had received a divine rhema, revealing that Israel had tested God's patience and that His judgment would be fulfilled at a specific time. The prophet based his prayer on the Scriptures and on the rhema he'd heard from God. Three-and-a-half years later, Elijah again heard God's voice and knew he had to return to King Ahab to declare that the drought would end. Before Elijah prayed, and before the rain began to fall, the prophet told the king that rain would soon be coming. The revelation of the word and the power of the Holy Spirit operated at the same time in the life of Elijah. (See 1 Kings 18:1, 15–46.)

> *By the word of the* LORD *the heavens were made, and all the host of them by the breath of His mouth.* (Psalm 33:6)

The entire universe came into existence by the joint operation of two entities: the Word and the Spirit. God released the same creative power through Elijah that brought the world into being! On this basis, who was really ruling in Israel: Ahab or Elijah? The solution to ending the drought was the people's repentance, and Elijah had to pray before the rain would return. King Ahab was powerless to challenge God's sovereignty. Clearly, Elijah was in charge through his prayers. Who rules your life: you or your circumstances?

In the New Testament, we read how the prayers of believers ruled over a situation of persecution in which King Herod had imprisoned Peter. Herod has just killed James, the brother of John, so Peter's life was in jeopardy.

> *Peter was therefore kept in prison, but constant prayer was offered to God for him by the church.* (Acts 12:5)

While Peter was in jail for preaching the resurrected Christ, the church in Jerusalem was praying in one accord. Their prayers paved the way for God to send an angel to deliver Peter from prison in a supernatural way. (See Acts 8:6–17.) Sometimes, one person's prayers are not enough, and the Holy Spirit will lead a group of people to pray in unity until a spiritual breakthrough occurs.

Not long after Peter was freed from prison, Herod died under the judgment of God.

> *So on a set day Herod, arrayed in royal apparel, sat on his throne and gave an oration to them. And the people kept shouting, "The voice of a god and not of a man!" Then immediately an angel of the Lord struck him, because he did not give glory to God. And he was eaten by worms and died.* (Acts 12:21–23)

Who was in charge: Herod or the church? Herod was resisting the purposes of God, and he was taking for himself glory that belonged only to the Lord. An angel struck him down, and he suffered a terrible death. Herod was on his throne one day and in his tomb the next. Through prayer, the rule of the church was superior; its intercession in the Spirit caused Peter to be released from prison, and it may also have caused their persecutor to be removed from power. Who rules your life: you or your circumstances? Who rules your thoughts: you or the enemy? Who rules your body: you or the sickness?

In Venezuela, a doctor named Betty Martínez was diagnosed with a cancerous tumor of the thyroid gland that was two-and-a-half centimeters (about one inch) long, and she underwent two surgeries. The first surgery showed that the cancer had metastasized to the lymph nodes in her neck. The second surgery, which should have lasted only one-and-a-half hours, lasted eight hours due to complications. The surgeries did not produce the desired results, and, worst of all, certain nerves in Dr. Betty's spinal cord were affected. Consequently, she was unable to raise her left arm and was quickly losing all feeling on the left side of her face. She spent torturous sessions in therapy that left her feeling terrible and from which it took her a long time to recover. To make matters worse, three more tumors appeared. She needed more surgery and chemotherapy!

Dr. Betty said, "My God, I won't be able to endure this!" Her heart gave out, and she had a heart attack. After her recovery from the heart attack, and as she was preparing to have the next surgery, she was invited to a House of Peace affiliated with our ministry, and she was told healing would be ministered to her. To this she said, "I have to see it to believe it." However, she was sick and tired of being ill and not finding a medical solution to her condition, so she accepted the invitation.

The entire group at the House of Peace joined in prayer for her, and the power of God enveloped her completely. She felt the three new tumors disappear instantly! Her joy was overflowing! Her life was radically transformed, so that she now testifies to her patients and prays for them in her office. She also preaches to her colleagues through her personal testimony. Many doctors are coming to the Lord through her witness and are imparting what they have received to their patients. Spectacular miracles are taking place. For example, cancer patients and people who are undergoing intensive therapy are being healed by the power of God.

Can we rule over our circumstances today? Of course! We are kings with God's authority and power to take dominion. Receive this word by faith! We must learn to rule over sickness and every evil thing through prayer.

Answer the Call to Be a King and Priest

*But you are a chosen generation, a **royal priesthood**, a holy nation, His own special people, that you may proclaim the praises of Him who called you out of darkness into His marvelous light.* (1 Peter 2:9)

In the above verse, Peter affirmed God's purpose for the church of Jesus Christ. Everyone—without exception—who has wholeheartedly repented and entered the kingdom of God is called to be a king and a priest. God, not man, chose us according to His purpose and grace. (See 2 Timothy 1:9.) And the time will come when we must answer His call. If we hadn't been called, we wouldn't have to give an answer. But Jesus died for this very purpose. By His blood, He cleansed, justified, and redeemed us to make us kings and priests with the power to continue His ministry on earth. We are His inheritance (see, for example, Deuteronomy 32:9), and we are all chosen to be a *"royal priesthood."* We must answer this call! Righteousness, peace, and joy must flow from our hearts to the world around us.

---

*In a kingdom of kings and priests,
the only ones allowed to enter are kings and priests.*

We must be aware that Satan attacks the spiritual priesthood of the church because, if the priesthood falls, there will be no one to offer sacrifices to God; and there will be no kings to exercise dominion and extend God's kingdom on earth, manifesting His presence. Dear friend, I challenge you to take your place in the kingdom and in this world as a priest of almighty God and as a king over the territory He has given you.

As you present sacrifices of praise, worship, offerings, service, and intercession through Jesus, our High Priest, God's fire will descend upon the altar of your life, and you will experience transformation as it fills you with His glory and power.

Once you establish your priesthood, begin to rule as a king over the territory that was assigned to you, from your position in Christ, seated with Him in the heavenly places. Rule in your home, business, ministry, church, neighborhood, city, and nation. You have a territory and sphere of influence in which you can reign from the spirit realm with the rod of authority that carries the name of Jesus. From that place, you can bring God's kingdom to earth, manifesting miracles, signs, and wonders to destroy the works of the devil and banish the kingdom of darkness. You can exercise dominion through prayer by declaring your territory holy—free of sin, sickness, curses, injustice, and death.

With this knowledge, we can dream of living in a city free of crime, bloodshed, witchcraft, and death because of the intercessory prayers of kings and priests who have taken their positions in God's kingdom and who exercise their power. If you accept this challenge, I invite you to pray the following prayer of commitment to seal your decision. Please say it out loud, wholeheartedly and with faith.

Jesus Christ, You are Lord, the Son of God, and the only way to heaven. You died on the cross for my sins and were raised from the dead on the third day. You paid the wages of my sins and redeemed me with Your precious blood. I surrender to You once more, Lord, and I present my body to God as a living sacrifice. I place myself at Your disposal. Do with me as You wish. Send me wherever You want me to go. From this day forward, I am Yours. Thank You for accepting me! Anoint me with authority and power so I can fulfill my calling as one of Your kings and priests who rules to expand Your kingdom on earth, today! I take my rod of authority and begin to use it right now. Amen!

8

Faith: The Currency of the Kingdom

Faith is to the kingdom of God what currency is for a nation. In today's society, the strongest currencies in the world are losing their strength, people's purchasing power is fluctuating, and most people do not feel financially secure. Only the kingdom of God is unshakable. Its currency is always strong, and it allows us to acquire everything we need from the eternal realm. However, if we are to receive from what is in eternity, we must understand what faith is, how it functions, and how to walk according to it.

Faith is the currency of the supernatural in the now.

Where Faith Originates

Without faith it is impossible to please God (see Hebrews 11:6), and if we fail to please Him, we won't obtain anything from His kingdom. Of course, faith is not the only thing that pleases God—obedience, holiness, reverence, worship, fasting, and prayer also please Him, but none of these things has value if it is practiced without faith.

Many people think faith originates with them, and they become discouraged when they feel they don't have enough faith and can't generate more of it in order to receive from God. Let me share with you an indispensable spiritual truth: *true faith originates in heaven*, and it operates from there. This is why, to have faith, we must be born of God's Spirit, which gives us access to the heavenly realm. (See John 3:1–8.)

It is impossible to be born again and not be activated in the supernatural.

When we first come to the Lord, most of us have only simple faith for salvation. We choose Christ after hearing the message of the gospel, and we confess Him as Lord and believe that God has raised Him from the dead. (See Romans 10:9–10.) At that moment, we cross over from the kingdom of darkness into the kingdom of light. We are also given a measure of faith from God. (See Romans 12:3.)

Here is the heart of the matter: This faith of which we are given a measure is a portion of God's own faith, which is supernatural. In Mark 11:22, Jesus told His disciples, *"Have faith in God."* A more literal translation of this statement is "Have God's faith." Jesus was telling us that God grants us a portion of the faith that belongs to Him. Therefore, we all start our Christian lives with a measure of potent faith already given to us. Yet, since faith is not tangible currency, as money is, you might ask, "How do we 'spend' it to receive what we need?"

Faith originates in heaven; it operates above and beyond the natural world.

How Faith Is "Spent"

Faith is "spent," or "put into circulation," by our words. The Bible says that life and death are in the power of the tongue. (See Proverbs 18:21.) Every time we speak, we activate a spiritual exchange. If we do not speak God's words of life, there is the danger that our words can bring forth something harmful.

For instance, the words "I can't" activate impossibility. When we speak according to this outlook, our mind, body, and spirit conform to our affirmation. This is not an expression of the faith of God; rather, it is a declaration founded in fear. It comes from a mind-set originating in the natural world and our carnal thinking. If we say, "It can't be done," we are, in essence, eating of the tree of the knowledge of good and evil, because the impossible came about as the result of the fall of man.

On the other hand, when we say, for example, according to God's Word, *"I can do all things through Christ who strengthens me"* (Philippians 4:13), we activate life and possibility. (See Matthew 19:26.) In Christ, all things are possible if we believe. (See Mark 9:23; Luke 1:37.) When our minds are renewed in faith, we remove the limitations we have placed on God, and it becomes easier to think as He thinks.

Are your words producing life or death?

The true atmosphere of faith is heaven. Faith is anchored in the invisible realm, which is superior to all that is visible.

Speak Faith from Your Position in the Heavenly Realm

The faith of God is in the now, because the power of the resurrection is in the now. We do not serve a dead Christ but a living Christ, and we are seated with Him in the heavenly places! On the basis of God's faith within us, we can speak, declare, decree, and pray from a position of absolute certainty. That for which we exercise our faith has already been provided by the work of Christ. This makes it possible for new believers—not just mature Christians—to do miracles. Many new believers are able to walk according to God's supernatural kingdom because they don't know any reason why something can't be done; they aren't blocked by religion or formality, because Jesus' work on the cross and His resurrection are fresh in their hearts. They have the passion of their first love, they believe what God has said, and they are willing to use the faith they have received. "Seasoned" Christians may be certain that what they believe does indeed exist in eternity, but many of them don't have faith that it can be manifested on earth, because they have conformed to religion or have grown apathetic or skeptical.

When we speak God's Word according to "now" faith, our words have spiritual "weight," or "matter." On occasion, persistence is necessary.

However, in the presence of God, one word is enough to bring into existence what He has pronounced and finished in eternity.

God gave us faith because it is the legal entrance to the supernatural. It "thinks," "hears," and "sees" what is in heaven.

We must declare what God has promised, so it can come into being. The Calderons, a family in our church, exercised their faith in God's Word when they underwent a financial crisis. The husband was working in construction in Miami, but his hours were reduced, making it impossible for the family to meet their mortgage payments. So, the bank began the process of evicting them and auctioning off their property. "We were very sad because it was our home, but we began to declare a miracle from God," they said. They had heard testimonies of the financial miracles experienced by various people in the church, and they were determined to receive their own miracle. During a "firstfruit" service, in which the congregation presented offerings to God, they presented their covenant for a home, certain that the Lord would provide. Not long after that, a friend of the family was praying for them and heard God say, "They will not be left homeless, because you will give it to them." This person called them, shared what God had said, and gave them $95,000 for the purchase of their home—the only condition being that they buy the house debt free. Today, the Calderon family is very happy because they have seen God's hand at work in their lives; they have experienced firsthand His great provision and His faithfulness to the covenant. Their declarations for their financial miracle had great spiritual weight because they were full of "now" faith.

Declaring by faith, from eternity, brings things into existence.

God's Word feeds our spirits and builds an atmosphere of faith around us. Jesus said, "*It is written, 'Man shall not live by bread alone, but by every word that proceeds from the mouth of God'*" (Matthew 4:4). We make transactions with the spiritual currency of God's kingdom by declaring His Word in faith.

Let me caution you not to confuse faith with the act of confessing God's promises. In today's church, faith is often turned into a formula, so that some Christians tend to believe they will find a solution to their problems by simply repeating Bible verses. Faith is thereby reduced to "positive confession" rather than something activated by the *"living and powerful"* Word of God. (See Hebrews 4:12.) Remember that confessing what God has said feeds our faith, but it is not faith itself.

Let us further explore the meaning of faith and how it functions.

What Is Faith?

Now faith is the substance of things hoped for, the evidence of things not seen. (Hebrews 11:1)

The word *"faith"* in the above verse is translated from the Greek word *pistis*, among whose meanings are "credence," "moral conviction (of religious truth, or the truthfulness of God or a religious teacher), especially reliance upon Christ for salvation," "assurance," "belief," "faith," and "fidelity" (STRONG, G4102). *Pistis* comes from the root word *peitho*, which means "to persuade" and "to have confidence" (NASC, G3982). When we move in the spiritual realm, there is no natural, tangible evidence; we operate by internal spiritual discernment rather than physical proof or intellectual understanding.

God stakes His reputation and integrity on every word He has spoken. This means that when we place our faith in something He has said, the responsibility to carry it out rests on Him, not on us. Our approach to God should simply be, "Lord, You said it, and I believe it!" God will answer us, "It shall be done; amen!"

God gave us faith as the avenue from the unseen world to the seen world.

People often define eternity as a long period of time, but eternity is essentially a state of being, which is why we can exist in the eternal realm in Christ Jesus and access His treasures.

[God] has made everything beautiful in its time. Also He has put eternity in their hearts.... (Ecclesiastes 3:11)

While everything in eternity is already finished and in a mature state, everything on earth must be declared before it comes into being. As we approach the end times, an acceleration of this process is taking place. We can declare something by faith and receive it instantly. The more we declare what we need, the less time we will have to wait to receive from God. In this way, the future becomes now. Therefore, if we continue with our traditional mind-set of hearing the Word, processing it, reasoning it out, and analyzing it, so we can eventually believe it and perhaps act on it, it may be too late. Respond and receive your miracle now!

---

*The realm of faith existed before time was created—
it is eternity in the now.*

After studying Hebrews 11:1 comprehensively, I developed the following as a summation of what I believe is its essential meaning:

Now, faith is; and it is the reality of the main foundation on which hope rests, the conviction of all that truly exists and the controller of the things we do not see.

Let me expound on this statement according to its various parts, as we continue to explore the question "What is faith?"

1. "Now..."

Man has placed in the future what God has placed in the present. In the mind and realm of God, the present and the future exist together, and faith is the currency with which we obtain the future *now*. I don't believe He ever wanted there to be a delay between the will of heaven and the manifestation of that will of earth—*"Your kingdom come. Your will be done on earth as it is in heaven"* (Matthew 6:10). God did not "try" to create light on earth by saying, a hundred times, *"Let there be light..."* (Genesis 1:3). He said it once, and there was light.

Through faith, we enter into the "time zone"
of the kingdom in the "now" of God.

When Jesus manifested the supernatural, His faith worked according to the leading of the Holy Spirit and the rhema of God for that moment. (See Matthew 4:4.) He said,

> *The Son can do nothing of Himself, but what He sees the Father do; for whatever He does, the Son also does in like manner.* (John 5:19)

In the same way, we must daily rely on God to show us what He is doing in heaven so that we can do it on earth. (See Romans 8:14.) This is how we receive immediate manifestations from the eternal realm and avoid getting into trouble by trying to declare something on our own. Notice that when Christ ministered on earth, there was no delay between His declared word and its manifestation. We see examples of this reality in the deliverance of the Syro-Phoenician woman's daughter (see Mark 7:29–30), the deliverance of the demon-possessed man (see Mark 9:25–27), the calming of the storm at sea (see Mark 4:38–39), and the resurrection of Lazarus (see John 11:43–44).

Christ operated in the revealed faith of the here and now.
Every miracle He did was in the now.

Jesus did not confess a hundred times, "Lazarus, come out!" He called Lazarus once, and a man who had been dead for four days came out of his tomb alive. Jesus had received a rhema from the Holy Spirit pertaining to that situation and the time when Lazarus would resurrect. Note also that Jesus never prayed for the sick or the demon possessed when He cured them—nowhere in the Bible does it say that He prayed for them. Neither did He say to anyone, "You will be healed sometime in the near future." Rather, Jesus declared the sick healed, and they were healed! He simply made declarations, such as *"Be healed of your affliction"* (Mark 5:34), *"Rise, take up your bed and walk"* (John 5:8), and *"Your faith has made you well"* (see, for example, Luke 18:42). Likewise, He cast out demons, and they immediately fled!

Jesus spoke based on the truth rather than the facts as they appeared in the natural world. Every miracle He performed came to pass because He spoke with faith from the eternal realm as a result of a revealed word in the present. If Jesus Christ did this, we can do it, also. (See John 14:12.) Read through the book of Acts, and you will see that there was no lapse of time between the apostles' declarations and the visible manifestations of God's power. In my own ministry, the most powerful miracles I have witnessed have taken place the moment the word left my mouth. We will witness the most extraordinary miracles of all time when we receive and practice the revelation that faith is now. As our old mind-set is renewed, everything we say, decree, declare, and pray will no longer be for the future but in the now.

---

*In Christ, all things are in the now. Outside of Him,
all things are subject to time.*

Melina García of Colombia had suffered from alopecia areata (hair loss) since she was twelve years old. The doctors could not find the underlying cause or a cure. They thought her condition might have been triggered by stress or a vitamin deficiency, but no corresponding treatment worked. She lost a significant amount of hair every time she combed it. People would stare at her, and this made her uncomfortable, so she would attempt to arrange her hair to hide the bald spots. Her condition had caused her self-esteem to plummet.

Melina then attended CAP (Apostolic and Prophetic Conference) Colombia, sponsored by King Jesus Ministry, and she prayed for a miracle. During one of the sessions, as I declared healing over different illnesses, the Holy Spirit led me to decree that hair was growing on people who were bald. Instantly, Melina felt a supernatural weight come upon her, and she fell to the floor. When she got up, she checked her head and felt new hair! Every place where there had been a bald spot was now covered! She went back to the doctor, who could not explain what had happened. Her miracle was not for the future but in the now.

The future is the eternal present postponed.

I witness miracles like Melina's everywhere I go, and the entire church of Jesus Christ can witness similar miracles multiplied many times over as we expand the kingdom of God on the earth. The only condition is that we constantly exercise the measure of faith God has given us. When we do this, our faith will increase exponentially, because the more we use our faith, the more faith we will be given.

> *I am God, and there is none like Me, declaring the end from the beginning.*   (Isaiah 46:9–10)

Many of us have been trained to pray and then wait an indeterminate amount of time until something happens, but God is the God of the here and now. He declares *"the end from the beginning."* So, if we declare that something will take place in a week, a month, or a year, we delay its manifestation or materialization in the present. When we believe miracles "will" take place, "sometime," they are like an airplane stuck in a circling pattern over an airport, unable to land. However, we can remove all delays when we live in the now, so that the miracles can "land," and we can receive them.

People often prefer to believe for healing rather than for miracles, because healing is usually progressive (see, for example, Mark 16:18) and demands less risk to our faith. In contrast, miracles take place instantly, so they require an immediate response from those receiving them. If we don't respond instantly, we may lose them. Some blessings in our lives are being detained because we have established a future due date for their arrival. When we combine a rhema with "now" faith, we can receive them today.

Faith takes something from the eternal "future"
and materializes it in the present.

2. "Faith Is…"

Before we were born on earth, we existed in eternity. In God, we first "are" in the spiritual realm, and then we manifest in the physical realm.

This is because God determines the purpose for something before He creates it, and He finishes everything before He starts it. Our job is to discover what "is" in God's eternal realm so that we can bring it into our physical realm through faith.

In Western culture, most people reverse this process. Rather than starting with who they are, they "do" things to try to gain acceptance by others, so that they can "be" someone. This is how people become slaves to public opinion and never really know who they were born to be.

The Scripture says,

> For as [a person] *thinks in his heart, so is he.*   (Proverbs 23:7)

To operate in the kingdom of God, we begin with who we "are" in eternity. When we know that we are God's beloved children, chosen from the foundation of the world (see Ephesians 1:4), and discover who He created us to be, we will think and act from that perspective. Everything else will develop from our identity and existence in Him. Our "being" will lead to our "doing," and not the other way around. We will not aspire to "become" something, because we already "are"!

You are a child of God with a unique purpose; and because you are in Christ, you receive every spiritual blessing in Him. (See Ephesians 1:3.) God designed you to be saved, righteous, holy, at peace, joyful, blessed, healthy, free, prosperous, and more. You don't have to wait for someday in the future to be saved, healed, prosperous, and so forth, because you "are" those things! Receive them now!

Faith enables us to remain in the state of "being"
supernatural, in the now.

---

3. "The Reality of the Main Foundation on Which Hope Rests…"

The above phrase reflects the following portion of Hebrews 11:1: "the substance of things hoped for…." The Greek word translated "substance" is hupostasis, which means "a setting under (support)." In a figurative sense, it means "essence," or "assurance." Among its other indications are "confidence" and "substance" (STRONG, G5287).

Basically, to exercise faith means to "sit upon" the Word that God gave us; to rest on it, or submit to it, knowing that God will keep it. When we rest, we are in faith. When we worry, we are not in faith; as a result, our hope—in the sense of confident expectation—has no substance. Faith is the assurance that what we believe is real and legally ours. No one can have a legal deed to a nonexistent property. Faith is the authentic or reliable proof that guarantees the existence of what we believe for. Even though we have yet to see it with our natural eyes, it is a reality, because has God promised it.

Faith "is," and we do not hope for something that "is" but something that will be. (See Romans 8:24–25.) Hope is for the realm of time, but faith is for now. If salvation, healing, and deliverance exist now, then why are we still waiting for them? To wait is to apply hope to matters where faith should be in operation. For example, hope enables us to wait for the second coming of Christ in His glory, but faith enables us to expect and receive health, salvation, prosperity, and miracles in the here and now.

Faith acts and stands on what God has already predetermined, generating expectation.

God is releasing supernatural expectation in believers. During a leaders' conference in Argentina, I met Oliver Inchausti, a seven-year-old who had been deaf in his right ear since birth because the ear had not developed properly and was deformed, having no orifice. Oliver's deafness considerably affected his ability to interact with his surroundings and to develop language skills. His mother had consulted many doctors, who gave a variety of advice. Some said they didn't even know if Oliver really had an eardrum, because it was very small. One specialist suggested that she take him to Cuba for surgery. Brazilian doctors said they could do surgery that would enable him to hear through his bone. Other plastic surgeons said they could do nothing until he became an adult.

When Oliver and his mother attended the leaders' conference, they came to the altar when I called all those who were deaf to come and demonstrate faith in the now. This young boy had spent years yearning for a miracle, so he was expecting something to happen. I placed my hand on his deaf ear and declared the miracle. His mother then placed her hand over his good ear, and one of my doctors tested him from behind his deaf ear. As soon as the doctor said a word, Oliver repeated it clearly and without hesitation. He heard perfectly! The doctor examined his ear and saw that the small orifice had increased in size.

Can you imagine what would happen if an entire congregation expected to receive something from God? In my ministry travels, I often experience the demand of faith upon the mantle of miracles God has given me from people who have great expectations. When this happens, miracles, signs, and wonders are released among them.

4. "The Conviction of All That Truly Exists..."

This part of the summation of Hebrews 11:1 refers to *"the evidence of things not seen."* The Greek word translated *"evidence"* is *elegchos,* among whose meanings are "proof," "conviction" (STRONG, G1650), and "test" (NASC, G1650).

When we doubt, it shows that we are not convinced, or persuaded, of the reality of the invisible supernatural realm. True faith is a "knowing" that originates in the heart; it is an ardent conviction of the eternal reality of the invisible world. When you experience problems, what do you "know"? Can you stand like Job and say, *"I know that my Redeemer lives"* (Job 19:25), or like Paul and say, *"I know whom I have believed"* (2 Timothy 1:12)? Many people possess mental knowledge of God and the spiritual realm, but they are not persuaded to the point where they act on their knowledge. When people are persuaded, they move in a greater dimension of faith. Those who don't move in faith will die in the same place.

We cannot think like God unless we possess internal "knowing." Faith "sees" the invisible, believes the incredible, and receives the impossible.

---

5. "The Controller of the Things We Do Not See"

The supernatural rules the natural, and faith in the now determines what we will see manifest in the physical world. From the invisible realm of the kingdom of heaven, faith exercises dominion, lordship, and authority over creation. We have the ability to control even nature and death by a word spoken in faith. Raising the dead will become commonplace if we receive this revelation. Your faith is the controller, or gatekeeper, of what you need. Exercise your faith and open the gates!

Faith affirms the invisible as its reality.

Once we understand the meaning of faith, as I have described it above, our preconceived ideas and arguments concerning what God can and can't do will be put aside. "Now, faith is...." The only thing left for us to do is to act on the dominion God has given us. Receive your identity as a child of God. With the knowledge that you belong to Him, activate your measure of faith and bring the invisible realm to yourself, your family, your church, and other people, right now! Declare a time limit for the answer to your need or circumstance, according to the leading of the Holy Spirit. For example, declare that you will receive a phone call from an employer; a contract from a client; healing, salvation, transformation, or anything else you are expecting to receive.

Faith is the continuation of the invisible realm in the visible world.

How to Live and Move in "Now" Faith

If you are at a standstill in your faith, it means you have done everything within your own power or knowledge but have run out of your own resources. You need new resources, which God is providing today. Step by step, you can go *"from faith to faith"* (Romans 1:17). God wants to move you into the dimension of faith that is in the here and now—for miracles, signs, wonders, and acceleration in the advancement of His kingdom.

What I am about to teach you are principles and revelations I have observed and experienced over the course of twenty-plus years in ministry. If you believe them and put them into practice, I promise that you will do the same things that I have been doing, and even greater things. Walking, living, and moving in "now" faith requires the following steps:

1. Operate Your Faith from a Place of Righteousness

Behold the proud, his soul is not upright in him; but the just shall live by his faith. (Habakkuk 2:4)

We were saved and justified by faith, and it is only by faith that we can live and function in God's kingdom. Righteousness is the foundation of faith. We may have faith to believe and to declare a manifestation from the eternal realm, but if we are not right with God in any area of our lives, our faith can be nullified. For example, if we don't tithe or give offerings to God, our faith for finances or a job will not work, even if we believe with great zeal, because we are robbing God. We won't have access to the benefits that God has promised to those who tithe. In the family, if one spouse abuses the other, his or her faith becomes ineffective. (See 1 Peter 3:7.)

This principle is applicable in every area of our lives and ministry. Even though God wants to back up our belief and declarations, He is unable to do so because it would mean going against His Word and righteousness.

Does the kingdom of darkness know when we are not walking in righteousness? Of course, it does! Demons know when we are not exercising our faith properly, because they live in the spirit realm and are aware when our faith has substance and when it lacks the integrity of righteousness. We should pause right now and ask ourselves if there is unrighteousness in any area of our lives. If so, we must repent and allow the blood of Jesus to cleanse us. This will activate the righteousness of the kingdom in us, and God will be able to bless us according to His promises.

The law of righteousness makes faith operative; unrighteousness makes it inoperative.

2. Walk by Faith, Not by Sight

For we walk by faith, not by sight. (2 Corinthians 5:7)

"*Sight*" represents the limitations of our natural environment, surroundings, circumstances, difficulties, obstacles, sicknesses, lack, impossibilities, and more. Such things are the opposite of faith. In order to rise above them, we must acquire a different perspective and reality. If our thoughts are consumed by a hard situation, problem, or obstacle, we are not living by faith. The natural world is unstable, insecure, and temporal, but God does not change. When we walk by faith and not sight, our reality no longer depends on our environment or circumstances but on His eternal reality, and we become everything He has called us to be.

Everything that is not eternal is subject to change.

Some people walk according to a "neutral optimism" rather than by faith. For example, they say, "If a miracle happens, it is God's will, but if it doesn't happen, it is not His will." Jesus did not preach or act according to this mind-set, but much of the church seems to have adopted it, thus conforming to a "probability" mentality. If we pray for healing but nothing happens, that's okay; if we pray for provision and nothing happens, that's okay, too. This detached attitude reveals our apathy and demonstrates our lack of expectation to receive from God.

Other people walk according to trust instead of faith. Sometimes, these terms are used interchangeably. However, trust is generally a feeling that operates in relationships, whereas faith is a heavenly substance that operates in the spirit realm and doesn't depend on emotions or circumstances. Trust works on the basis of our mental knowledge and emotional experience of a person's prior faithfulness and competence, but faith operates on the basis of revelation knowledge in the now, given by the Holy Spirit to our spirits. Therefore, in spiritual matters, our trust will not operate beyond what we personally know and have experienced of God. It won't lead us to believe in what we have not yet received from Him. It takes faith to move from what we have already seen, heard, or felt to what is newly revealed by the Holy Spirit.

Faith is a continuous, supernatural walk with God in the now.

Decide right now to rise above the places, people, and things that keep you from walking and growing in faith. Begin to edify a new atmosphere of faith in your life and home. Do not conform to the temporal; enter the spirit realm, where faith can change your reality. Sickness, problems, adversity, and trials were never ordained to be permanent. Yet we have learned to tolerate them, and we have turned them into something permanent by saying, "*My* sickness; *my* cancer; *my* pain; *my* lack; *my* depression...." We speak of these things as if they belonged to us, but they don't! Rebuke them right now!

Everything to which we conform will become our reality and mind-set.

3.   Rise Above Human Reason Through the Spirit and the Word

The things that are possible in heaven are rejected by human reason because they are outside our natural experience. We will not find faith until we rise above reason, because God will continually ask us to do things that do not make sense to our finite intellect. Miracles, signs, and wonders go beyond the ability of our natural mind to comprehend because their purpose is to demonstrate and manifest the supernatural.

If we use reason to evaluate an illness, situation, adversity, or calamity, it could turn deadly. What does a doctor usually do when explaining to a patient that he has a fatal illness? He tries to convince the patient to own the sickness and to make the best of it, because nothing else can be done. The doctor may have the best intentions toward the patient, but he is weakening that person's faith. If the doctor tells someone he has only a short time left to live, the patient's faith is the only thing that can break that word, because faith is able to enter eternity and pull from it whatever he needs in the now. I appreciate doctors and medicine; they are useful to humanity. I also know that sickness is a fact. I don't tell people to negate the facts, but I affirm that there are eternal truths, such as divine healing, that are above temporal facts, such as sickness.

The truth that exists above the reality presented by the doctor is that Jesus' death on the cross provided for our healing. Knowing this, we must decide whom we will believe. Will we believe the doctor or God? The diagnosis or His Word? Sickness or faith?

Faith is the ability to believe what reason finds nonsensical.

The Holy Spirit enables us to rise above our reason and common sense. When we receive the baptism of the Holy Spirit, we are given the gift of speaking in spiritual tongues, or languages, not understood by our reason. (See, for example, Acts 10:44–47; 1 Corinthians 14:2.) God gave us tongues to enable us to bypass our minds so that we could communicate with Him and receive from Him in the spiritual realm. If you have not yet been baptized with the Spirit, ask God to give you this gift of His supernatural power and presence. Then, stop paying attention to circumstances and begin to declare and obey, by faith, the rhema you receive from the Spirit. Also, don't lose the blessing just because it may be hard to understand. Understanding is not a requirement for obeying God, and living by faith always entails an element of risk.

Correspondingly, our reality should be determined by the truth—the Word of God—which operates beyond human reason as the highest level of reality. My job as a teacher of the Word includes dealing with people's disbelief as they try to "reason things out." I work alongside the Holy Spirit and the truth of the Scriptures to demonstrate to people that their reason makes no sense according to the laws of the supernatural realm. As their spiritual eyes are opened, they set aside reason and fill the void with the logic of God. The supernatural begins to make sense to them, because they see from His point of view.

Pastor David Alcántara of Honduras, one of my spiritual sons, reported that "a man named Manuel, who is a chauffeur to the president of our country, suffered from a terrible attempt on his life. One day, after he had dropped off the president, killers for hire followed him, assuming that he was the president, and they riddled the car with bullets. Manuel was taken to the hospital on the verge of death. His wife, desperate, called a leader in our ministry asking for prayer. One of Manuel's legs was so badly damaged that the doctors decided it needed to be amputated. His wife made a covenant with God, and, that night, as I ministered in supernatural power, the Holy Spirit placed in my heart that I should send the healing word for Manuel's life. I declared that God was going to create new bone, flesh, arteries, veins, nerve endings, and so forth, in his leg. The next day, the doctors had their surgical tools ready for the amputation, but when they removed the bandages from Manuel's leg, to their surprise, they found he had a completely healthy leg. It even had new skin!"

When reason is present, faith is absent, and the impossible will never be possible. But when faith is present, reason is absent, and the impossible is possible!

4. Renounce the Spirit of Religion and Be Activated in God's Faith

We have seen how religion enslaves us by raising mental strongholds—structures of thought that are rigid, as hard as cement, preventing the new in God from entering our hearts and minds. When we stop flowing in revelation, our minds can become closed by man-made rules and tradition, and we can become legalists. In this state, we may grieve the Holy Spirit, so that He becomes distant.

It is very hard for people to break free from the spirit of religion. If they do try to free themselves from that bondage, other religious people often call them troublemakers, transgressors, or even traitors. To break the dominion exerted by religion, we must cut loose the man-made rules and traditions that bind us and allow the power of the Holy Spirit to destroy all mental strongholds, regardless of any criticism we may endure from others.

Are you merely observing traditions, or are you living according to faith in the now? If you are not seeing God's power manifest in your life and ministry, you are probably not walking by faith. You must learn to wait on the Holy Spirit and hear what He is saying. As you wait, the rhema will come, indicating what you should do in a particular situation and moment. God gave you faith so you could keep up with Him and never miss the next wave of the move of His Spirit.

There is movement and life in faith but stagnancy and death in religion.

Many leaders and believers think that as soon as they are aware of their religious spirit and decide to reject it, they are free from it. However, just because they have turned their back on religion doesn't mean that religion has completely left them. Moses was raised in Pharaoh's house, where witchcraft, magic, Egyptian wisdom, and control and manipulation abounded. This future leader of Israel had to spend forty years as a shepherd in the desert so that the Egyptian traditions and religion could be removed from his mind and heart. Moses left Egypt in one day, but it took forty years to take Egypt out of Moses, so that he was totally dependent on the power of God. Only when this process was complete did God call Moses and send him back to Egypt to deliver His people.

I invite you to renounce the spirit of religion in your life by praying the following words. Remember that your prayer must come from your heart.

> Dear Jesus, I repent of observing rules and traditions that nullify the effect of Your Word and keep me from intimately knowing You and advancing to greater levels of faith. Forgive me and cleanse me with Your blood. I renounce and cast out, of my own free will, every religious spirit of tradition! I declare myself free, and I receive the spirit of faith in the now. Through You, I am baptized into the faith of God. Amen!

Religion might have deactivated you from genuine faith, but today, as an apostle of God, I reactivate you in God's faith to receive your miracle right now. Each day, continue to renew your mind; reject tradition and religion as you seize true faith!

5. Continually Walk in the Revealed Knowledge of God

Faith comes by hearing, and hearing by the word of God.

(Romans 10:17)

We cannot operate in "now" faith without "now" knowledge. Revelation, or revealed knowledge, takes our faith to another level, and our increased faith takes us to another revelation. This cycle cannot be stopped, because, if we were to reach the end of our spiritual knowledge or revelation, we would also reach the end of our faith. There would be nothing more to believe and manifest. Our faith should be in continuous movement; this is why we go *"from faith to faith"* (Romans 1:17).

Faith is based on knowledge. The only parts of the Bible that will work for us are the ones we know.

We must continuously receive fresh knowledge through rhema from the Spirit that illuminate our hearts to spiritual truth. Since faith works with knowledge, we will experience difficulties in those areas of our lives where we have not applied God's Word in faith. We cannot claim a promise with "now" faith if we don't know it exists or even if it belongs to us. Therefore, if we don't receive a word from God, we will not have present knowledge with which to work out our faith. I have downloaded hundreds of Scriptures and biblical teachings to my iPod, which I continuously listen to, in order to feed my faith and spirit.

Leaders cannot take their disciples above their level of knowledge or enable them to believe beyond their level of faith.

6. Stand Firm on the Truth, Not on Facts

And you shall know the truth, and the truth shall make you free.

(John 8:32)

Facts pertain to conditions, environments, and situations, but such things are constantly in flux. In contrast, truth is absolute; it is a reality that never changes. (See Hebrews 13:8.) In the midst of the facts—and after the facts—faith takes hold of the truth!

Facts are temporal, but faith is eternal.

It could be a fact that you are out of work right now, that you are sick, that you are facing problems in your family, or that you are experiencing other difficulties. Yet the truth is that God supplies all of your needs *"according to His riches in glory by Christ Jesus"* (Philippians 4:19), that by Jesus' stripes you were healed (see 1 Peter 2:24), that God is the restorer of relationships (see, for example, Ephesians 2:14–18), and that our difficulties are "*working for us a far more exceeding and eternal weight of glory,*" while we look to what is eternal (see 2 Corinthians 4:17–18). The decision is yours: Will you accept the facts or the truth?

Faith is based on the truth. As long as you think you have another option or alternative, you will not commit to believe.

When times get hard, some believers compromise the truth. Yet God doesn't have a "plan B" in reserve, because, if He did, He would no longer be sovereign or eternal, and His kingdom would not be unshakable. We must stand firm and believe what God has said. In the midst of a crisis or problem, we can be certain that He never alters His thoughts, plans, or power toward us and toward our purpose, provision, healing, and deliverance. God doesn't change in regard to these things, and neither should we!

If the doctor declares sickness or death over you, do not accept it. Use God's faith and seize your healing. If you accept the doctor's words, you are conforming to the enemy's desire to destroy you. What the doctor is saying is true and is a temporal fact, but it is not God's *truth* for your life. Our inheritance in Christ is kingdom health. Therefore, cancel the influence of those words with the power of God's faith. Use kingdom currency to seize the miracle and say to the doctor, "I don't accept this diagnosis."

When facts change, feelings also change;
but faith is firmly planted on the truth.

Vene Labans of South Africa was diagnosed with HIV six years ago. A couple of days prior to our conference on the supernatural in East London, South Africa, a friend of Vene's invited her to the meetings. She was reluctant but decided to go. On Sunday, I preached on "The Gospel of the Now," saying that, if you believe, you will receive your miracle. Then I made an altar call for those who were HIV-positive or had cancer. Vene approached the altar, willing to use her faith to be healed. One of my ministers declared healing over her, and she felt heat flowing through her body. The following day, she was scheduled to go to the clinic to obtain her monthly medication, but a friend insisted she should be tested, instead, to confirm her healing. So, Vene asked for a new test. To the glory of God, the results were negative!

In one day, Vene's life was completely transformed. Her sickness was temporary; it came to its end when she encountered the power of God. "This conference has completely changed my life; it has given me joy, health, and everything I needed!" she said.

Faith is where the supernatural begins.

If we conform to what the natural world says, we will accept it as being the last word, and it will rule over us. When such thinking becomes established in our hearts, we are not able to receive the supernatural, and we become magnets for sickness, poverty, lack, depression, and pain. We must establish in our hearts the truth that goes beyond all temporal reality. Receive everything that Jesus provided on the cross, right now!

Truth is the only thing that can defy facts because it is the highest level of reality and operates beyond facts.

7. **Discern and Maintain the "Rhythm" of Your Faith**

God established that everything in life should have a continuous rhythm. The earth orbits the sun, and the moon orbits the earth, according to perpetual patterns. Plants and animals maintain certain cycles of life. Every year is made up of four sequential seasons. Crops require a cycle of planting, nurturing, and harvesting. Human beings have biological rhythms in their bodies. For example, we inhale oxygen and exhale carbon dioxide with regularity. The human heart beats at a steady rhythm, constantly pumping blood to all parts of the body. These rhythms cannot be interrupted if the body's life is to be sustained.

Similarly, I believe there is a "rhythm" to our faith that must be kept in motion; if it ceases, the life of God's kingdom is hindered. For example, when we receive revelation or guidance by the Holy Spirit but fail to implement it, the cycle of revelation is broken. (See, for example, James 1:22.) Faith stops, and the word dies out because it is beyond our level of obedience. Each time we receive a fresh revelation, therefore, we must put it into practice and experience it. We must maintain the rhythm of faith in all areas of our lives.

8. Exercise Your Faith Through Love

For in Christ Jesus neither circumcision nor uncircumcision avails any-thing, but faith working through love.   (Galatians 5:6)

The Greek word translated *"working"* is *energeo*, which means "to be active, efficient" (STRONG, G1754), or "to be at work, to work, to do" (NASC, G1754). While righteousness makes faith operative, love energizes and ac-tivates it. Faith works through love because it functions according to the character of God. Faith that doesn't originate in love is like a clanging cym-bal—pure noise without substance. (See 1 Corinthians 13:1.)

The love of Christ is immeasurable (see Ephesians 3:18–19), and it is available to all of us through the Holy Spirit (see Romans 5:5). We can take the risk to go beyond what seems reasonable according to the natural world, our intellect, our religious background, and our selfish motivations by acting on our faith—based on our love for God, His kingdom, and the people who need to see His power manifested.

Every miracle and healing that Jesus performed was motivated by compassion.

---

9. Commit to Using, Exercising, and Investing Your Faith

We each received a measure of God's faith at salvation, but we need to intentionally exercise it. Let me suggest that you start by believing for small things. Give your faith a specific assignment. For example, believe for a small amount of money, healing for your headache, or something else you need. If your faith is mature, go beyond these small requests and risk praying for creative miracles, deliverance, profitable business contracts, the salvation of souls, transformed hearts, the multiplication of the gifts of the Holy Spirit, supernatural favor with people in authority, and more. The most important thing is to live by your faith and to exercise it continuously so that you will maintain its rhythm and keep moving to greater levels of faith.

Don't treat faith like an emergency kit, using it only when problems arise, because you will be "out of practice." When you have only one month to live, when your business is bankrupt, or when your marriage is broken, you don't want to start learning how faith works—and there is no time to wait for help to come in the future! Faith is "now" to provide practical solutions to the problems we face every day. But we also have to exercise it daily. We must make the decision to employ our faith purposefully right now.

Enter the Dimension of Faith in the Now

If you have never asked Jesus Christ to be the Lord and Savior of your life and received your measure of faith, or if you have wandered away from God and need to be reconciled with Him, I invite you to say this prayer out loud so that you can dwell in the realm where faith lives:

Heavenly Father, I recognize that I am a sinner and that my sin separates me from You. Today, I believe that Jesus died for me on the cross and that You raised Him from the dead. I repent of all my sins and, of my own free will, confess Jesus as my Lord and Savior. I renounce every pact I have made with the world, with my flesh, and with the devil, and I now make a new covenant with You. I ask Jesus to enter my heart and change my life. If I were to die right now, I know that You would receive me into Your arms. Amen!

Perhaps you have been exercising your faith and have witnessed the power of God to some extent, but you want to enter the dimension of faith in the here and now in order to revolutionize your environment. I invite you to pray the following prayer out loud:

Heavenly Father, I confess that Jesus Christ is my Lord and Savior. I believe that He is seated at Your right hand, that I am seated with Him in the heavenly places, and that I have received Your faith. Therefore, from this day forward, I will live and walk in the divine supernatural. I have legal access to the invisible realm, and the supernatural is normal to me because I have Your perspective, in which anything is possible. Signs, miracles, and wonders are my lifestyle. I declare that I am an ambassador of the kingdom of God and, by faith, I bring Your kingdom to earth. I call the eternal realm to the physical realm! I heal the sick, cast out demons, release prophetic words, deliver the captives, and preach the gospel of the kingdom with power. Father, I make a covenant of commitment, right now, knowing that You give me the grace to do these things until Jesus' return to earth. Amen!

9

Demonstrations of Kingdom Power Here and Now

Jesus taught His disciples to pray, *"For Yours is the kingdom and the power and the glory forever. Amen"* (Matthew 6:13). Jesus came to earth to reveal God as our heavenly Father—and the kingdom, the power, and the glory belong to Him.[9] Although each facet of God's dominion is distinct, it always works in conjunction with the others: the kingdom is the rule of heaven, the power is the ability of heaven, and the glory is the atmosphere of heaven. God is calling us to exercise His kingdom rule, demonstrate His power, and manifest His glorious presence on earth—here and now!

Our model for demonstrating the kingdom is Jesus. When He walked the earth, He carried the presence of God everywhere He went, and He announced the arrival of the kingdom in two essential ways, which are indicated in Acts 1:1: *"The former account I made, O Theophilus, of all that Jesus began both to **do** and **teach**...."*

+ *"**Do**"*: Jesus did the works of the kingdom.

+ *"**Teach**"*: Jesus taught about the kingdom.

If we don't teach people about the kingdom, it won't advance. And if we don't do the works of the kingdom, it won't be demonstrated with

---

9. For further reading on the topics of God's power and glory, see *How to Walk in the Supernatural Power of God* and *The Glory of God* by Guillermo Maldonado, published by Whitaker House.

power. At present, we have many teachers but few "doers." Why is there a discrepancy in the church between teaching and doing? Many believers are doctrinally correct and precise in what they teach, but they reject the manifestations of the supernatural. They declare truths, but they don't live according to the faith of God, which brings His power in the now. The saying "Knowledge is power" is only a half-truth. If knowledge is not put to use, it won't bring about change, and its potential power will be lost.

We have a generation of young people who are seeking an experience with something beyond themselves—something they have not found in religion, education, sports, music, business, technology, sex, fame, and so forth. In actuality, they are looking for an experience with the living God. Many of them use illegal drugs, practice witchcraft, and engage in other harmful practices while seeking this experience of God, and the enemy ends up destroying them. Can the church offer these young people—and people of all generations—a personal encounter with God and His kingdom? It can—when believers have an ongoing experience with God and His kingdom. We can do this when we transition from mere head knowledge to knowing God and His power through the Holy Spirit.

Once, our ministry sponsored a conference on the supernatural in Chile where a man named Pastor Ulises gave his testimony. He explained that, years earlier, he had decided to leave the ministry because he was tired of dealing with the problems in his congregation and was frustrated by a lack of fruit—there were no miracles, salvations, or other spiritual evidence to justify his continuing in the ministry. About that time, I held a conference in Argentina, which Pastor Ulises attended. There, he received a prophetic word: the Lord told him not to leave his congregation, because an unprecedented wave of miracles was about to take place. Two years later, during CAP in Miami, I prophesied to him, saying that he would be named president of the pastors' association in his city. Four months later, that word came to pass. Since then, the Lord has used him to manifest all types of miracles, the most impressive of which have been three resurrections.

The first resurrection occurred when Pastor Ulises' own daughter suffered a fatal heart attack. When he saw his daughter die, he began to pray with anguish and desperation. The Holy Spirit led him to rebuke death and to declare the spirit of life over her. To the glory of God, when he did this, her eyes opened, and she began to breathe normally. Overwhelmed with emotion, he embraced his daughter and thanked God for His power and mercy. This miracle filled him with the faith to rise to a higher level of belief.

The second resurrection happened during a baptismal celebration by the river. A young lady who attended the ceremony drowned. When they pulled her out of the water, her body was swollen and her skin had turned blue, and she was declared dead. When Pastor Ulises arrived on the scene, he was told that nothing more could be done. However, he heard the same mandate from the Holy Spirit that he had heard on the day his daughter was resurrected. So, not caring what other people said, he began to declare life over the young woman in the name of Jesus—and she came back to life! She looked as if she had suddenly awakened from a deep sleep. Her skin regained a healthy color because her blood was again circulating throughout her body. Everyone rejoiced and praised God.

The third resurrection took place at a mall, where a girl had suffered a heart attack. Once more, the pastor heard the command of the Holy Spirit, and, without hesitation—convinced that God would do the miracle—he began to pray for her, declaring life and health. Immediately, her vital signs returned, and she recovered within minutes.

Pastor Ulises cannot stop thanking God for the impartation of the Holy Spirit that God sent him. That impartation has transformed his heart and mind. He had been about to turn his back on his ministry when the supernatural power of the kingdom came into his life. Today, he is a man of spiritual warfare who establishes the kingdom by force, taking back souls from the grip of death.

Spiritual Knowledge Comes Through Experience

While it is important for us to teach people about the kingdom, it is even more powerful to demonstrate that message. If we fail to act on what we teach, then we are not being true to ourselves or to others. Jesus Christ demonstrated the kingdom by both teaching and acting with power. And He gave us the ability to do the same through the Holy Spirit.

To the Hebrew way of thinking, true knowledge comes through experience. We will not be able to understand many of God's truths unless we have a personal experience of them. Knowledge doesn't come just by studying the Bible. If this were true, theologians would be among the most effective instruments for manifesting the kingdom. And yet, a number of them seem stuck in spiritual stagnancy. They study the Bible from cover to cover but fail to achieve an accurate understanding of God, because they reject the idea that His power operates in our world today. If we turn God into a theological concept—one limited by human reason—we will never know Him intimately.

God has not called us to be religious or apathetic Christians but rather His true sons and daughters who are able to manifest His presence and power on earth. We must present a gospel with supernatural proofs demonstrating that Jesus lives and that His resurrection power is for today! Most people are not interested in us, our great knowledge, or the nice words we speak. They are interested in the bottom line: Do our words lead to supernatural works? Does our knowledge lead to an experience with God? Does our revelation produce a manifestation of His power? Does our theology bring healing to the sick, deliverance to the oppressed, prosperity to the poor, and repentance to the sinner? Does our testimony transform lives?

Many people do not want to hear a message—they want to see one.

Knowledge Should Lead to Supernatural Experience

Our experience with God should lead us to gain real knowledge of Him, or intimate relationship with Him. The reverse should also be true. Whenever we receive information or knowledge about God, through either the written Word or a rhema, this should result in an encounter with Him. Each time God gives us knowledge or revelation, He wants us to have personal contact with His kingdom and power. Therefore, when we receive a word that inspires us, challenges us, and encourages us to seek more of Him, we are not to remain where we are but to take the next step and experience the reality of that word, which always leads us to Him. The renewal of our minds is meant to transform our lives. People who accumulate knowledge without practicing it become merely religious.

Revelation knowledge is divine enlightenment for demonstrating the presence and power of the kingdom.

When anyone hears the word of the kingdom, and does not understand it, then the wicked one comes and snatches away what was sown in his heart. This is he who received seed by the wayside. (Matthew 13:19)

The *"word of the kingdom"* is like seed. When we receive a revelation from God, allowing it to be implanted within us, it imparts the power that enables us to obey it. But when we do not understand or accept a word from God, it cannot be implanted within us. Instead, it is like seed that gets scattered on the side of the road; it lands on shallow soil and is vulnerable to being eaten by birds and animals passing by. In a spiritual sense, this is what happens when the enemy comes and steals the word away from us.

The word *"understand"* in the above verse is translated from the Greek word *suniemito*. It literally means "to put together" and indicates mental comprehension that leads to godly living. (See STRONG, G4920.) In other words, it is an understanding of the knowledge of God that leads to a transformed life.

A believer who has a kingdom mentality is one who obeys the voice of God, putting into practice the truths he learns about the kingdom. This leads him to have experiences with God that enable him to further understand the implications of those spiritual truths.

We must know God to demonstrate His works.

[God] *also made us sufficient as ministers of the new covenant, not of the letter but of the Spirit; for the letter kills, but the Spirit gives life.*
(2 Corinthians 3:6)

When we don't enter into an experience with God based on what we learn from His Word or from a rhema we have received, then we have just the *"letter"* of the Word, not the *"Spirit,"* which *"gives life."* We simply have knowledge of something that should be or might be but does not occur. However, when we have an experience with that knowledge, our perspective changes. We gain greater spiritual depth, and we are able to explain God's Word with better clarity and insight. We no longer describe God and His truths as external observers. It's almost as if we are within the truth itself, or a part of it. In contrast, people who are mired in religion do not undergo transformation or gain such clarity of knowledge, because religion is void of experience. They develop spiritual numbness, which leads to self-deception. Consequently, the power of the kingdom does not manifest in their lives. (See James 1:21–25.)

Revelation knowledge is the basis for manifesting the supernatural.

Let me balance what I have just said with this warning: We should not base our spiritual lives on manifestations alone, or we will likely fall into error. We might get out of order and refuse to listen to wise spiritual counsel because we believe that the manifestations themselves are evidence that we are right with God and have His perspective. Instead, we must live—and, just as important, we must disciple other Christians—on the basis of the revelation of God's Word combined with demonstrations that support its teaching.

God's kingdom, power, and glory are not just theoretical ideas or historical facts to remember. As they are experienced on earth through supernatural manifestations, they bring about transformed lives! Since the Western mentality is so prevalent in our culture, I must emphasize again how important it is for us to break free from mere theoretical knowledge so that we may move on to have experiences with the power of God. The human mind is much too limited—it cannot embrace the greatness of God. We must allow Him to demonstrate in visible form what we believe and proclaim.

The reality you claim to experience in the invisible realm must have physical manifestations.

As I wrote earlier, God may choose to give fresh revelation not only of spiritual knowledge but also of natural knowledge, such as in the areas of science, engineering, or art. Various scientific inventions, medical breakthroughs, and technological developments have come from people who have had a fear of the Lord, a sanctified mind, and an understanding that all knowledge is meant to serve humanity. If we want to be intellectual giants, we must start with revelation from God given by the Holy Spirit. (See, for example, Ephesians 1:17–19.)

Let me state again that I am not opposed to the mind, but we need to regain the proper spiritual order, so that our spirits—guided by the Holy Spirit—can direct our souls and bodies. The Spirit is above the mind; He can take us to places in God where reason cannot enter. The mind must follow, not lead. When the mind is renewed by an experience with God, it is able to follow the direction of the Holy Spirit.

All knowledge and wisdom come from God's knowledge and wisdom.

People under the influence of the Western mind-set overemphasize the intellect, lose their spiritual sharpness, and find it difficult to accept and receive miracles. Yet I have found that people in Africa, Asia, South America, and the Caribbean find it easier to see and receive miracles because they still believe in the spiritual realm.

During a pastors' association meeting in my city of Miami, a pastor told me about an extraordinary miracle that God had done in his life. Pastor Favio had been at a church service in West Palm Beach where I ministered. He said I had declared that many miracles would take place, including supernatural weight loss. He appropriated that word because he weighed 300 pounds, and it had been impossible for him to lose weight on his own. He was truly suffering because of his obesity—he had difficulty bending over, walking, and breathing while speaking, in addition to other health problems.

Three days after the meeting, Pastor Favio got dressed in the morning, and his wife exclaimed, "Look at your pants. They are falling off!" He looked and was amazed at how baggy his pants and shirt looked on him. Then he decided to try on some of the old suits of various sizes that he had saved but hadn't been able to wear for years because of his weight gain. He started with a suit that was size 48 and kept trying on smaller suits until he reached size 38. That suit fit him! When he got on the scale, he saw that he had lost seventy pounds.

But the miracle did not stop there. He lost additional weight, so that now he weighs 185 pounds. His transformation was so radical that people were amazed and asked him if he had been sick. His mother asked if he'd had liposuction! When he shared his miracle, she couldn't believe it. Pastor Favio is a healthy man who is a good steward of the miracle God gave him. He shares his testimony everywhere he goes and prays for people who are obese, declaring the same miracle over their lives.

Pastor Favio did not lose weight through diets or medical treatments—neither of those methods worked for him. Rather, the power of God touched his life, and it transformed him. This was a demonstration of a spiritual reality manifested in the natural world.

There can be no demonstrations of kingdom power without fresh revelation knowledge from the Holy Spirit regarding how to manifest them.

The Balance Between the Word and the Spirit

Jesus was able to teach and demonstrate the message of God's kingdom because He was continually in contact with the Father. His words and actions had the life of God in them. God's pattern in Scripture is to send His Spirit before sending His word, because His word has power on earth only if it originates from the atmosphere of His presence—otherwise, it will be lifeless. Again, it is the difference between the *"letter"* and the *"Spirit"* (2 Corinthians 3:6) of His word. For example, when a believer gives forth a "prophetic" word that did not originate in God's presence, those who accept that word can be pulled out of the realm of His presence and become spiritually dry. However, when the Holy Spirit is in the equation, He brings life and induces spiritual movement.

Some people live in stagnant waters. The waters might be deep, but there is no movement of the Spirit in them. God did not begin to create anything on earth until the Holy Spirit moved over the waters. (See Genesis 1:2–3.) There is nothing worse than a person who is submerged in his own knowledge, having no spiritual motion. If we preach, but the Holy Spirit doesn't move, we are speaking mental knowledge that we have yet to experience. Our knowledge lacks revelation; therefore, it is absent of spiritual life.

People will spiritually dry up and die unless the Holy Spirit moves in them.

Jesus responded to a question posed by some religious leaders by asking them, *"Are you not therefore mistaken, because **you do not know the Scriptures nor the power of God?"** (Mark 12:24). God's word and His Spirit work together. Both are essential; when one is missing, there is imbalance. A word of God operates when He speaks (either a word from the written Scriptures or a rhema) and the power of God operates when He acts. If all we do is emphasize the word and ignore the Holy Spirit, we risk making mistakes. People who emphasize the word alone usually do not recognize the presence of God when it arrives.

All believers can demonstrate the kingdom of God in the here and now. Yet, to do so, we must go beyond the "letter" of God's word to the Spirit who gives it life and power. The Pharisees knew the letter of the law very well, but when the ultimate Revelation of God came to them—Jesus, the Word made flesh—they didn't receive Him. (See, for example, John 1:1–14.) A word from God will not demonstrate the kingdom until we receive a revelation of it.

Biblical words alone will not produce supernatural manifestations— they need to be combined with revelation from the Holy Spirit.

Manifestations from God are revelation that may be discerned by the natural senses, so that we can see or hear tangible evidence of His kingdom, power, and glory here and now. The Holy Spirit is the Agent of these manifestations.

> *The wind blows where it wishes, and you hear the sound of it, but cannot tell where it comes from and where it goes. So is everyone who is born of the Spirit.* (John 3:8)

God the Holy Spirit is an invisible Being who dwells in our hearts. While there may be many works of the Spirit taking place today that we cannot perceive, see, or feel, the Holy Spirit reveals God the Father and God the Son in many ways. As the above verse indicates, no one has ever seen the wind, but we know when it is blowing because we see trees sway, dust swirl, and so forth. Wind is invisible, but its influence is perceptible. In a similar way, no one sees the Holy Spirit dwelling within a believer, but His manifestations in and through the life of that believer are perceptible.

The Holy Spirit manifested Himself in the lives of the disciples on the day of Pentecost, shortly after Jesus' resurrection and ascension:

> *And when this sound* [the disciples speaking with other tongues] *occurred, the multitude came together, and were confused, because everyone heard them speak in his own language.* (Acts 2:6)

No one should argue or doubt that these tongues were a manifestation of the Holy Spirit, because they drew a multitude of people to hear Peter's sermon about Jesus, and over 3,000 of them were saved in a single day! (See Acts 2:41.) Without this manifestation, as well as the sound of *"a rushing mighty wind"* and the sight of *"divided tongues, as of fire"* (verses 2–3), people would not have realized that the Holy Spirit had arrived, because He makes Himself known by His manifestations. The gifts of the Holy Spirit, including tongues, are primary ways through which He manifests Himself to our natural senses: *"But the manifestation of the Spirit is given to each one for the profit of all"* (1 Corinthians 12:7).

In the above ways, and more, we can recognize the movement of the Spirit and live in His power here and now, with the ability to rise above our human problems and conflicts and expand God's kingdom on earth.

Purposes of Demonstrating God's Kingdom Here and Now

Let us now turn to the purposes of demonstrating God's kingdom, to make sure we understand the main reasons why He desires to manifest His eternal realm on earth and why it is essential for us to seek first His kingdom. (See Matthew 6:33.)

1. So Our Faith Will Be Founded on the Power of God

And my speech and my preaching were not with persuasive words of human wisdom, but in demonstration of the Spirit and of power.
(1 Corinthians 2:4)

It was not through eloquence or education that Paul produced great results for the kingdom; rather, it was through the visible demonstrations of the work of the Holy Spirit in his ministry. Our faith must be founded on the power of God, not on abstract theories or human abilities. Sermons, biblical training, educational degrees, theological arguments, and the like cannot accomplish what an experience with God can.

Experiencing God and seeing His manifestations changes our mindset, attitude, and behavior. Doctrine or theology is not enough to base our faith on, regardless of how sound it may be. It is hard to live in victory unless we walk in the power of God. This is not a luxury for us—it is an absolute necessity! I urge you to make the decision today to experience the supernatural in your life. I pray that the power of the kingdom be released over you and that it manifest to your physical senses. Receive it, right now!

We can demonstrate God only when we have experienced Him.

2. To Establish a Kingdom Context for God's Power

In the first chapter of Acts, we read that Jesus taught His followers *"things pertaining to the kingdom of God"* (Acts 1:3) during the six weeks between His resurrection and His ascension to heaven. In the second chapter, God poured out the promised *"power from on high"* (Luke 24:49) on Jesus' disciples at Pentecost (see Acts 2:1–4), leading to the disciples being baptized with the Holy Spirit and thousands of people entering the kingdom of God. In the third chapter, the glory, or presence, of God fell, manifesting in the healing of a man who had been lame since birth. (See Acts 3:1–9.)

Jesus knew that He needed to prepare His followers to receive the outpouring of the Spirit. If the Holy Spirit had descended *before* Jesus had given His disciples the revelation of the kingdom, they would have lacked the spiritual context for the power they received. The power of God always comes with these purposes: to build and expand the kingdom. Likewise, we must understand—and teach—the context for the power God wants to pour out in our lives. If we ignore the reason for which the Holy Spirit comes upon us, we can dry up or burn out spiritually, mentally, and emotionally. However, if we operate in God's power from His throne in the heavenly realms, for the right reasons, we will never dry up or burn out. In His presence is the realm of rest and *"fullness of joy"* (Psalm 16:11).

Power without purpose brings confusion and burnout.

A related reason why Jesus taught His disciples about the kingdom after His resurrection was that He was aware of the governmental and cultural environment of His time. The religious Pharisees and Sadducees had always questioned and persecuted Him during His ministry on earth, and He knew that from the time He resurrected, great persecution from the religious establishment would be released on His church, and His disciples would need power for boldness and effectiveness in ministry. These same religious leaders would try to eliminate all evidence of Jesus' resurrection in order to destroy His credibility. Yet the proof that He was raised from the dead would come from His Spirit-endowed disciples, who would perform miracles and wonders in His name and in the power of His resurrection.

In many Christian circles today, people are taught that the sole purpose of being filled with the Holy Spirit is to be enabled to *"speak with other tongues"* (Acts 2:4). Tongues are the language of heaven, and they are a sign of the supernatural. However, to open blind eyes, unseal deaf ears, and give strength to the lame requires more than just speaking in other tongues—although we can receive spiritual strength, guidance, and empowerment as we pray in our heavenly languages. We must realize that the main purpose for being baptized in the Holy Spirit is to receive power. (See Acts 1:8.) When people fail to realize this, they continue to be sick, depressed, and tormented by demons, even though they may have already been baptized with the Spirit.

The purpose of being baptized with the Spirit is not to magnify the sign of speaking in other tongues but to receive God's power.

God gave us the power of the Holy Spirit so we could defeat the devil and all his works, overcome temptation, rule over the fleshly nature, and triumph in the midst of adverse circumstances. I believe that society accepts sin as the norm today because the church has not manifested the power of the Spirit to deliver people. This means, for instance, that homosexuals and lesbians must settle for living in sin because few believers are demonstrating that God can truly change them.

Odalis Lozano had practiced a lesbian lifestyle all of her life. As a young girl, she wore her hair short, dressed in men's clothes, and used a masculine wallet. At eighteen, she began to have relationships with women. She rejected men because they disgusted her.

According to Odalis, her life was a living hell. Her heart was full of anger, hatred, bitterness, and rancor against her parents because they never taught her that her lifestyle was harmful. She also drank too much, was trapped by addiction, practiced masturbation, and spent much time in casinos because she was obsessed with gambling. She was terrified of doctors, thinking that they touched her sexual parts without medical cause. Her lack of personal identity led her to live with a partner for eleven years, even though she was unhappy. They fought constantly over money. The situation became so bad that Odalis's partner threw her out of the house, and she found herself homeless.

Desperate, she began to cry out to God, screaming, "Lord, help me! I can't go on with my life!" Then she came to King Jesus Ministry, and God's love began to minister to her. She went to a retreat led by my wife, where she received inner healing and deliverance. When the spirit of lesbianism was rebuked and cast out of her, Odalis cried and vomited. She also experienced what felt like fire burning in her abdomen. Since that day, the Holy Spirit has changed her life completely—spiritually, as well as physically. Today, she feels like a woman. She wears women's clothes and has let her hair grow. She has more self-confidence and has not shed another tear of pain. Odalis is happy because she now has inner peace.

A few months after her deliverance, her former partner came to one of our services and she, too, was delivered from the spirit of lesbianism, which had held her in bondage for forty years. Today, she feels like a child of God, with identity and purpose. The Father's love transformed her! Odalis now uses her own testimony to help other women walk away from the lesbian lifestyle and be delivered by the power of God.

Satan's defeat can be truly understood only from a kingdom perspective.

To live victoriously in difficult times and to spread the kingdom, bringing transformation to society, we need real power. When the Holy Spirit comes upon us and fills us, we are enabled to "explode" the dynamite power of God through manifestations that come from the invisible world to the visible world to meet the many needs of the people around us.

If Pentecost has come upon us, it should be the norm for us to manifest the power of the resurrection daily! Everyone can have a permanent Pentecost experience. In our ministry, if a demon manifests, we cast it out. If anyone is sick, we heal him through the power of God. You can do the same.

Receiving "Pentecost" without kingdom power is merely one more Christian experience.

Jesus' disciples were common people who did extraordinary deeds by the power they received in the upper room. The coming of the Holy Spirit was not just a historic event in the first century. It can take place in the here and now, if we have the faith to receive it. God is not looking for religious leaders, and He is not necessarily looking for "great Bible scholars" to build

His kingdom. He is looking for common people whose minds are open to the reality of His power and glory and who can bring these facets of His dominion from the invisible realm to the here and now—people who believe in His Word and act upon it.

"Pentecost" is the kingdom in motion here and now.

---

3. To Establish Order

Another purpose of demonstrating the kingdom is to restore the "territory" of a person or place to God's original design. Suppose someone suffers from scoliosis, and the power of God heals that person, straightening his back. With this act, God has restored the person's back to the way He originally intended it to be. He has reestablished the order of creation. The following is the testimony of a woman for whom God performed such a restoration.

Mafe Regetti's sense of smell had not operated for approximately twenty-one years. She had been shot in the right side of her head, and the bullet had become lodged in her frontal lobe, affecting normal neurological function and leading to her inability to detect smell. Then, Mafe attended a CAP Conference in Miami with the conviction that God's supernatural power would manifest in her life. During a ministry session, the glory of God descended over the meeting and, suddenly, she began to detect different smells all around her. She then confirmed her sense of smell with various perfumes and other scents. God had restored what had been damaged! Medical science had no solution for her problem, but God had given her wholeness by His supernatural power.

4. To Establish Kingdom Structure

I define the term *structure* as the process through which something is carried out or the way in which something is built. The Spirit of God establishes a structure for us in which to carry out God's works and build His kingdom. There is no order, or restoration of God's purposes, without structure. Structure must first be established for God's power to be used in the correct way. When His power is released on believers before they have been established in kingdom structure and context, or when the power comes upon believers who have forgotten its purpose, that power can become difficult to handle and therefore dangerous to have. I believe this is the reason why revivals eventually die out over time. For example, some of them end because the people involved fall into strife and division, and some end because the leaders succumb to sin.

What is the structure with which the Holy Spirit establishes and builds the kingdom? It is the structure of relationships—not rules, traditions, or statutes established by denominations or churches. Christianity is not a religion, but we have often turned it into one by being led by human criteria rather than by the Holy Spirit.

When the church was birthed, it was an organism—not an organization. What is the difference? The dictionary defines *organization* as an "association," "society," or "administrative and functional structure (as a business or a political party)." An *organism* is defined as "a complex structure of interdependent and subordinate elements whose relations and properties are largely determined by their function in the whole." There is nothing wrong with establishing an organization, as long as it is based on relationships.

The members of the church—the body of Christ—are meant to be interdependent as they exercise their stewardship of the power and presence of God's kingdom on earth. However, for the most part, the church has fragmented into a multitude of independent parts, so that it operates more like multiple organizations than one organism. This fragmentation prevents the Holy Spirit from moving as He did in the days of the early church. Today, when a spontaneous manifestation of God's glory descends upon a congregation, it must "submit" to the vote of the elders and deacons to see if it will be welcomed or not! It is incredible that God has to "ask permission" to manifest in His own church. This is like a steward or butler calling a meeting of the domestic staff to decide if they should allow the owner of the home to enter it, or what the owner is allowed to do on his own property.

When Jesus ministered on earth, He taught and established a flexible structure for the kingdom based on relationships. He said that the Father was in Him, and He was in the Father. (See John 17:21.) He told His disciples, *"I am the vine, you are the branches"* (John 15:5), *"If you abide in Me, and My words abide in you, you will ask what you desire, and it shall be done for you"* (John 15:7), and *"You know* [the Holy Spirit], *for He dwells with you and will be in you"* (John 14:17). Jesus prayed, *"That they* [His disciples] *all may be one, as You, Father, are in Me, and I in You"* (John 17:21). And Paul wrote, *"For as the body is one and has many members, but all the members of that one body, being many, are one body, so also is Christ"* (1 Corinthians 12:12). The kingdom of God is about relationships.

As the Administrator of the kingdom, the Holy Spirit is always moving; He doesn't adhere to rigid structures. Today's church is full of strict structures that cause people to act in independent ways rather than developing relationships through which the power of God can work. For instance, a spirit of independence can cause leaders to deal harshly with people instead of nurturing them. They can grow insensitive to other people's pain and, most seriously, to the voice of God.

I believe that patience and compassion are rare today. Ask yourself these questions: "Am I able to work with difficult people?" "Can I love people even when I feel negatively toward them?" If we don't establish a relational structure through the Holy Spirit, we will reject our fellow believers instead of working in unity with them. Sometimes, it seems that what keeps believers together despite their problems is the organization of a church or ministry, not the kingdom and its eternal purposes. When we have a kingdom mind-set, we recognize the worth of each person and his contribution to the body of Christ. We welcome the diverse people whom God has sent into our lives.

When Jesus ministered on earth, He taught and established a flexible structure for the kingdom based on relationships.

Therefore, we must endorse a flexible structure for God's kingdom on earth based on relationships, so that we may maintain the order He has established. Such a structure will include leaders who can uphold other pastors and believers by offering them the benefits and blessings of spiritual fatherhood and covering. I am aware of certain churches that do not function on the basis of relationships and who lack spiritual covering. As a result, the leaders feel alone and unprotected. They are missing the vision, training, and tools that would help them to establish the kingdom in their territory. This was the case for the pastor in the following testimony.

Pastor Guillermo Rubalcaba, from Mexico, has served God since he was very young. A few years ago, he started a small church in his backyard with only six people, and the congregation grew to 120. "My wife and I served with the desire to please God, but we lacked vision and identity. We knew nothing about spiritual fatherhood or the apostolic and prophetic ministries. We didn't know how to disciple people or how to increase our membership.

"Our church was founded on good intentions. We desired the supernatural, but we settled for having only praise and worship services and preaching—nothing beyond that. More people left the church than stayed. We felt alone and without support. We were a church with few resources: our building had a weak metal structure and a tent for a roof, and we sat on plastic chairs. One day, my wife dreamed that she had ascended to heaven to request payment, and she was asked, 'Under whose name are you registered?' Since we were not registered, they could not give us anything! We needed spiritual covering!

"During that time, we would watch Apostle Maldonado on television, and we admired his ministry, but we thought it was too far away. By a divine connection, we were invited to a meeting of his apostolic network. When we arrived, he prophesied to us and accepted us as his spiritual children. From that day, our personal lives began to change. God healed old wounds, and we no longer felt alone. The teachings we received impacted our lives. We received identity and began to implant vision in the church. After this, the church grew to 2,000 people. We established an apostolic government, and we now provide spiritual covering to two churches in Mexico and a House of Peace in Spain. Pastor Ana Maldonado prophesied that God would give us land for the church. Afterward, two pieces of land were donated!

"Furthermore, supernatural power for miracles was released, and the testimonies are too many to count. For example, Mario Gonzalez had a debt of half a million dollars because his accountant had not paid his taxes. We prayed, believing for the cancellation of the debt, and the miracle took place! First, he was notified that the debt had been reduced by half. A month later, he received notification that the rest of the debt had been canceled. He didn't have to pay anything.

"There is also the testimony of Joel, who was born with a heart defect. By the time he was fifteen, he could not walk, and it was hard for him to catch his breath. He had open-heart surgery, after which he was told there was nothing more that could be done. Joel was connected to an oxygen tank twenty-four hours a day and needed a wheelchair to get around. This was his life for ten years! One day, he heard me preach on the radio, and he attended one of our miracle crusades. After I prayed for him, he felt great heat, and he was shaking. Then, he removed his oxygen tank and felt air entering his lungs. He stood up from the wheelchair and walked! He was healed for the glory of God. Today, Joel lives a normal life. He serves in church and has gone back to school.

"Another case involved a woman named Guadalupe. When she went to the doctor to be treated for a stomachache, she was diagnosed with peritonitis and admitted to the hospital. After doing some tests, the doctors told her that her condition was worse than they had originally thought. Guadalupe's intestines were so swollen that they were protruding through her skin. Then, her stomach burst due to the pressure exerted on it from the intestines. When the doctors performed surgery, they discovered cancer, and they had to remove about five feet of her intestines. She was in a coma for fifteen days. She also had four additional surgeries and a colostomy. During the last surgery, the doctors noticed that her organs appeared blackened, as if they were rotten. Guadalupe's condition was terminal. The doctors stapled her abdomen closed, and she was sent home to die.

"During a miracle service, we anointed pieces of cloth with oil. Guadalupe's aunt took a piece and went to her niece's house, where she lay unconscious, and anointed her with it. When Guadalupe woke up, she testified that she felt peace and well-being. Within days, the swelling in her stomach went down, the staples came out by themselves, and the wound healed miraculously. God healed her! This is a powerful miracle! When she walked into the hospital for further testing, the doctors could not believe it. By their estimation, she should have been dead. They tested her and confirmed that all of her internal organs were healthy and cancer free!

Guadalupe had also been barren because she had no ovaries, but God created new ovaries. Today, she cradles her baby in her arms."

The fruit of Pastor Rubalcaba's ministry speaks for itself. Once he established a kingdom structure by coming under the covering of a spiritual father and reordering the relationships in his church according to kingdom principles, everything that had been held back was activated. Today, he pastors a church that is alive, prosperous, and full of supernatural power.

I know churches and ministries that have strong structures based on rules and laws but lack power. This is because they elevate order—founded on human ideas and purposes—as their supreme goal. If a structure is rigid, it will lead to extremes that prevent the Holy Spirit from moving. At that point, God will leave, and the only thing left will be formality. Every kingdom manifestation must be demonstrated within a structure of relational order and purpose.

It is dangerous to stay where God no longer is.

---

5. To Confront and Bind Satan and His Demons

Each time we cast out a demon, we bind the enemy. Satan is defeated when the power of the kingdom comes into a place and seizes the territory he has been occupying illegally. Some Christians confuse the power of God with dancing and yelling. As a result, if a demon were to manifest in someone nearby, they would have no idea how to cast it out. Their perception of the power of God dwelling within them through the Spirit is very limited! In fact, some Christians have the impression that if they rebuke a demon, it will jump on them and hurt them, similar to what happened to the itinerant Jewish exorcists, as recorded in Acts 19:13–16. This fear causes many people to reject the practice of casting out demons. In essence, some Christians have taken one incident from the book of Acts that depicts demons having the upper hand and have established it as a norm for believers. Yet those itinerant Jewish exorcists were not believers. They were operating according to their own initiative—not according to the power of Christ.

Most Christians who do accept the practice of casting out demons believe that it has to be done during special church services presided over by pastors or other spiritually prepared leaders. They either don't know or don't remember that the Bible says *they* have power and authority over the enemy. (See, for example, Luke 10:19.)

The subjugation of Satan always occurs in conjunction with the arrival of God's kingdom. When we don't understand the purpose of the king-dom, we overlook our ability to defeat the enemy, and we fail to cast out demons. The church is in a position to cast out demons because Jesus has already won the victory! We don't have to host an annual "miracle crusade" and bring in special preachers to cast out demons from people. We have the power of God within us. While the demons may first try to resist us, they have to flee when we expel them in the name of Jesus and the power of His Spirit.

6. To Bring Judgment and Mercy

Demonstrations of God's kingdom can bring either judgment or mercy, as people variously reject them or accept them. (See, for example, 2 Corinthians 2:15–16.) When Moses delivered the Israelites from slavery, the power of God brought judgment on Egypt and mercy to Israel—destruction for one and freedom for the other. It is important that the motivations of our hearts be pure, and that we be open to God when He moves in our midst, because we want His mercy rather than His judgment. And yet, when we are in Christ, there is mercy even in His chastisement of us. His mercies are new every morning. (See Lamentations 3:22–23.)

7. To Confirm That We Are Legitimate Witnesses of Christ

We believers are credible if we can produce the same spiritual fruit that the early church produced. God confirmed their testimony of the risen Christ with mighty demonstrations of His power. We can bring salvation to people when we ourselves have been saved. Similarly, I believe we will be able to deliver people when we ourselves have been delivered. We will be able to heal others when we ourselves have been healed. Our fruit will validate our testimony, wherever we are—at the office, at school, at the gro-cery store, anywhere. If we have not been delivered or healed of something, then we cannot be credible witnesses. But when we release the same power through which we have been delivered or healed, we can create a spiritual revolution.

Let me encourage you to begin at the beginning: tell people what happened to you the day you were born again. Next, tell people how you have changed since that day. No one else can communicate your testimony like you. I cannot testify to your experience because it did not happen to me. Only you can speak with absolute certainty about how you have been transformed. When you do, the power of God will manifest, because you will be a legitimate witness. Decide to share your testimony today—right now!

The more you respond in faith to the revelation God gives you, thereby experiencing His presence and power, the more you will grow in your ability to testify with manifestations of the kingdom to support your words. Refuse to settle for giving ineffective testimonies. Show people a demonstration of the power of God that dwells within you so that they, too, can be transformed, healed, and delivered!

8. To Establish Kingdom Expansion by Spiritual Force

The kingdom cannot be established without forceful demonstrations of the power of God. As we have seen, such power is necessary to uproot and cast out the kingdom of darkness from a person or a place. In chapter 10, we will look more closely at how to establish kingdom expansion by spiritual force. Then, whenever we encounter someone in need, God can speak to us and lead us to manifest His transforming power—here and now!

If you are willing to commit to demonstrating God's kingdom, please pray the following:

Dear Jesus, I recognize You as my Lord and Savior. I am willing and available to go and demonstrate Your kingdom here and now. I ask You to give me Your supernatural grace to take risks and be bold in order to manifest Your power and glory. I ask Your Holy Spirit to come upon me and empower me now to do the works of the kingdom. Lord Jesus, by faith, wherever I go—to my school, to my job, to a restaurant, to a sporting event, to the mall, on a vacation trip, or anywhere else—I will pray for the sick, the oppressed, and the captives, and I will deliver them in Your name. Those who haven't received salvation or the baptism in the Holy Spirit will receive it by Your power! I submit my will and my heart to You right now. In Your name, amen.

10

Kingdom Expansion by Spiritual Force

G od gave human beings two global commands. The first was to exercise dominion over the earth, which Adam and Eve did not carry out. After Jesus resurrected, He gave the church the Great Commission of expanding God's kingdom on earth—extending its borders and frontiers and exploring new territories, dimensions, and realms. (See, for example, Matthew 28:18–20.) As the church fulfills the mission of the second command, it also returns to exercising dominion over the world.

Jesus Gave Us a Global Vision

Of the increase of His [Jesus'] *government and peace there will be no end....* (Isaiah 9:7)

Jesus exhorted the apostles to go the whole world with the gospel of the kingdom. (See Mark 16:15.) Through the power of God, Jesus' followers had an effect on many aspects of their society in just a short time—without modern communications systems like television, radio, or the Internet. One reason they pushed to expand the kingdom was that they believed Jesus would return within a short period of time. The apostles preached each sermon as if He were coming the next day, and they did it with the fear of the Lord. They operated in holy zeal, and they proclaimed the gospel with righteousness and demonstrations of kingdom power.

Many people responded to their message of salvation through Christ and wholeheartedly surrendered their lives to God.

If we know how to interpret the signs of the times, we will recognize that Jesus will soon be returning, because evil has multiplied and the hearts of many people have grown cold. (See Matthew 24:12.) Expanding God's kingdom throughout the earth is an urgent matter! On September 11, 2001, when the Twin Towers in New York City were attacked and destroyed, many people ran back to the church, afraid that the end of the world was near. When we see judgments, earthquakes, tsunamis, and more, we must proclaim the kingdom of God with true conviction and demonstrations of His power. Manifestations from the invisible world will cause people to develop a hunger for the things of God—a genuine desire to worship Him, to seek holiness, to overcome sin, and to become vessels through which He shows His presence and power on earth. They will have a passion to reveal the living Christ to others in a tangible way.

We Must Have a Revelation to Go to All the World

The early church proclaimed the gospel with remarkable results. However, most of the believers stayed within a limited sphere for the first few years. Many of them were situated in Jerusalem, growing in numbers and perhaps thinking that this would give them political strength in the eyes of Rome.

What were they doing in Jerusalem when their commission was to go to the whole world? Looking at their situation from a contemporary perspective, perhaps they were waiting to mature a bit more or to have one more deliverance session. Maybe they thought they should acquire more spiritual knowledge and experience, and so they were taking discipleship classes and leadership courses and attending conferences and meetings. It could be that they were collecting offerings to make sure they had enough funds to cover their travel expenses. Or, perhaps they were waiting for their children to get married or for the time when they could comfortably retire from their jobs.

I believe the early Christians stayed where they were because they lacked the revelation to go—the revelation that the Great Commission was global. It was to start in Jerusalem, but then it was to extend to Judea, Samaria, and the whole world. The same lack of revelation is hindering the church from fulfilling its mandate today. Believers are holding back for all of the reasons I mentioned above—and more. Apparently, many of us do not feel spiritually ready to proclaim the gospel of the kingdom with visible manifestations. In the meantime, the world remains lost, and people are dying and going to hell.

There may be periods in our lives when we will need to take time out to focus on building Christlike character. Yet, for the most part, character and the exercise of spiritual power grow together. Sometimes, people say, "I will ask God to fill me with power when my character is mature enough to receive it." However, if we wait until we are "mature" before we demonstrate the kingdom, we will never be ready, because there will always be one more thing in our lives that needs to change.

If we are in the place spiritually where we can receive God's revelation, power, and glory and demonstrate them with visible manifestations, our lives will surely change. What we really need is a revelation of Jesus' global commandment. As we discussed in the previous chapter, we are baptized in the Spirit for the purpose of receiving power—and we receive power to enable us to go and demonstrate God's kingdom in the now!

If you are waiting for your character to be fully mature before you go to the world with the gospel of the kingdom, you will never be ready to go.

We are citizens of God's domain, kings and priests who rule on earth from the heavenly realm, representatives and ambassadors of the kingdom. Christ commanded us to be concerned with the world, not just the immediate circle of our family, friends, and church. The enemy wants to keep us contained so that we won't reach out in ever-expanding ways. To extend God's domain, the church as a whole must function like a kingdom embassy in every town, city, and nation as we go to every tribe, race, and ethnic group in the world.

When you have an encounter, or experience, with the power of God, it will transform you within and without.

Moving from Occupation to Expansion

Now Saul was consenting to [Stephen's] death. At that time a great persecution arose against the church which was at Jerusalem; and they were all scattered throughout the regions of Judea and Samaria, except the apostles. (Acts 8:1)

Most of the believers in the early church stayed in Jerusalem until strong persecution came, forcing many of them to flee the city. It was then that they began to carry out the global plan that Jesus had given them.

It has never been God's intention for us to just "occupy" the earth or exist on it. His plan has always been for us to actively extend His kingdom. Spiritually speaking, it is unhealthy to settle in one place and feel that you have arrived. The instant you settle for that place, you stop advancing because when your passion declines, you begin to die.

Expansion is vital for the advancement of the kingdom of God. And expansion is a process. God did not give the Promised Land to the Israelites all at once, because the people could not occupy all the territory immediately. He gave them whatever territory the soles of their feet touched. (See Deuteronomy 11:24; Joshua 1:3.) This is how He positioned them for expansion. He will do the same for us.

The purpose of war is victory. The purpose of victory is occupation. And the purpose of occupation is expansion.

Then [Elisha] said, "Take the arrows"; so [King Joash] took them. And he said to the king of Israel, "Strike the ground"; so he struck three times, and stopped. And the man of God was angry with him, and said, "You should have struck five or six times; then you would have struck Syria till you had destroyed it! But now you will strike Syria only three times." (2 Kings 13:18–19)

The prophet Elisha had wanted the king of Israel to strike the ground five or six times, but he struck it only three times. As a result, he gained only three temporal victories over his enemy. His error cost him a complete breakthrough against the enemy nation. King Joash did not have enough passion to carry the anointing that God wanted to give him.

If a leader loses his passion for expansion, it will cost him his ministry, his business, his organization—whatever he rules over.

Anointing and passion go together because when we have passion, we strike with all our strength and take risks in order to expand. When we move into a new realm, we typically face all types of problems and inconveniences, and we will not be able to obtain the victory if we are simply trusting in past victories. We have to fight fervently to enter into all that God has given us. *"We must through many tribulations enter the kingdom of God"* (Acts 14:22).

We were born for expansion! Every human empire has had to fight to conquer new territories. Are you willing to do as much for God's kingdom? As we have seen, when we stop moving forward in God, we become spiritually stagnant. We stay at the same level, with the same measure of faith, so we stop being transformed *"from glory to glory"* (2 Corinthians 3:18). Are you willing to push forward so that you may enter into greater dimensions of anointing, glory, power, authority, financial provision, revelation, and more? Are you willing to expand the influence of your family, ministry, business, or organization through revelation for the sake of the kingdom of God? Decide today!

God will always ask us to expand—even if we think we have a successful ministry or abundant wealth or a peaceful community to live in. The poverty mentality says, "It is enough," but God wants us to extend and multiply the kingdom without delay. An expanded and multiplied kingdom gives glory to God as *El Shaddai*, "the Almighty" (STRONG, H7706).

Every kingdom principle is rooted in the law of increase and multiplication.

Pastor Guillermo Jiménez had a congregation of 1,500 in Las Vegas. Many pastors would have been satisfied with a church of that size, but he and his wife knew that something was missing from their ministry. After several years of maintaining the same number of members, they visited our ministry seeking help to overcome their stagnancy.

"We were an active and motivated congregation but also very methodical," Pastor Jiménez said. "When I met Apostle Maldonado, the first thing he said to me was, 'You need the supernatural power of God.' After we received spiritual covering and were activated in this power, the congregation grew to 3,500 in three years. There was great enthusiasm among the people to win souls and train leaders. We have introduced classes for new believers, formed mentorships for the purpose of discipleship, and established miracle services, deliverance retreats, and a school for leaders. We have learned to conduct spiritual warfare and to pray—we have over 100 intercessors. During a financial crisis, we decided to obey God and build a 50,000-square-foot modern building. It is completely paid for because the tithes and offerings from church members doubled.

"Since we adopted this vision, we have faced criticism and opposition. Some congregations refuse to accept the supernatural, but it is worth moving forward. The ministry has gained a certain reputation. Pastors from other churches visit us to learn about and be activated in the supernatural power of God. The Supernatural Fivefold Ministry School and CAP have been a great help. Every time we take our associate pastors and leaders to these conferences, they return on fire, activated, and aligned with the vision of the church and the pastors. We are grateful for these events that equip those who truly want to learn. The city of Las Vegas is being impacted by the supernatural power of God!"

All this has taken place because one pastor refused to conform to a number and decided to move beyond his comfort zone, knowing that God's mandate is ongoing expansion.

Today, much of the church seems afraid to expand into territories it has never been to before. This reluctance among believers is a great challenge to leaders. Yet, if a leader wants to move people into a greater dimension, he must already have gone there himself.

When someone teaches and demonstrates a truth,
it is because he has experienced it.

It is often said that the best defense is a good offense. To expand the kingdom means to go on the offensive—continually entering territories that are in the grip of the enemy as we start new churches, ministries, businesses, and other ventures that demonstrate God's supernatural power. It means to always be moving forward and aggressively attacking the kingdom of darkness. Then, the gates of hell will not prevail against us. (See Matthew 16:18.) We cannot wait for the enemy to assault us before we take action against him. Instead, we are to be in permanent "attack mode."

The operative mode of the kingdom is offense,
because the kingdom is continually expanding.

Expanding Our Eden Here and Now

At the same time that God blessed the first human beings, He gave them the mandate to multiply and have dominion over the earth: *"God blessed them, and God said to them, 'Be fruitful and multiply; fill the earth and subdue it; have dominion…'"* (Genesis 1:28). To bless means to affirm and to empower with the ability to succeed. This means that expansion and dominion are the first signs that God has blessed us. He releases His blessings in stages of increase: thirty, then sixty, then one hundred. (See, for example, Mark 4:8.)

God gave Adam the territory of Eden from which to expand and fill the earth. Likewise, He will give each of us our own "Eden," which represents the territory, grace, anointing, favor, measure, realm, authority, power, finances, gifts, talents, influence, and more that we are called to exercise and expand. Depending on our faithfulness and our stewardship of what He has given us, He will increase our blessings or take them away.

Our faithfulness and stewardship determine
the level to which our blessings will increase.

How do we know we need God's increase? When He calls us to a vision that is beyond ourselves, that surpasses our current level of blessing, and that is for the purpose of expanding the kingdom. If we are continually on the offensive in terms of spiritual growth and movement, God will give us the increase. His responsibility as a Father is to give us what we need. When He gives us more than that, it is for the purpose of blessing others with it. If we want increase solely for the purpose of supplying our own needs (or wants), and nothing more, God will not grant it, because that is not a good enough reason in His eyes—it does not align with His character and His kingdom purposes. Often, the church's mind-set is to keep what it has, but those who are operating according to a kingdom mentality will invest and multiply everything God gives them.

Increase comes while we are in the process of expanding the kingdom.

Jesus taught the following parable to illustrate how we are stewards of the resources God gives us.

> For the kingdom of heaven is like a man traveling to a far country, who called his own servants and delivered his goods to them. And to one he gave five talents, to another two, and to another one, to each according to his own ability; and immediately he went on a journey.
>
> (Matthew 25:14–15)

A steward is one who administers the assets of another; he is not the owner of the assets. In the parable of the talents, the money did not belong to the servants; they were merely the managers of it, and their faithfulness and stewardship were tested. (See verses 16–30.) Whenever we feel that we own our gifts, money, ministry, or anything else that God has given us, we usually do not want to give back anything to Him from the results they produce. Yet, when we acknowledge that we are God's stewards, it is easier for us to give His "goods" back to Him and to invest them in further service.

I believe that as we expand the kingdom, our first rule of business is to be good stewards of our time. In the passage from Matthew 25, the owner gave each of the three servants a business mandate, and *"after a long time"* (verse 19), he returned to settle his accounts. In a similar way, God will come to us during certain seasons of our lives and ask, "What have you done with what I gave you?" We are meant to multiply and expand what we have, *"each according to his own ability"* (Matthew 25:15). "According to our own ability" doesn't necessarily mean that we will accomplish less if we have less ability. Those who use what they are given are given more— God may grant us additional abilities and resources. Moreover, He is not limited by our human abilities. He gives supernatural power to each of us, including the *"power to get wealth"* (Deuteronomy 8:18).

The servant in the parable who received one talent didn't do anything with it. Instead, he buried it, and when his master discovered this, he said, *"You wicked and lazy servant,…you ought to have deposited my money with the bankers"* (Matthew 25:26–27). The servant was unproductive and worthless because he never tried to be a good steward of what he had been given. He didn't even try to gain interest with the money. The owner was very hard on this servant. Not only that, but he also ordered the following:

> *Therefore take the talent from him, and give it to him who has ten talents. For to everyone who has, more will be given, and he will have abundance; but from him who does not have, even what he has will be taken away.* (Matthew 25:28–29)

We must multiply what God gives us. Otherwise, we will lose it.

We should not take for granted what the Lord has given us. If we merely hold on to it, never exercising it or increasing it, we will lose it. It will be given to someone else who *will* use and multiply it. I have seen evidence of this principle throughout my years of ministry. I know leaders, ministries, and churches that once had anointing, revelation, abundant finances, favor, grace, and much more, but, after a time, they lost it all because they failed to be good stewards of those blessings. God judged them and gave their blessings to those who would invest them and gain increase through them. We cannot live in the kingdom without producing increase.

Regardless of how many excuses we give the Lord for not getting a return on what He has given us, the result will always be the same. People hide behind the excuses of fear, lack of time, the idea that God expects too much of them, an insistence that numbers aren't everything, and so forth. However, no matter what diverse callings and territories God has given us—we may be farmers, pastors, lawyers, doctors, mechanics, artists, scientists, or businesspeople—we must always yield dividends for the kingdom.

The excess God gives is to be used to expand His kingdom.

Thus says the LORD, your Redeemer, the Holy One of Israel: "I am the LORD your God, who teaches you to profit, who leads you by the way you should go."   (Isaiah 48:17)

God's kingdom never has a deficit; it always has a surplus. If we start a business, only to end up with an operating deficit, we are not kingdom businesspeople. This doesn't mean we won't have financial challenges and even temporary setbacks. However, if we don't take the initiative to invest what we have and to expand, God will essentially say, "Take away from the one who fails to produce and give to the one who yields dividends."

It works the same way in the realm of ministry. We must continually expand by winning souls, making disciples, healing the sick, delivering the oppressed, and helping those who are in need. Regardless of the size of your church, it is never enough for the kingdom! God's heart is for the whole world, for the globalization of His gospel. Years ago, most of my conferences operated at a loss, until God taught me the principle of dividends, or return: I must produce "earnings," not only financially but also in souls saved, disciples trained, revelation imparted, and anointing exercised, in order to continue investing in the expansion of the kingdom. When I followed this principle—relying on the Holy Spirit to bring about these results as I moved forward—I stopped experiencing loss.

The three levels of God's provision are:
sufficient, abundant, and superabundant.

Pursue Your Purpose, and Your Needs Will Be Provided

The parable of the minas (see Luke 19:12–27) is another illustration about "doing business" in the kingdom: "[A nobleman] *called ten of his servants, delivered to them ten minas, and said to them, 'Do business till I come'"* (Luke 19:13). People in the world know how to make a profit, and companies expect their employees to be productive. Paradoxically, much of the church doesn't have a mind-set of increase, even though its mission is one of expansion.

Kingdom expansion requires that we pursue our purpose in God rather than focus on our personal needs. When people become preoccupied with their needs, they often develop a mind-set of limitation and poverty. Jesus already paid for our physical, emotional, material, and spiritual needs at the cross. God supplies everything we need through Christ and gives us abundant provision as we seek first His kingdom.

When we find our purpose, we find our prosperity.

This reminds me of a powerful testimony from a Supernatural Fivefold Ministry School held at our church in Miami. Paul Galindo from Los Angeles had started his own company, called Go Green Consultants, to provide ways to use alternative energy through natural sources. His business was going very well, and his contracts were worth millions of dollars. Then, Paul lost everything when someone in the company embezzled the money. He became discouraged and wanted to give up. At the same time, his father, a pastor of a church in California, suffered a heart attack, and Paul had to step into his ministry to help out. A woman told him about my ministry and gave him my books and teaching CDs. He received the impartation of revelation knowledge through these materials and wanted more, so he came to the Supernatural Fivefold Ministry School.

At the conference, I released a word of knowledge that there were businesspeople in attendance who were currently in the process of signing multimillion-dollar contracts, but lawyers were getting in the way. Paul had indeed been in the middle of negotiating a contract for a little over $18 million, but it had been canceled because of lawyers. Suddenly, I noticed Paul in the meeting and asked Dr. Renny McLean to prophesy over him. Dr. Renny told him that he was in a transition process and needed to keep his hands clean and to take care of himself. A short time later, Paul received a call from an investor who told him, "I don't know what it is about you, Paul, but I am going to invest in your project!" And a contract was signed for one million dollars!

Once Paul returned to Los Angeles, many doors began to open for him, and he was able to sign an $18-million-dollar contract! Paul said, "When you're on fire for God, the money becomes irrelevant. If I had received the breakthrough before the conference, I would've left the ministry for the business. The prophetic word transformed my heart. I am more excited about what God will do than about how much money I will gain." Now, Paul invests his business profits in expanding the kingdom, because he understands that it was for this purpose that God performed such amazing financial miracles for him.

Many people are happy just to be members of a church, but God's great purpose is that we should be His kings on earth, ruling and expanding into new territories for His kingdom.

We will know when we are operating in the right territory and dominion because we will be productive.

The Enemy's Plan to Contain the Kingdom

Satan has a plan of containment to stop the advancement of God's kingdom, and he is always implementing it in some way. This means that we are in a continuous war against a spirit of suppression. We should not be surprised when every forward movement we make for the kingdom is countered by difficulties, obstacles, and persecution. The enemy will try to bind us and hold us back. He will confine us to one place, situation, or circumstance—in our personal lives, our ministry, our business, or any other arena where we are actively involved in extending the kingdom. We must learn to counteract this opposition.

Have you been spinning your wheels in one place for a long time? Do you feel restricted? Have you lost the vision you once had for your life? Have you seen your finances, business, or ministry begin to decline? Are you feeling stagnant? It is dangerous to be where God is not—this is why we must continue advancing, no matter what the cost.

If you have reached a point in your life where you have come up against an immovable wall, perhaps you think you have done something wrong. It is always important for us to check our motivations and to ask God to reveal anything for which we need to repent. Yet, it may just be that Satan has constructed a wall in order to contain the advancement of the kingdom that you are making or are about to make. This is when you need a spiritual breakthrough.

First, you must learn to detect the main schemes of Satan's plan of containment and how to deactivate them. Primarily, the enemy tries to confine us by tempting us to succumb to complacency and passivity.

+ *Complacency* refers to self-gratification—pleasing the desires of the flesh or seeking personal gain with egocentrism and selfishness.

+ *Passivity* refers to the state of being totally indifferent when evil takes over. It is an attitude of tolerance in which we allow the enemy to gain ground for his kingdom of darkness, never doing anything about it. (See, for example, Revelation 3:16.)

A brother in our church had to fight hard against the enemy's schemes to contain him. "I was facing bankruptcy and the loss of a million dollars," he said. "Some weeks, I wouldn't even earn a dollar. I was desperate and even thought about taking my own life. One Sunday, all I had was forty dollars, and I gave them as an offering at church. During the service, the apostle called to the altar the businessman who had lost everything. I went forward immediately, and he prophesied, saying, 'The Lord says that at the beginning of next year, He will return to you everything that the devil has stolen.' The enemy wanted to stop me because he knew that my desire was to provide for the advancement of the kingdom.

"Time passed, and we were tested emotionally and financially. The enemy would always whisper in our ears not to return to church and to leave it all behind. He would tempt me to take my own life. But we persevered by serving and by giving offerings—often giving what we didn't have. At the beginning of the year, one of my businesses began to grow supernaturally. We went from invoicing $300 a week to $15,000 a week. Shortly afterward, another business of mine, which had gone dry even though we had tried everything, began to bring in $5,000 a month without much effort. We started to sell via the Internet, and, overnight, our profits came to $10,000 a month. We were constantly running low on inventory because the volume of sales was greater than our purchases. This was completely supernatural!

"A year later, while I was praying for creative ideas, God gave me the idea to form a company that would do business between the United States and Latin America. I joined two other corporations, and we literally went from zero to $100,000 per month in sales. We know this is a miracle from God because we had tried everything in our own strength, without Him, and had spent much money to no avail, and we had lost it all." This brother broke through the enemy's plan of containment by his faithfulness to God, his covenants, his prayers, his offerings, and his hard work. He did not give up but persevered until he experienced the breakthrough he needed.

Spiritual Breakthrough Is the Key to Expansion

We can begin to deactivate Satan's schemes and experience spiritual breakthrough by discovering the answers to two essential questions: "What is a spiritual breakthrough?" and "Why do we need spiritual breakthroughs?" Then, we must learn the steps to personally receive a spiritual breakthrough.

What Is a Spiritual Breakthrough?

A breakthrough is a sudden intervention of God that takes us through—and beyond—whatever is preventing us from crossing over into new territory for the kingdom. Receiving a breakthrough requires a "breakthrough anointing," or a "spirit of might," from God, which enables us to increase, multiply, expand, or enlarge what He has given us.

> *Finally, my brethren, be strong in the Lord and in the power of His might.* (Ephesians 6:10)

The word *"might"* in the above verse is translated from the Greek word *ischys*, meaning "forcefulness." In addition to "might," *ischys* indicates "ability," "power," and "strength" (STRONG, G2479). This concept of might can be compared to the military strength and resources of a great nation. A "breakthrough anointing" or a "spirit of might" uses the strength of the kingdom of heaven and its almighty God, whose arsenal, strategies, and advance forces are deployed to destroy the enemy's plan of containment and extend the territory of the kingdom on earth.

"*Samson said: '…With the jawbone of a donkey I have slain a thousand men!'*" (Judges 15:16). Samson was a judge and warrior in the Old Testament. When the spirit of might came upon him, he was able to kill a thousand enemy Philistines with only a jawbone, as well as to carry away on his shoulders heavy city gates and to push down massive columns in the Philistine temple, killing three thousand additional Philistines. (See Judges 16:2–3, 21–30.) When he operated under God's power, he could not be contained. God will give us the strength to remove and destroy the walls of sickness, poverty, and oppression that try to contain us.

The power of God in the area of spiritual warfare is called "might."

Why Do We Need Spiritual Breakthroughs?

We need spiritual breakthroughs because only God can shatter the limitations that Satan imposes on us, releasing us from what binds us. The enemy entraps us so that, even if we move, we never advance—like a person jogging on a treadmill or a hamster running on a wheel. Our efforts are futile, and we are continually frustrated. Until God intervenes with a supernatural event, we aren't able to cross over into new territories for the kingdom or progress to the next level of faith.

When we fight with utter futility against something, it testifies of our weakness. Only God can disarm what binds us and holds us back.

Henry and Claudia González are pastors of a church in Colombia. When they attended our Supernatural Fivefold Ministry School, their leadership was passive, and they felt spiritually weak. People seemed to leave their church as fast as they came, so their congregation was not growing. They also had been unable to break through in the area of miracles. In the Fivefold Ministry School, they received spiritual fatherhood and covering for their church. This resulted in a radical transformation in their ministry. They started with 600 people, and 120 of them left the church. However, after that, the congregation grew to more than 1,000 members with the addition of new believers. The church continues to grow, and the congregation's spiritual gifts have been activated. Furthermore, the church was able to pay off its mortgage in only six months!

During their regular services, God heals people who are suffering from cancer, leukemia, pulmonary disease, and many other sicknesses. One of the miracles that had the greatest impact was the resurrection of an eight-year-old named Denis hours after he was declared dead. His father had taken him to the doctor because he was complaining of pain in his leg. He was diagnosed with a malignant tumor on his femur. After further testing, the medical personnel discovered that his lungs had also been affected. The hospital called for a medical consultation, and they decided the femur had to be replaced. During the surgery, a complication arose, causing significant blood loss. The boy went into shock and died in the operating room. Two hours after all of Denis's vital signs had disappeared, the orthopedic surgeon, who was a Christian, prayed for him and rebuked the spirit of death. To the glory of God, he came back to life! Denis testified that while he was dead, he could see himself floating through the clouds with God the Father. New tests revealed that the metastasis in his lungs had reversed. God had not only breathed life back into Denis but also healed him of cancer.

Another remarkable testimony was reported by a member of their church whose brother had crashed his motorcycle against a car and died instantly. The man prayed for his brother, rebuking the spirit of death, and the man resurrected! There was also the miraculous healing of a child with autism who spent his days rocking back and forth, apparently unaware of reality. A week after this boy received the impartation of the supernatural power of God, he was walking, eating on his own, and in full contact with reality. In addition, a leader in the church prayed for a twenty-day-old baby who had been born with cancer, and the baby is now healthy! Praise God!

As part of their church's multiplication, Henry and Claudia González have planted seven churches on donated land. At one of those locations, they had a warlock for a neighbor. The pastors decreed that the warlock would leave in one month. After a month, the wife and son of the warlock came to Christ, and, a month later, the warlock was also saved. Today, he is a transformed man, free of witchcraft.

These pastors testify, "Spiritual fatherhood released the inheritance of the supernatural and gave us security in God's purpose for our lives. It uprooted from us and from the church the passivity, the discouragement, and everything else that was holding us back, and it established His kingdom in our territory."

The enemy tries to deceive us by keeping us focused on our problems and adversities. He wants our circumstances to become our reality because, that way, we will further empower the negative situations as we repeatedly confess them. He wants us to forget that all circumstances are temporary and have an "expiration date." (See, for example, 1 Peter 1:6–7.) Your difficulty has an expiration date because your breakthrough exists beyond time; it is supernatural and is brought forth by faith.

If we focus on our circumstances,
we will never know how far we are meant to go.

Steps to Receiving a Spiritual Breakthrough

Many people want a spiritual breakthrough because they are unhappy about a particular situation in their lives. However, receiving a breakthrough requires more than just a desire to activate God's spirit of might in order to destroy Satan's wall of containment. We must take the following steps:

1. Refuse to Tolerate the Situation

We must overcome the passivity and compliance in our lives if we are to fight back against the enemy. When we become sick and tired of a certain situation—when we realize that enough is enough and we choose not to tolerate the circumstance any longer—we will desperately seek God. We will recognize that we are at the end of our own strength and ability and will rely only on His. This is what happened with the ten lepers whom Jesus healed, particularly the Samaritan leper who came back to thank Jesus and give glory to God. (See Luke 17:11–19.) If lepers can say "This is enough," make a decision to live, and seek deliverance from God, why can't we? When we find ourselves in bondage to a problem, habit, addiction, or difficulty, we must begin to say, "Enough! It ends here! No more! This was the last time!"

2. Be Filled with Righteous Indignation

When King David was a young man, he was filled with righteous indignation against the enemy of Israel, so he challenged Goliath, the Philistine giant, killing him with God's spirit of might. (See 1 Samuel 17:26, 32.) When three Hebrew young men who were living in exile in Babylon were threatened with their lives if they did not practice idol worship, they were filled with holy zeal, and they declared to the king that they would not worship false gods or kneel before the golden image. God rescued them after they were thrown into a fiery furnace, and He also silenced their enemies and gave them favor with the king. (See Daniel 3:13–30.) Similarly, when we are confronted by sickness, financial lack, marital discord, sin, bondage, or anything else that threatens to destroy us, then we, too, can be overcomers and receive our breakthroughs by responding in righteous indignation. The enemy knows when we are serious and full of holy zeal, just as our children know when we are serious and will not allow them to overstep their boundaries.

3. Exercise "Spiritual Violence"

When we seek God, and He gives us the spirit of might, or breakthrough anointing, we must begin to push forward what has been contained. We are to become spiritually violent, not physically violent. We are to become angry with the devil and his demons, not with God or other people. Otherwise, our violence will neither be from God nor be holy. Holy indignation fights against injustice, sickness, poverty, depression and all the other works of the devil.

> *From the days of John the Baptist until now the kingdom of heaven suffers violence, and the violent take it by force.* (Matthew 11:12)

A more literal translation of this verse might read, "From the days of John the Baptist until now, the kingdom of heaven has been governed by force, and only those in power control it." God is in control of everything, but He has given us authority and power to exercise dominion in the territory to which He has assigned us. Why do we need to be *"violent"* in our governance? Because we are in a constant war with the kingdom of darkness, fighting over who will have dominion over various territories on earth—whether physical places, people, or areas of influence. God has given dominion to His people, and dominion is the highest territorial power. This is the reason Satan has fought against human beings from the beginning of creation and why he continues to fight against them to this day.

Jesus taught us that to defeat the *"strong man,"* or Satan, we must bind him. (See, for example, Matthew 12:29.) We begin to do this is by confessing Jesus Christ as the Lord of our lives, because the phrase "Jesus is Lord" is a territorial expression—the word *Lord* meaning absolute authority and Master.

To establish your authority in any place, you must always declare the name of Jesus.

Let us now take a closer look at the implications of Matthew 11:12:

+ **"From the days of John the Baptist until now…"**: John the Baptist was the first one to preach the gospel of the kingdom. The battle against the realm of darkness started then and has continued throughout all succeeding generations.

+ **"The kingdom of heaven suffers violence…"**: Why would the kingdom of heaven suffer violence? Every time we manifest the kingdom by rebuking an illness, delivering someone from the bondage of drugs, or setting someone free from mental or emotional trauma, we win back a territory for Christ and remove the kingdom of darkness. As we have seen, when we begin to take dominion over a territory where Satan has been ruling, he will fight back. Moreover, when the enemy loses a territory, he will never give up trying to retake it. This is why we must always be alert to his schemes and resist his attacks. (See Luke 11:24–26.)

+ **"The violent take it by force"**: The kingdom of God is not advanced by timid, passive, or weak people who have settled for doing nothing. Earlier, we learned that the devil has spread a lie throughout the church that we aren't responsible for doing anything because Jesus has already accomplished it all on the cross. Many people believe that

God gives us everything for free, without the need for any effort on our part. It is certainly true that God gives us grace in Christ, which is indispensible for forgiveness and for receiving all His blessings. We don't deserve our redemption, and we never could pay for it. However, if we are to possess everything that Jesus won for us, we must still fight the enemy in the power of God's might! When we received Jesus, He gave us His Spirit, His strength, and His supernatural weapons to retake what Satan has stolen from us—establishing the kingdom of God by spiritual force.

If we want a breakthrough, therefore, we must be militant in exercising kingdom principles. This is a spiritual matter, and it applies to all of us—whether our natural personality is to be assertive or quiet. Passivity will leave us spiritually wounded instead of securing our breakthroughs. We must be ruthless with the enemy—he wants to destroy us! Demonic strongholds will tremble and fall away as we push against them in God's power.

There are some people who have learned how to break bricks with their hands or feet. They are able to do this because they see beyond the bricks. Likewise, we must be able to see beyond our circumstances in order to break through them. To use another illustration, a hen does not facilitate the birth of her baby chicks by breaking the outsides of the shells in which they are encased. The chicks themselves must break free by pecking at the insides of the shells with their beaks. Otherwise, they will not gain the strength they need to live once they are outside of the shell. Similarly, we are the ones who must push against the enemy's containment! But God gives us His strength by the indwelling Holy Spirit to enable us to do this. In the process, we will grow stronger to fulfill our role in the kingdom.

Until the spirit of might descends upon us, we will not be able to push through the enemy's walls of containment.

To be spiritually violent doesn't necessarily mean to make a lot of noise or to yell at the top of our lungs. It means to exercise God's authority and power. Jesus was the most compassionate Man who ever walked the earth, but He was also the most spiritually violent through the power of the Spirit. He was strong and firm, and He never tolerated religiosity, sin, sickness, or death. Likewise, God's spirit of might will come upon us, empowering us to aggressively push past the things that have kept us stagnant. In the Scriptures, we see that when the spirit of might came upon the Israelites after they entered the Promised Land, the walls of Jericho came down (see Joshua 6:20), and when the spirit of might came upon the apostle Paul, he rebuked the spirit of divination (see Acts 16:16–18). For each breakthrough we experience, spiritual violence will be manifested.

We can seize and control territory for the kingdom when we have power, but we cannot exercise power unless we are under spiritual authority. This is a kingdom principle. The key is obedience! No one can expand the kingdom by force, casting out demons and healing the sick, unless he submits to kingdom government, and the devil knows this well. He recognizes those who speak with the weight of authority and those who don't.

Authority is something that must be recognized and received.

Today, in some Christian circles, people argue among themselves about the proper method to cast out demons. As a result, when demons manifest, it usually takes a long time for them to be driven away. In the early church, the casting out of demons was accomplished quickly and efficiently, because the demons recognized the government of God in Jesus' disciples. The demons were forced to obey, knowing that the disciples spoke in the name of the King of Kings.

This is why, to expand the kingdom, we must establish the authority of God in our homes, businesses, churches, ministries, communities, and nations. If we do not establish God's authority and submit to His superior rule, we have no legal right to exercise His power. When the enemy doesn't see God's government in us, he challenges our authority and refuses to leave. Could this be the reason he often won't go when we tell him to? Could it be that we have granted him the legal right to remain because we are not submitted to God and His delegated human authorities? Let us therefore submit to God and advance His kingdom with authority and force.

If you are not in submission, you are not in government.

4. Offer Glorious, Spontaneous Praise to God

"Sing, O barren, you who have not borne! Break forth into singing, and cry aloud, you who have not labored with child! For more are the children of the desolate than the children of the married woman," says the LORD. (Isaiah 54:1)

Like the barren woman depicted in the above verse, many people are not producing fruit in various areas of their lives due to a spirit of infertility that is robbing them of expansion and blessing. For example, each time they are about to find a job, close a business deal, get married, or finish an important project, a spirit of barrenness or miscarriage causes them to lose their blessing. The solution to fruitlessness is spiritual breakthrough, and the final step in the process of receiving breakthrough is to offer glorious, spontaneous praise to God.

Rejoice, give shouts of jubilee, offer God exuberant praise, sing a new song to the Lord! We must praise God in the midst of our pain, even if it seems abnormal to do so. As we seek a breakthrough, the process doesn't have to make sense to our human reason, because reason doesn't produce faith. The kingdom principle here is to invade the kingdom of darkness through songs that are inspired by God's Spirit. This manifestation of the Spirit can come upon us suddenly. I'm not referring to the regular songs we often sing in church, although we may begin with those songs. I am referring to what I call "sudden bursts" of song. It is not a matter of our singing one song, stopping, and expecting the breakthrough but of continuing to sing out loud until the spirit of might comes upon us. We must continue to push against the kingdom of darkness through song because we are in the process of birthing something in the Spirit.

High and spontaneous praise births supernatural breakthroughs.

Don't stop singing—sing heavenly songs; burst through the darkness with praise to the Lord. Rejoice, because you were once sterile but are now fruitful. Shout with the voice of jubilee, right now! Wherever you are, the breakthrough is on its way. It will lead you out of your spiritual, personal, vocational, or ministerial stagnancy so that you can bring down the enemy's walls of containment, advance the territory of God's kingdom, and destroy the works of the devil.

Establish the Kingdom in Your Area of Influence

Enlarge the place of your tent, and let them stretch out the curtains of your dwellings; do not spare; lengthen your cords, and strengthen your stakes. (Isaiah 54:2)

When the spirit of might comes upon us, we will extend to the north, south, east, and west. The barriers that were hindering us will be broken down—the limits that were imposed on us will fall. Then, we will expand the kingdom by multiplying our ministries, churches, businesses, and gifts. The spirit of might will be upon us to bring forth great breakthroughs. Today is the day of expansion in our lives!

This is what happened to a pastor from Venezuela. During a youth conference that our ministry sponsored in his country, Pastor Gregory testified that I had given him a prophetic word sometime earlier and that it had since been fulfilled. God had shown me that Pastor Gregory would establish a school and a radio station. Both words came to pass. They have the school, and they also were given approval for a commercial radio station. A while later, Pastor Gregory attended the Supernatural Fivefold Ministry School, where I released a financial breakthrough to everyone in attendance, under the direction of the Holy Spirit.

After Pastor Gregory's return to Venezuela, a businessman sought him out and said, "The Lord has not allowed me to sleep but has urged me to sow four million bolivars into your ministry." Later, another businessman sowed $1.5 million dollars and then another half a million dollars. A wave of supernatural provision had been released! Someone else gave Pastor Gregory a new SUV and even paid the airfare for his entire family to travel. His church has experienced creative miracles and healings, which have made a great impact. This pastor joyfully testified that his congregation is now a megachurch! The influence of God's supernatural power is evident in his life and ministry. When he finished sharing his testimony,

I embraced him and ministered the presence of God and spiritual fatherhood to him. Pastor Gregory was visibly and deeply touched by God.

> ### *The purpose for a spiritual breakthrough is the expansion of the kingdom.*

Jesus said, *"You did not choose Me, but I chose you and appointed you that you should go and bear fruit, and that your fruit should remain..."* (John 15:16). If your life is not bearing fruit for God, or if your ministry is ineffective, ask yourself questions such as these:

+ To what territory, or sphere of influence, have I been assigned by God?

+ Why am I in my present territory? Did I let circumstances lead me here? Did I come by my own choice? Or did God plant me here?

+ Is my purpose connected to this territory?

+ Who is my delegated authority—for example, my pastor or apostle? Am I allowing him to train, disciple, and guide me according to God's Word?

+ Am I bearing the kind of fruit that lasts?

When God calls us, He also enables us—giving us the resources we need to accomplish His purposes. In contrast, when we have not been assigned to a certain territory, or when we have not been properly sent to it by God's delegated authority, we will not have dominion over it. Again, the enemy and his demons know how to recognize men and women who are functioning outside of their spheres of influence or authority.

Sometimes, our assignment from God will involve being in full-time ministry; however, God calls believers to many fields, such as law, government, education, the arts, science, and engineering. If God has assigned you to bring reform to your city's educational system, for example, He will support you, regardless of how impossible the task might seem, because that is your territory. God placed you there, and His power will back you up.

We must all be in the process of fulfilling our assignments. Each of us needs to seek God earnestly to discover our particular assignment. Through the parables of the talents and the minas, Jesus explained that when we are faithful in what God has given us to do, exercising good stewardship of the gifts He has given, He will reward us with greater territory and responsibility. Moreover, as we are faithful on earth, we will be rewarded in eternity.

If God has planted you in a place, then you should see the evidence of it by your fruitfulness. I believe that if you are prosperous where you are, then you are in the right territory, because when you find your purpose and pursue it with integrity, God's prosperity will be with you in every area of your life.

When a spiritual breakthrough takes place,
our old mentality of limitation changes to a mentality of expansion.

Demonstrate the Kingdom of Power Here and Now

The challenge of the kingdom is in the here and now! God's kingdom is the atmosphere, government, and culture of heaven brought to earth so that Jesus can be King and Lord of our lives and Satan can be removed from our midst. When a heart is transformed, when a sick person is healed, when someone suffering from oppression is delivered, we see demonstrations of God's kingdom power. Bringing such manifestations from heaven to earth is what we were born to do; this is why God gave us empowerment, gifts, and abilities.

Through this book, you have been equipped with the revelation of the kingdom of power here and now. When the Holy Spirit comes upon you, then you will receive God's power and baptism of fire, igniting you to manifest His kingdom wherever you go—ruling over sickness, sin, demons, poverty, and death. This is the season for the manifestation of God's children on earth. God created you to go into the world with all the gifts and blessings He has bestowed on you so that you can expand and multiply the kingdom on earth. As you do these things, He will increase your faith, power, and blessings, enabling you to continue extending His kingdom in the world.

Are you ready to expand God's kingdom here and now? If you have not yet received Jesus as your Lord and Savior, I want to give you another opportunity to do so right now. You will not be able to receive breakthroughs and expand the kingdom if you are not yet a citizen of the kingdom. Don't wait any longer!

> Heavenly Father, I recognize that I am a sinner and that my sin separates me from You. Today, I believe that Jesus died for me on the cross and that You raised Him from the dead. I repent of all my sins and, of my own free will, confess Jesus as my Lord and Savior. I renounce every pact I have made with the world, with my flesh, and with the devil, and I now make a new covenant with You. I ask Jesus to enter my heart and change my life. If I were to die right now, I know that You would receive me into Your arms. Amen!

If you just prayed this prayer, or if you had previously accepted Christ but have not yet received the baptism in the Holy Spirit, pray the following so that you may be filled with the Spirit, with the evidence of speaking in other tongues. Remember that the purpose of being baptized with the Spirit is to receive supernatural power to overcome sin, temptation, sickness, poverty, demons, and death, and to have victory in any other adverse circumstance of life.

> Heavenly Father, I am Your child, and I ask You to fill me with Your precious Holy Spirit. As the Spirit gives me utterance, I now start speaking in other tongues.

Continue praying with expectation that, right now, you will speak in a heavenly language.

If you have received Jesus and been baptized in the Spirit, and if you want God to use you in ever-increasing ways for His kingdom, please pray the following:

> Heavenly Father, I am Your beloved child. I am a king and priest under Your authority who rules over my territory in Your kingdom. I am a warrior, having Your spirit of might to break down Satan's walls of containment and receive Your breakthroughs for the greater expansion of Your kingdom. Live in me today, and let Your Spirit move in my life. Let my heart always be receptive and obedient to Your purpose and will. May Your kingdom come and Your will be done on earth as it is in heaven—in the here and now, and for all eternity. Amen and amen!